D1631173

fortitude

ALSO BY BRUCE DAISLEY

The Joy of Work

fortitude

Unlocking the Secrets of Inner Strength

Bruce Daisley

Cornerstone Press

3 5 7 9 10 8 6 4 2

Cornerstone Press
20 Vauxhall Bridge Road
London SW1V 2SA

Cornerstone Press is part of the Penguin Random House group of companies
whose addresses can be found at global.penguinrandomhouse.com.

Penguin
Random House
UK

First published by Cornerstone Press in 2022

www.penguin.co.uk

A CIP catalogue record for this book is available from the British Library.

ISBN 9781847943651 (hardback)
ISBN 9781847943668 (trade paperback)

Typeset in 12/14.75 pt Dante MT Std
by Integra Software Services Pvt. Ltd, Pondicherry

Printed and bound in Great Britain by Clays Ltd, Elcograf S.p.A.

The authorised representative in the EEA is Penguin Random House Ireland,
Morrison Chambers, 32 Nassau Street, Dublin D02 YH68.

www.greenpenguin.co.uk

Penguin Random House is committed to a sustainable future for our
business, our readers and our planet. This book is made from
Forest Stewardship Council® certified paper.

With love to my family

Contents

PART THREE

FINDING FORTITUDE

Prologue

F**k Resilience! We Just Want to Live!

Beirut is a real wake-up for the senses. Visually, the skyline is dominated by unspooled nests of phone wires and power cables – an unpredictable series of metallic threads that weave chaotic patterns up buildings and across streets, and that often obscure an unparalleled scrapbook of architectural styles: from delicate wrought-iron balconies that would grace a Parisian street, to details and flourishes that evoke an Ottoman past. Your ears are assaulted by the sound of traffic that doesn't so much hum as growl, as the locals tear around the narrow roads with clear irrepressible intent. Everywhere there's a sense of bustle and chaos. Stuck nose-to-tail on a two-lane highway, you may well detect some audacious driver ambitiously attempting to squeeze his slightly weathered Mercedes into what he's designated as a new, third lane between the two official ones. It's an improvisatory approach that is another hallmark of life in the city. Almost every household, for example, has a home-made solution to the daily power cuts that have been a feature of life here for decades.

It wasn't love at first sight for me, but during the course of more than half a dozen visits to see my partner's family, I've fallen for the charms of Bayrūt – or Beyrouth, as it's known to its French speakers. The city has more life, more gloriously hectic vitality than anywhere else I've ever been.

So if there's one place where the strangeness of 2020, mid-coronavirus, was particularly marked, it was the Lebanese capital. Suddenly the roads were clearer, the adrenalised city was a little calmer than usual. Social media before-and-after shots clearly documented a lift in the fug of smog that normally shrouds the messy metropolis, revealing its underlying beauty. *Nature is healing*, as people took to saying that spring.

The Lebanese have never had life easy, and even this moment of regeneration had been soured by months of hyperinflation and economic precarity. First the Lebanese pound had collapsed, causing people to lose their life savings. Then prices in the collapsed currency had soared several hundred per cent. All the while the country's rival governing cabals, which were collectively responsible for the mess, bickered and finger-pointed. The city I found myself in on 4 August 2020 was both calmer than usual and badly bruised.

The first indication I had that something untoward was happening that Tuesday evening, as I slouched in my chair after a day in the Beiruti sunshine, was an initially shallow rumble that made the pictures on the wall tremble, the crockery chink and what was left of my coffee splash against the sides of the cup. I glanced at the clock. It was 6.08 p.m. I set my cup down on the floor to wait out what I assumed was an earthquake. Maybe 5.0 on the Richter scale? Not huge, but certainly something to talk about at dinner that night.

Our building in Jnah proceeded to shake for thirty seconds. That may not sound long, but as I can testify from once experiencing a stretch of 'dead air' on a flight back from Barcelona, even ten seconds can seem an eternity when you don't know what is going to happen next. Eventually the building stopped shuddering. Then the apartment's windows were blown in. I was witness to the chilling sound of the air inside the flat being sucked out, a screeching, shrieking noise that set my pulse racing. By now, the rest of the family had gathered in the lounge. We scanned each other's faces, trying to conceal our own emotional tells while taking in the repressed reactions of everyone else. *What was that?*

Within minutes WhatsApps started to arrive. 'It was a bomb.' 'It was an explosion.' 'Look at this, it was an attack.' One video we received showed a violently raging sooty fire in the city's port being subsumed first under a perfectly hemisphered canopy of dust and then by a vast radiating bubble of debris, which swept outwards across dozens of streets. Gradually the bubble dissipated, giving way to a mushroom cloud that towered for minutes over the city, like a noxious cumulonimbus genie.[1]

Unbeknownst to us, 2,750 tons of ammonium nitrate, carelessly stored in a portside warehouse for almost a decade, had ignited and generated a bigger blast than that which had destroyed Chernobyl back in 1986. Indeed, the explosion had been powerful enough to shake the windows in Cyprus, 150 miles across the Mediterranean.[2] The shockwaves caused death and destruction across the whole city, leaving 200 people dead, seriously hurting 6,000 more and damaging tens of thousands of buildings. Injuries caused by shattered glass and collapsing construction left many with injuries that would transform the remainder of their lives.

The next day, news reports from around the world streamed live from the rubble of Beirut's port. The BBC reminded viewers that this small nation of under seven million people (including one and a half million Syrian refugees) was special. 'The Lebanese are famed for their resilience' was the BBC's take.[3] A correspondent for the *New York Times* concurred: 'Anyone who knows Lebanon has heard this: The Lebanese are resilient.' The roving focus of international news teleported millions of viewers to Beiruti streets to witness the devastation on a disaster-movie scale. And then, within hours, it inevitably moved on to other stories.

Narrative established: the Lebanese are resilient. Now, other news.

We love resilience stories. They have a fairy-tale quality that gives them a timeless appeal. And we love resilient people. When we hear of star athletes who, far from being demoralised by setbacks, seem to draw strength from them, we venerate them as we would movie superheroes. One moment we're watching the gymnastic prowess of Simone Biles, the adopted child of an addict parent. The next we watch Peter Parker, cared for by his aunt after the tragic deaths of his family, who acrobatically keeps New York

in order as Spider-Man. When we can't be entranced by the endeav-
ours of LeBron James, one of the most celebrated basketball players
of all time – raised by a troubled mother amid domestic fragility
and the sound of police sirens – then we celebrate Bruce Wayne,
son of murdered parents, who enacts his cold-tempered revenge on
law-breakers under the guise of the vigilante, Batman.

These are our favourite sportspeople and these are our society's
most successful fictional heroes. We love the redemption of resilience plotlines. They provide a satisfying narrative twist,
transforming undeserving victim into celebrated victor.

Such images of resilience hardly seemed apt as we walked
through the broken ruin of Beirut the day after the blast. There was
a caustic bite to the air that had a fortunate few upgrading their
COVID-era face coverings to medical-grade N95 masks. The hum
of traffic might have diminished, but in its stead came the crunch-
ing sound of glass, either as tiny shards of it were trodden underfoot
like fresh, icy snow, creating a musically scratchy *tinkle-tinkle*, or as
it was swept up; or, more orchestrally, as it poured on high from
buildings into makeshift skips below. Everywhere around us,
weary-eyed Beirutis brandished brooms as if their shattered city
could be healed by dogged sweeping.

It was a Turkish news outlet, TRT World, that first seemed to
capture a more accurate sense of what locals were really feeling
and saying. TRT quoted one Beiruti: 'I really thought I'd seen
everything in this godforsaken country. How much more are we
supposed to take? If I hear one more person referring to us as
"resilient", I will lose it. Fuck resilience. We don't want to be resilient. We just want to live!'[4] A Lebanese writer, Lina Mounzer, spoke
for many when she addressed the superficially charming fantasy of
resilience. 'We have finally come to recognise that a myth is poor
consolation for a half-lived life, no matter how attractive that myth
might be.'[5]

I'm ashamed to say that until that moment I'd never thought of
resilience like this – as a myth or fairy story, or as a substitute for
a life well lived. I'd assumed it was something admirable that we

should all deploy – something halfway between a trait ('the Lebanese are resilient') and a mindset to be emulated ('We're calling on people to be resilient'). Now my mind throbbed with the contradictions embodied in the word.

Shortly after I returned from Beirut I was invited to participate in a radio discussion about the mess of COVID-cancelled exams in the UK and the botched grades that pupils had initially been awarded. As we talked about children whose years of study had, hours before, been downgraded by a depersonalising algorithm, my fellow panellist, the broadcaster Robert Peston, offered a breezy assessment. The young people involved, he said, 'just need to be more resilient'.[6]

There it was again. That call for resilience; that suggestion that things would be so much better if only people toughened up a bit. Of course, I thought, listeners might very easily find themselves nodding along: 'OK, their exam results have been randomly plucked from a tombola after thirteen years of full-time education, but kids just need to deal with it.' After all, throughout history each generation has shown a tendency to assume that those following in its wake lack some of the backbone they displayed at the same age. On the other hand, I thought, it was possible that some of those tuning in might be experiencing the dash of scepticism I now felt.

As I pondered this, I recalled friends wearily telling me of the fruitless resilience-training courses their employers had sent them on – courses that, if anything, made them feel *more* helpless. I remembered how one friend said that the R-word elicited scornful resentment among colleagues in her big public-sector organisation. And I considered how resilience has not only become something of a buzzword now, but has become political. As the radio discussion demonstrated, there seems to be a widespread belief not only that we have witnessed an erosion of the innate strength that characterised our forebears, but also that we are currently witnessing a *snowflake generation*, an enfeebled breed of youngsters who are less equipped for the struggles of life than any previous cohort. We've countered by demanding that they show inner toughness. We don't empathise with them. We instruct them. And to society as a whole we throw out a series of challenges:

- You failed to get recruited for a new job (because of systemic discrimination)? *Solution*: be more resilient.
- Your city is decimated by an explosion (caused by governmental corruption and ineptitude)? *Solution*: be more resilient.
- Your tap water is polluted with lead (as a result of civic incompetence)? *Solution*: be more resilient.

Alongside the burden of expectation laid on the unfortunate, we're bombarded with headline-grabbing stories about heroes who have been resilient. We're invited to get in on the act: I can vividly recall hearing a bestselling author pronounce, 'Whatever your life brings you, respond with creation – this is the engine of resilience' (whatever that means). But the stories and the injunctions are invariably vague and hard to pin down. It's no wonder that, when we're struggling, a call from others to be resilient is less than helpful.

When I was growing up in the 1980s I barely ever heard discussions of resilience in school or on the news. Now it's become ubiquitous. Google's Ngram project (which tracks the deployment of specific words in books and literature over the last two centuries) suggests that in the course of the twentieth century, use of the word 'resilience' rose sixfold. Between 2000 and 2020, the year of the Beirut explosion, its use quintupled again. In other words, between 1900 and the era of TED Talks and viral video hits, its frequency rose almost 3,000 per cent. True, there have been a few sceptical voices. The author of an article in the *New York Times* magazine remarked on 'the profound emptiness of resilience', noting that it was increasingly the go-to word to buttress mission statements, to strengthen the published philosophies of educational institutions, and a trait whose absence we were bemoaning in others.[7] The novelist Jami Attenberg once pondered whether it was another way of saying 'Let those who are suffering take care of themselves.' 'Is [the word] an act of subterfuge for those most powerful?' she asked pointedly.[8] But such questioning has been the exception rather than the rule.

As my own scepticism grew, I decided to dedicate myself to finding out more. I wanted to know what resilience actually is. I wanted to discover whether it is more than something we simply encourage others to embody – whether it's something we can summon up in ourselves. I wanted to understand precisely what forms it takes. I therefore proceeded to track down experts, speak to victims of misfortune and work through the findings of hundreds of academic papers. And I set myself the task of answering the questions that were bubbling up inside me. If, by the very nature of the law of probability, not every child can succeed, what distinguishes those who forge ahead from those who remain behind? If the people of Lebanon truly are resilient, what can we learn from them? If resilient people have particular traits in common, what are they, and can we emulate them?

My journey of discovery has turned out to be full of surprises. I have found that many of the notions of resilience that have become very popular recently rest on questionable research. I have also come to realise that even the words used – 'resilience', 'grit', 'self-reliance', 'determination' – require close and critical scrutiny. Above all, I have come to appreciate how, when presented with a particular problem or issue, it's worryingly easy not just to misdiagnose it, but also to hold the wrong people accountable for it, turning villains into heroes, and heroes into villains. I've even asked myself whether resilience is actually a thing or whether it's just a convenient myth for those who, as Jami Attenberg suggested, believe that the 'system' is a fair one and that it's down to the individual to find their place within it. 'Resilience is made up by our capitalist overlords, lol,' the novelist Sara Nović told a friend.[9]

Perhaps the best way to explain the pitfalls of assigning responsibility for displays – or non-displays – of resilience is by analogy with another story of the modern world: the story of plastic.

In the 1980s the world was gradually waking up to the fact that it had a plastics problem. The material was so astonishingly versatile and cheap that it was becoming ubiquitous; and, as a result, it was also becoming a waste nightmare. Discarded plastics lay everywhere. They were filling home rubbish bins, they were turning up by the side of roads and in rivers and seas.

In the US the plastics industry was worried. If it didn't do something, it realised, it faced the risk either that politicians would start to impose tough regulations or that someone would come up with a replacement material. According to Larry Thomas, then president of the Society of the Plastics Industry (now known as the Plastics Industry Association), 'The image of plastics is deteriorating at an alarming rate, we are approaching a point of no return ... We've got to do what it takes to take the heat off because we want to continue to make plastic products,'[10] he said.

Stopping manufacture was not an option – at least as far as those invested in plastics were concerned. Instead, the owners of the plastic manufacturers, the giants of the petroleum industry, set about reframing the problem.[11] From the 1990s they began spending their way out of a PR disaster, investing millions of dollars each year to promote the benefits of plastics. At the same time they tried to improve the material's image by pushing the notion of recycling. As Sian Sutherland, founder of the campaigning organisation A Plastic Planet points out, plastic recycling is actually 'a red herring'.[12] Even today less than 10 per cent of waste plastic is recycled. Most ends up in landfill sites or is incinerated. What is repurposed has a tendency to degrade when recycled, rendering it of limited use. The process is also complex, costly and slow. But for the plastics industry, pushing the idea that this wonder material could be reused was irresistible. The packaging of billions of plastic products was therefore set to work as in-home advertising space for the new propaganda message. Duly stamped with a confusing range of arrow logos, it promoted the illusion that everything could be reused, even though a careful decoding of the recycling symbols showed the opposite. 'If the public thinks that recycling is working, they're not going to be concerned about the environment,'[13] Thomas later said.

And here's the thing: as the recycling campaign got under way, the role of culprit shifted. Now it was no longer plastics manufacturers that created the material who were at fault, but the consumers who failed to recycle it. The problem was no longer that there were too many plastic items around; it was that households weren't doing their bit to ensure reuse. As Sian Sutherland says, 'it behoves the plastic industry to confuse people. Plastic recycling is bullshit – a fig leaf on consumerism – it's simply a way to appease our guilt.'[14]

For recycling, now read *resilience*. The highly respected psychologist Professor Alex Haslam suggests that, in its current form, this is a fairly new phenomenon. 'Resilience really emerged as a construct around about ten years ago,' he explains. He argues that there was a particular trigger for this. 'Organisations started getting tired with what you might call the "stress agenda". People like [the psychologist] Professor Cary Cooper had done a good job raising people's awareness of stress and the idea that the way work was fashioned was leading to dramatic increases in workplace stress.'[15] Haslam cites one particularly noteworthy episode in 2003 when the UK's Health and Safety Executive issued a 'Stress Improvement Notice' to West Dorset general hospitals NHS trust to resolve stress issues there.[16] As he explains, this move – and others like it – demonstrated to employers that they were expected to resolve the stress they were causing. And it worried them. 'Major employers like the NHS and big companies got quite nervous because here was this thing stress, which in a very clear way they were responsible for creating, and they had them being charged by the then Labour government with tidying up.'[17]

The response such organisations adopted was not dissimilar to that employed by the plastics industry: responsibility for stress was shifted from the manufacturer to the consumer. Or, as Professor Haslam puts it, 'One way they did that was rhetorically by saying "OK, we've had enough of talking about this bad stuff. So let's start looking on the positive side and talking about resilience." Of course the point of that,' Haslam adds, 'was really to take the spotlight off organisations and what they were doing and to focus on the people and effectively have a psychological analysis which said, "The real problem here is that people just aren't resilient enough."' In the process, a true understanding of the factors at play was lost.

This individualistic concept of resilience is now big business. As one boss of a British well-being organisation that works with companies in both the public and private sectors sighed to me, 'Yes, resilience has become productised' (he then directed me to his firm's own online tool, branded with a trademarked name). You can subscribe to courses and schemes that will 'fix' workers (the implication being that if they don't end up 'fixed', you'd be within your rights to write them off as defective). If you're at college, you may well be taught a resilience module. If you're in the military, you may be supplied with coping mechanisms that draw on resilience teaching. You may buy one of the many bestselling books that enable you to do it for yourself. The irony, of course, is that you're living in a world that is simultaneously awash with resilience programmes and convinced that we're all becoming less resilient.

I have spent the past few years making podcasts about business and popular psychology in general, and about work culture in particular, and I've also sought to help firms improve their workplace culture. And as I've done so, I've become acutely aware that a consensus can build up around a topic that parrots the views of a small number of experts and ignores the inconvenient contrary voices of others. I also know that it's all too easy for a simple, powerful narrative to take hold that silences more nuanced ones. In the case of resilience, that narrative involves celebrating the stories of individuals who have managed to turn trauma into triumph – who have displayed an inner toughness that overcomes all odds and who, so the argument goes, should serve as a model to us all. I've also become wary of people who peddle one-size-fits-all solutions to complex human problems or who offer simple injunctions. A friend told me once that 'Never in the history of calming down has someone calmed down by being told to "calm down".' So it is with resilience. Never in the history of resilience has someone become more resilient by being told, 'Be more resilient.'

As well as becoming wary of the dangers of group-think, I've also come to appreciate the leaps forward that can be taken when ideas from different fields cross-fertilise: when social scientists start talking to clinical practitioners, when psychologists talk to anthropologists. So much of what we learn sits in discrete silos. But how would we know about the nature of trauma, had the curiosity of a weight-loss expert, Vincent Felitti, not come into contact with the doubts of an epidemiologist, Robert Anda? How would we have discovered essential truths about recovery from medical procedures, had Alex Haslam not looked at the issue from the perspective of group psychology? Connecting different ideas and thought processes is essential if we are to advance our understanding. And there are few areas where this connectivity of disciplines and ideas is more essential than in the field of resilience. As I've explored the subject and talked to experts from different fields, I've really come to appreciate how remarkable breakthroughs seem to happen when big thinkers step out of their lane.

In the chapters that follow, I've drawn on the research and insights of a wide array of people from various disciplines and walks of life to dissect current notions of resilience and point out what, for me, are the many deficiencies of those notions. At the same time I have come to appreciate what I believe is a far more compelling model, based on what psychologists would describe as a *social-identity explanation of resilience*. To differentiate this from classic 'resilience', I have decided to call it by the synonymous term 'fortitude'. In the book I set out to answer the many questions that crowded in on me in the days and weeks after the Beirut explosion. Why do some people appear to be emotionally tougher than others? Does success depend on the ability to overcome personal setbacks? What is a *growth mindset* and what are the challenges regarding the claims that its adherents make for it? Finally, is resilience – or, rather, fortitude – something that we either have or don't have, or is it something that we can develop? And, if so, how?

A note on endnotes

You'll notice that the text that follows is littered with endnote numbers. I have to confess I'm ambivalent about their inclusion. When I am simply reading for pleasure, I find those superscript numbers distracting and unrewarding. When I want to delve deeper, I find them an invaluable source of evidence and proof. I would urge readers who don't intend to dive into the subject in greater detail to ignore the notes (everything of substance appears in the main text). However, those whose curiosity is piqued, or who are sceptical about particular lines of argument, will find that the Notes on pp.231–282 serve as useful guides to further reading.

PART ONE

Decoding the Myths of Resilience

Chapter 1

I Get Knocked Down But I Get Up Again
The Doctrine of Resilience

To watch Simone Biles at the peak of her powers was to be lost in wonder that a human could use her body to paint such impossible patterns in the air. Biles unquestionably brought a balletic beauty to gymnastics. Such was her aerial sorcery that, while we all tried visually to rewind and untangle the knots that she tied in fast-forward, gravity itself ceased to be an enemy to be overcome, but was rendered a spectator.

Not only did she display unmatched artistry, but she transmitted joy in the process. She looked like the happiest sprite in the world, her radiant smile lighting up auditorium screens once her two feet were planted – a beam that confirmed we'd just witnessed something extraordinary. Linda Stone, a tech executive, once coined the term *email apnea* to describe the way that 80 per cent of us unconsciously hold our breath when responding to an email. *Biles apnea* was something even more potent: our lungs froze while she remained skyborne.[1]

If ever there's a human who embodies triumph in the face of adversity, it's Simone Biles. Winner of seven Olympic medals, she had a tough upbringing in Columbus, Ohio. Her birth mother – about whom Biles has always spoken respectfully – 'got caught up in drinking and drugs' and, as small children, Biles, her brother and her two sisters frequently went hungry. 'Growing up, me and my siblings were so focused on food because we didn't have a lot,' she later recalled. 'I remember there was this cat around the house and I would be so hungry. They would feed this cat and I would be like, "Where the heck is my food?" And so I think that's [why] I don't

3

like cats … because this freaking street cat, she always fed it. But she never fed us.' Eventually social services were called and three-year-old Biles and her siblings were taken into foster care.[2]

As the children navigated their uncertain new lives together, she and her protective older brother, three years her senior, found escape in physical activity. Simone recounts how she would build exhilarating momentum on a back-yard swing at their foster home, back-flipping from its apex, soaring through the air, exalting that she could fly. This energetic physicality was her release. 'I had these miniature six-pack abs and lightning fast legs … I was always running and jumping, cartwheeling and somersaulting.'[3] Biles felt her muscle strength to be part of her identity (her classmates called her out for having bulging biceps by the age of eight); even today, she describes herself as 'a four-feet-eight-inch ball of nonstop energy'.[4] Not being permitted to use the trampoline in her foster parents' garden (imagine trying to explain personal-accident insurance to a heartbroken four-year-old), she would gaze longingly at the acrobatics that her carers' own children were permitted to perform.

A promise of stability came when her grandparents took her in: 'the knots I usually felt in my tummy were gone', she has said. But that promise was soon snatched away. Biles's mum was intent on winning the children back and they were placed once again in the foster-care system while the authorities waited to see whether she could free herself from her drug dependency. Regular visits from Biles's grandfather became Simone's sole positive experience. 'Whenever we had visits with my grandpa, I was so excited. That was the person I always wanted to see.'[5] Otherwise, she recalls her time in foster care as being characterised by 'always being hungry and afraid'.

Eventually she was moved with her younger sister to be with her grandparents again (her older siblings chose to stay with an aunt nearer to Ohio). Weary from a year in foster care and vividly aware that she'd seen this movie before, Biles was at first guarded with those around her. It took a while for her to relax. Over time, though, she came to regard her adoptive parents (her grandparents) as her real mother and father. Today, she speaks glowingly of her love for them and credits them for having helped to define her – for having 'made' her.

Biles's family situation may have finally reached a point of equilibrium, but her troubles were not over. While in the care of USA Gymnastics she was a victim of sexual assault by the team doctor Larry Nassar, who has since been convicted of molesting more than 250 young women and girls.[6] Adding to the trauma, in her view, was the fact that, rather than make the welfare of young girls their priority when accusations of misconduct were first made against Nassar, USA Gymnastics sought instead to defend itself.[7] In the lead-up to the delayed Tokyo Olympics Biles felt frustrated by her prolonged association with an organisation she couldn't forgive.

Her achievements are so extraordinary that it is worth briefly recalling them. She has won more medals and titles than any other gymnast. She has invented new manoeuvres that now bear her name: one on the beam, two on the floor. In 2021 she added a fourth, when she achieved the Yurchenko Double Pike from the vault. It is now known as the *Biles (vault)*. Insiders acknowledge that she has redefined what is possible in gymnastics.

And she has done all this in the face of early trauma, sexual abuse – not to mention physical suffering (she won national championships with broken toes, and a World Championship while suffering from a kidney stone) – and family stress (her brother was charged with, and later acquitted of, murder).[8]

In other words, Simone Biles exemplifies the trajectory of resilience that we hear about. She has not only overcome profoundly negative experiences, but has somehow channelled them to achieve greatness. She is far from being the only sportsperson to have done so. Footballer Paul Gascoigne experienced the trauma of seeing his best friend run over and killed while in his care. He went on to become an iconic figure for club and country. The Auckland childhood of rugby-union star Jonah Lomu was scarred by domestic abuse perpetrated by his father, and by a violent local gang culture that saw his uncle and cousin murdered when he was twelve. He went on to become the youngest ever All Black and a star adored by millions.[9]

Tennis player Andre Agassi was bullied to play by his emotionally distant father, causing him to assert in his autobiography, 'I play tennis for a living even though I hate tennis, hate it with a dark and secret passion and always have.'[10] He ended his career as an eight-time Grand Slam winner, additionally picking up the 1996 Olympic gold medal. Middle-distance runner Kelly Holmes, who was born to a seventeen-year-old mother and an absent father, was first placed (much to her mother's anguish) in care, and then often racially bullied in her village school. She won medals at the Commonwealth Games, World and European Championships. Siya Kolisi, who grew up in the Black township of Zwide, Port Elizabeth, experienced the traumas of seeing his mother being regularly beaten up, his grandmother dying in his arms when he was ten, and then, two years later, witnessing a neighbour being stoned to death. In 2019, as the Springboks' first-ever Black captain, he led them to victory in the World Cup.[11]

It's not just sport that has such stories to tell. Take Marie Curie – or Maria Salomea Skłodowska, as she was born in Russian-occupied Warsaw – who remains the only person to have won Nobel Prizes in two different scientific disciplines. Curie's life was beset by tragedy. Her father, suspected of harbouring pro-Polish sentiments, lost his teaching job and the family had to take in up to twenty student boarders at a time to make ends meet. Her mother was a long-term sufferer of tuberculosis, then an incurable condition. To protect the children she withdrew from them, avoiding hugging or kissing them or even using the same eating utensils, for fear of passing on her sickness. She was often absent from the family home, spending months in mountainous retreats where, sometimes accompanied by her eldest daughter Zosia, it was hoped the fresh air and rest would help her.

When Curie was nine, her sisters Zosia and Bronia caught typhoid from one of the boarders. Bronia survived, but fourteen-year-old

Zosia died. Curie's other sister Helena wrote: 'Our sister's death literally crushed our mother; she could never accept the loss of her oldest child.' Three years later, enfeebled by TB and tortured by grief, Curie's mother also died.[12] Curie, who was a keen correspondent throughout her life, wrote in her autobiography that her mother's death was 'the first great sorrow of my life and threw me into a profound depression'.[13] Her sister described how the loss devastated the teenager: 'She would often sit in some corner and cry bitterly. Her tears could not be stopped by anybody.'

Although Curie's schooling ended when she was fifteen – the mandated limit for girls – she was able to secure a place at the Sorbonne in Paris when she was twenty-four and married, and then, in 1903, at the age of thirty-six, she earned her first Nobel Prize (jointly with her husband, Pierre Curie, and the French physicist Henri Becquerel) for discovering radioactivity. She was the first woman ever to receive a Nobel Prize, although she secured it only because Pierre threatened to decline the award that was offered to him when he discovered that the intention had been not to recognise Marie's contribution. Three years later her beloved spouse slipped while crossing the rue Dauphine in Paris and was run over by a horse-drawn carriage. His death left Marie heartbroken. She nevertheless went on to win a second Nobel Prize in 1911.[14]

The psychologist Mihaly Csikszentmihalyi, who is best known for his concept of *flow* as a positive mental state, once argued that there is more than coincidence at work here, and threw some other names into the mix to illustrate the point: 'Leonardo da Vinci was illegitimate and grew up scarcely knowing his mother. Michelangelo's father was a failure and he had to be apprenticed in the shop of the artist Ghirlandaio at the age of thirteen.' He went so far as to argue for a relationship between childhood trauma and the development of genius, an argument that evokes memories of the saying credited to the French existentialist philosopher Jean-Paul Sartre that the best favour a father can do for his son is to die early (a favour that Sartre's own father had conferred).[15] Others have concurred with

Csikszentmihalyi's view, and a number of peer-reviewed studies and articles have appeared on the subject to support it.

Perhaps the most ambitious of these studies has been one commissioned by UK Sport, the government-funded high-performance sports agency responsible for investing in Olympic and Paralympic sport. By the early 2000s the agency had undergone major expansion, moving from a funding level of £59 million in 2000, when Team GB won eleven gold medals at the Sydney Olympics, to a budget of £265 million in preparation for the London 2012 games. Keen to ensure that money was being spent where it would be most effective, and simultaneously very aware of the uplift in national pride that medal success brings, the organisation – under the aegis of its director of performance, Chelsea Warr – put out a call in 2009 to academics to seek their help, as it sought to ensure that future Olympic Games appearances would be transformed into medals.[16]

Among those who applied for the research funding on offer were Professor Tim Rees, professor in sport at Bournemouth University, and his long-term collaborator Lew Hardy, one of the first creators of a sport science course in the UK. Rees was surprised, and somewhat impressed, that UK Sport should be thinking about elite performance in a process-orientated way: 'the thing that really struck me in the first meetings with UK Sport,' he told me, 'is that they talked about there being a global arms race in terms of winning medals and about trying to win market share.'[17] He and Hardy therefore got to work, seeking to understand what goes on in the minds of professional athletes and, in particular, what elevates an athlete from what they termed an Elite level of performance to a Super Elite level.

The researchers were only too aware that there were lots of theories about elite performance floating around – often anecdotal, often chalked up on blackboards or committed to coaches' notebooks. 'There are many ways to reach the top,' Tim Rees told me, 'and it's really important to base your decisions on evidence and not on opinion, popular wisdom and misinformation. We often find that there are people out there who shout the loudest who get listened to, and that's not always the best advice to take.' Rees and Hardy took a far more empirical approach, appreciating from the start that the answers might well be multifaceted. 'I always think of the quote by H. L. Mencken,' said Rees. '"For every complex problem there is an answer that is clear, simple and wrong."' The fact is that every athlete is unique and complex. There's nothing linear or predictable about their careers. Less than a quarter of winning medallists at the Olympic Games and World Championships, for example, had previously reached similar heights as juniors.[18] What faced the researchers would be like cracking the Enigma Code of individual and team performance.

Rees and Hardy adopted a pairing approach to their research, seeking to establish the differences between those who were exceptional enough to make it through to the World Championships or Olympic Games (these finalists they styled Elite athletes) and those who would usually finish by triumphing with a gold medal around their necks (labelled Super Elite). Why was it, for instance, that Super Elite athlete Mo Farah had been able to take home a *Double Double* – two gold medals from two successive Olympics – while many of those competing against him had been unable to fulfil what had once appeared similar potential, but ended up coming home empty-handed? The research team therefore recruited sixteen former Super Elite athletes from UK sport, all of whom had won at least one gold medal and at least one other medal (gold or silver) at major championships.[19] And they compared each of their lives and records with that of a paired former Elite athlete of the same age and gender – an athlete who had participated in the same sport, but had never achieved the same success; 260 hours of intensive (and subsequently anonymised) interviews followed, as the researchers sought to build up complete biographies of these high performers. To create as rounded a picture as possible, they also talked to the athletes' coaches and parents.

As they did so, they exposed certain widely accepted truths as questionable assertions. One such was the '10,000-hours rule' – a concept coined by psychologist Anders Ericsson, who posited that accomplishment in any field is normally the results of 10,000 hours of careful, deliberate practice.[20] (It's worth saying that twenty years before Ericsson, Herbert Simon and William Chase had identified that becoming a chess grandmaster was contingent on ten years of dedicated practice.[21]) Popularised by the likes of the Canadian writer Malcolm Gladwell, and in the UK by the journalist and author Matthew Syed, the 10,000-hours rule has become part of popular wisdom – the assumption being that pursuing an interest is not in itself sufficient to make you a master of it: you have to adopt a diligent and specific focus on skills attainment and talent refinement if you are to excel.

Rees and Hardy found that – in the sports arena, at least – the 10,000-hours rule doesn't really stack up. In fact many of the Elite athletes they studied had reached the top having practised for only half that time. The Bahamian Donald Thomas was one extreme example. He took up the high jump in 2006. Two months later he finished fourth in the Commonwealth Games in Melbourne, his performance drawing attention because he was wearing the wrong shoes, failed to achieve the right run-up and then landed rather clumsily. The following year he won gold at the World Championships in Osaka, Japan. He also won gold at the IAAF World Athletics Final. He'd reached the top of the sport within sixteen months of first competing in it.

Another allied myth – or at best half-truth – exposed by the researchers was the belief (common among professional coaches) that young talent has to be captured and nurtured early. One coach at the velodrome in Manchester told Rees, 'If we don't get an athlete in by fourteen then there's no chance of getting them to the top.' Again Rees, Hardy and their team found no evidence to support such assertions. Indeed, there were some indications that such teenage programmes might cause more harm than good. It was the same with the argument that, in order to excel, youngsters must focus ruthlessly on one activity. The researchers found that those who pursued multiple passions tended to remain more motivated.[22]

Nor was excellence down to the actions of pushy mothers, fathers or carers. Indeed, many parents had to be prompted to acknowledge the transformations their children had undergone. As Hardy said, 'Often with the parents [of the athletes, in the research interviews] there was a moment of realisation that something they had done somewhere in their child's upbringing had had a major impact. Some athletes cried at the interview, but a larger number of the parents did – a moment of realisation, not necessarily good or bad, about what their son or daughter had become.'[23]

However, there was a common single factor that the researchers did unearth, and it was a show-stopper. Every one of the Super Elite athletes reported a negative critical life experience in their formative years – an experience that was usually coupled with a positive sports-related event. In terms of defining the forms that a negative critical life experience might take, the researchers stated that they included, but were not limited to: 'the death (or serious illness) of a significant family member, parental divorce, or serious relationship problems, unstable or unsettled home environment (e.g. witnessing, or undergoing personal experience of, physical or verbal abuse), frequently moving home (with a subsequent loss of friendship groups), the perception of being sent away from parents (e.g. to boarding school), and difficulty at school (e.g. low achievement, bullying and loneliness)'.[24] And the Elite athletes? Only four out of sixteen Elite athletes had experienced similar setbacks.

There it was. In one of the most thorough analyses of sporting performance ever undertaken, clear evidence had been presented that trauma can indeed end in, and lead to, triumph. What doesn't kill you *does* make you stronger. The Simone Biles story is not a one-off; it fits a pattern. So, too, does the life of Marie Curie. While 25 per cent of the Elite athletes studied by Rees, Hardy and their team could claim a life trajectory that took them from trauma to triumph, 100 per cent of the Super Elite could do so. Nor is this the only study to have unearthed such connections between setbacks and success. Nico Van Yperen's extensive fifteen-year study of top-performing professional footballers found that, at junior Elite level, academy footballers who went on to reach the highest Super Elite level had home lives that involved more than three times the divorce rate of peers who failed to reach the top.[25]

Such studies have shown the range of triggers that can be involved. Van Yperen's study, for example, noted that the best footballers were more likely to have a large number of siblings, and so potentially had to overcome rivals and competitors within their family. Another study has shown that the best performers in rowing are significantly more likely to have been sent away to boarding school at an early age – a suggestion that, for some, there was a need to overcome an experience that they found isolating and stressful.[26] It's perhaps worth noting in this context the observation that award-winning novelist Louis de Bernières made to the *Sunday Times* about his own time at boarding school: 'The cruelty scarred me for life. At seventy-five, I am still hurting.'[27]

As I have already mentioned, the Great British Medallists Project was at pains to anonymise every aspect of its report. But it's not hard to find sportspeople whose experiences chime with those of the study: competitors who have achieved extraordinary success after terrible suffering. Smaller negative events might not make it through to an athlete's biography, but major details certainly do appear in the narratives of some of the most iconic names in sport. A noteworthy example is former world number-one tennis player Andy Murray: one of the most successful British athletes of all times. A three-times Grand Slam champion, he is also the only tennis player – male or female – ever to win two Olympic singles golds. And sure enough he has also experienced significant trauma. As a nine-year-old in March 1996 he was witness to one of the worst mass shootings ever to take place on British soil, when a gunman stormed Dunblane Primary School in Scotland and killed seventeen people, as Murray and his classmates took refuge in the head teacher's office.

Murray has, understandably, always shied away from saying much publicly about that day, but he did open up to film director Olivia Cappuccini in 2019 for what became her film *Resurfacing*, touching not only on the Dunblane shooting, but also on a series of subsequent difficult moments in his life. 'Obviously I had the thing that happened at Dunblane, when I was around nine. I am sure for all the kids there it would be difficult for different reasons. The fact we knew the guy, we went to his kids' club, he had been in our car, we had driven and dropped him off at train stations and things. And within twelve months of that, our parents got divorced. It is a difficult time for kids, to see that and not quite understand what is going on. And then six to twelve months after that, my brother Jamie also moved away from home. He went away to train to play tennis. We obviously used to do everything together. When he moved away that was also quite hard for me. Around that time and after that, for a year or so, I had lots of anxiety that came out when I was playing tennis. When I was competing I would get really bad breathing problems. Tennis is an escape for me in some ways, because all of these things are bottled up and we don't talk about these things. Tennis allows me to be that child. That's why it is important to me.'[28]

Later in Cappuccini's film, Murray's long-time coach Jamie Delgado shares an instructive observation. 'I'll never forget the first week I ever worked with him, we did interval training. Coming towards the end of the session Andy was on his knees, he was completely dead. I said, "OK, we'll stop there, that's enough." He spoke to me, he said, "Look, I don't know what it is within me but I can keep going, I can keep going through the pain. When you think it's over for me, keep pushing me because I can keep going."'[29]

Another – this time American – Super Elite athlete who has opened up about the experience and impact of trauma is LeBron James, four-times NBA Player of the Year, whose accomplishments have earned him the right to be considered as one of the greatest basketball players of all time.[30] Interviewed for the documentary *More Than a Game*, the commandingly athletic six-foot nine-inch star describes the challenges of a childhood spent in the care of a mother who had her own demons to face. 'She was sixteen when she had me,' he recalls. 'The father figure I was looking for was never there, ever. It was constantly on the move for us, from five years old till eight we probably moved ten, twelve times. Three, four, five schools. The hardest thing was meeting new friends. New schools all the time. Finally getting comfortable with a group of friends at one school and having to leave.'[31]

He goes on to explain, '[You] definitely see things at a young age that you don't want your kids to see. Violence, drug abuse and police sirens. It didn't matter where we were, being with my mother was the only thing that mattered.' That much-needed constant contact could not always be guaranteed. 'I remember Mother sitting me down and telling me, because of certain situations, that she may be gone for a little while, that I was going to be living with one of my coaches. It was a challenge. It's all I cared about, when I was growing up, if I was going to wake up and whether my mother was alive or still by my side. Because I was already without a father and I didn't want to be without both of my parents. It was definitely scary and tough.'

Whether my mother was alive or still by my side – it's tragic that any child should experience such anxiety. Although James's background was very different from Andy Murray's, one can detect similar potential psychological triggers: separation anxiety, a sense of insecurity. And it's the natural human desire for security that James talks about when describing his growing basketball prowess at St Vincent-St Mary High School class of 2003: 'The thing I had on the court that I didn't have off the court was security,' he recalls. 'Every day we went to the gym, I knew I was going to get picked, we were going to win basketball games, we were going to win pick-up games, I've always said it's home-away-from-home for me.'[32]

One further example will suffice. The diver Tom Daley is a two-times World Champion ten-metre diver, who first won the FINA World Championships when he was only fifteen. He suffered the early loss of his father, who contracted brain cancer when Daley was just twelve. He was also bullied at school, both for his fame and his emerging sexuality. He grew through his teenage years fearful of being judged for being gay, but has spoken of how these negative experiences propelled his competitive focus. 'To this day,' he said on BBC Radio 4's *Desert Island Discs*, 'those feelings of feeling *less than* and feeling different have been the things that have given me the power and the strength to succeed in the other things that I've done, because you want to prove that you're not less than. You want to prove that you are something and that you are someone, and that I'm not going to disappoint everyone when they discover my truth.'[33] He has spoken of how his awareness of constant potential disapproval spurred him on: 'When actually those experiences of being like an outsider is going to be what ends up giving you that edge, giving you that feisty little thing inside of you to make you the best you can be.'[34]

So what's going on here? The temptation is to assume that, along with other factors that the researchers behind the Great British Medallists report note (personality, motivation, commitment, the ability to regulate emotion and pressure, and so on), the Super Elites possess or acquire a resilience that enables them to deal with the misfortunes visited upon them at an early stage, and that this resilience is then channelled into achieving excellence. But there's a bit more to it than that. Their experiences appear to push them towards what can only be described as obsessiveness and, in many cases, selfish obsessiveness. As Rees puts it, 'You see ruthlessness and selfishness, obsessiveness and perfectionism, need for success, wanting to win above everything else, the importance of sports, focus on the outcome and winning.' For such Super Elite athletes, it's not a question of sport *and* family, or sport *and* friends. It's sport *and* sporting success. 'You might think this person is not necessarily that well adjusted or all that happy, and you probably would be right,' Tim Rees says. And he adds, 'There were three hundred and seven golds available at the Rio Games, for a worldwide population of billions. These people are, by definition, abnormal, so we shouldn't expect them necessarily to conform to normal levels of behaviour.'

For the UK Sport researchers, this character trait was sufficient to explain the intrinsic difference between Elite and Super Elite athletes. As a rule, both groups started their careers well, but there always came a point when the upward trajectory stopped for the Elites and carried on for the Super Elites. The Super Elites were ruthless, single-mindedly obsessed with succeeding at all costs. They were in no doubt that sporting success was the most important thing – maybe the *only* thing – worth achieving, and their lives were (often selfishly) organised accordingly. They 'tended to be very difficult characters', as Lew Hardy told the writer Owen Slot: 'Super Elite athletes are amazing. But they aren't necessarily the most well-adjusted, happy people. If they were, they wouldn't do what they do.'[35] Or as Rees expresses it: 'I'm not saying world-class athletes have a mental disorder but the point is they may be different to other people and this drive could be the key.'[36]

Compare this with the observations of a coach who talked to the Great British Medallists study about a (less successful) Elite athlete: 'Happy kids don't make great sports people in my opinion … I feel really bad on one level, having been as honest as I have about [the athlete he worked with, who never reached the highest levels] because I do think that he is a victim of [his happy upbringing] and that fundamentally they [the family] are all driven by really good, lovely principles of having a nice family. Protecting those you love, wanting to keep [them] safe and providing the best for [them] are the intentions within that family which are astronomically brilliant, and lovely, and something I'd love to be part of.'[37]

Were it not for the remarkable accomplishments of the Super Elite athletes, we'd almost certainly be observing that, rather than being role models, there is something not right with them. Indeed, the athletes themselves recognise that they aren't necessarily the easiest people to be around: fourteen out of the sixteen Super Elites interviewed for the Great British Medallists report described themselves as ruthless or selfish.[38] In contrast, only two of the Elite competitors used those terms about themselves. The majority were far more likely to describe themselves as 'people pleasers'. 'In competitive situations,' one of them said, 'I felt like I didn't have that real aggression when I was [performing] against them to be able to divorce the fact that I was friends with them [as well]. I would be a bit too nice ... I should have been more ruthless and again that was something we talked about with [my coach]; trying to be more cut-throat whereas actually I was good at doing what was right for the squad.'[39]

Two things emerge from this. The first, as Rees put it to me, is that 'The Super Elite athletes wanted to win – but also winning wasn't enough. Winning became a defining quality in their lives.' He went on to elaborate: 'The athletes mentioned significant turning points in their lives, the Super Elite athletes just found that sport was the most important thing in their life above all else. Relationships were dropped. Everything was cast to the side in pursuit of going to the Olympics and then in pursuit of a gold medal.' Rees framed what this looked like, for the Super Elite athletes that he spent hours interviewing. 'It's interesting, it seemed to me (and it was backed up in the data) that with the Elite athletes they often had choices. Let's say it didn't work out at one Olympic Games, they've been dropped from a squad. They think to themselves, "Am I going to try four more years to hopefully make the squad for the next Olympics?" They tend to think, "I've got a life outside of this, I want to move on."'

Super Elite athletes, by contrast, felt that if they couldn't succeed in a field where they displayed real talent, then they had nothing. Exposure to traumatic adversity had changed them. It had created a void that they used to justify a ruthless perfectionism, which would probably never be satisfied. As one Super Elite athlete put it of another: 'He just desperately needed to win. I watched him. I can remember the noise that he was making on an Ergo Trainer next door at the last training camp. He was desperate to make it work and he was "Whatever it takes, whatever it takes." A very, very intense individual ... There are several people inside that head quite frankly. It is pretty nasty. Sport can do that. It is such an unreasonable thing to do that it is weird to witness people who desperately need it more than anyone else ... I think he thought that a gold medal in [the Olympics] would be the answer; that was going to make it all right and it didn't. So he has just wandered around for a few years wondering what to do.[40]

This is reminiscent of a story that novelist Kurt Vonnegut told when Joseph Heller, the author of *Catch-22*, died. Years before, the two writers had found themselves at a party hosted by a billionaire on Shelter Island, New York. Vonnegut remarked to Heller, 'Joe, how does it make you feel to know that our host only yesterday may have made more money than your novel *Catch-22* has earned in its entire history?' Heller told him, 'I've got something he can never have.' 'What on earth could that be, Joe?' 'The knowledge that I've got enough,' came the answer. Super Elite athletes are like the billionaire: seeking to fill the void of personal emptiness excavated during childhood with glittering treasures.[41] *Whatever it takes, whatever it takes.*

The second, much broader point to emerge from all this is the view that the toughness, the grit, that the Super Elite athletes displayed was not imbued or encouraged in them by others. It was not nurtured by carers or coaches. It came from within. It was a personal decision.

Outside the rarefied world of elite athletics, it's this second aspect of resilience that has come to achieve such prominence in the popular mind in recent years. The notion that one might have to give up personal happiness to achieve great things is an uncomfortable idea for some. But the belief that it's down to the individual to be strong, to pick themselves up when things go wrong and to use inner setback to create the strength that will propel them forward to success has become widely accepted. Not just that, but there's also a widely held conviction that what separates the successful from the unsuccessful is a lack of resilience or – as a previous generation might characterise it – a lack of backbone.

I was reminded of this when I met a senior business leader, whom I'll call Aisha, at a talk I gave for start-ups in East London. In her early forties, she had spent the two decades of her career mastering an understanding of leadership talent, and perfecting the art of moving around the human chess pieces at a top international clothing-retail business to ensure the best possible results. Gritty, determined and a high-flier, Aisha was famed for telling it like it was. She certainly had opinions on the views that I expressed, and came up after my presentation to say so.

In the course of our conversation it became apparent that her company had merged, rather chaotically, with a competitor a couple of years before.[42] She had been under no illusion things would be difficult, Aisha told me. The past few years hadn't been easy for the retail trade. She knew that a merger would inevitably result in job losses and political manoeuvrings and drama. What she hadn't expected was that the employees of Hotlooks (as I'll call the former competitor) would prove 'way less resilient' than those of her own company, Ztylish.

Intrigued, I tracked down Aisha some time later for a more extended chat and asked her to expand on her experience. I have to confess that I'm always a little sceptical when someone tells me that their workplace culture is 'special' or that 'our people are our best asset'. It makes me wonder how they managed to come up with a recruitment process that was clearly so much better than that of the competitors (spoiler: they didn't). That's not to say that I don't think company cultures can differ from one another, or that organisations attract different types of applicant or motivate their employees in a different way. It's evident, for example, that an advertised role for a trainee at a circus is likely to attract different applicants from those who might be thinking of applying for a traineeship at a steel mill. But unless the organisation in question has made specific decisions about identifying specific employee profiles, the outcome seems to be more down to self-selection than careful planning. Otherwise, it's like saying, 'Our people are our best asset, whoever they are.' For the purposes of our conversation, though, I suspended my doubts.

Aisha reiterated her view that Ztylish placed more value on resilience than Hotlooks did. I asked her to clarify for me what she meant by that term. 'Resilience is the capacity to re-energise yourself,' she said. 'We all cope with stuff, but it's that ability to re-up that energy that is critical.' I probed a little deeper, asking what made an organisation and its staff resilient. 'At its heart,' she replied, 'one of the things that gives people resilience is purpose. Ztylish had a wider sense of purpose beyond selling our clothing.' She acknowledged that there was nothing in Ztylish's recruitment process that differed substantially from that of its competitors, but she was adamant that there was a unique quality to the company's culture.

As we talked, Aisha also touched on a point that an increasing number of people have made in recent years. 'Look, I know it's not a cool thing to be heard saying, but fundamentally young people now just aren't as resilient as they used to be.' She suggested that this was the unfortunate outcome of well-meaning actions. 'Over the last decade,' she argued, 'we've valorised the idea that people's individual feelings matter – the effect has been that we've undermined their ability to handle knockbacks.' By way of example, she drew on a recent occurrence at the Tokyo Olympic Games. 'It's like what's happening with Simone Biles at the Olympics,' she said. 'Younger people just can't handle knockbacks and pressure like they used to.' At the time, of course, the poster child for resilience was in something of a downward spiral, having pulled out of first one, then two, and then all but one of her five events at the Games, citing mental-health issues.

Before we parted, I asked Aisha how the leadership team of Ztylish had sought – apparently successfully – to keep their sense of resilience alive. 'Some of it is about spending time together as a team, spending time being together,' she answered. 'Sometimes resilience is "space", the ability to put things in context. If you look at the ocean, it is hard to feel as overwhelmed by the day-to-day. We spent time to get that perspective. We went to a festival together, we got our families together. Space was vital to us, the ability to stand back and get perspective.' And how did Hotlooks differ? 'They had spent less time thinking about the human dynamics rather than the logistics. They thought that was a lot of nonsense and a waste of time. It affected our ability to integrate the teams.'

It's not difficult to detect a certain contradiction in Aisha's world-view. On the one hand, she was saying, organisations suffer because their staff lack the resilience to adapt and thrive in competitive environments, and because younger people are now so molly-coddled that they can't handle setbacks. On the other hand, achieving the culture of resilience that Aisha was so proud of at Ztylish appeared to be due not to individual displays of grit, but to a sense of togetherness, of shared goals. It seemed to me that she was mentally constructing an idea of resilience as a destination that her company collectively worked towards reaching, but was then being hijacked by a knee-jerk view that it was in fact an individual decision. Her paradoxical stance made me wonder, not for the first time, if resilience is everything it is cracked up to be.

Aisha defined resilience for me as 'the capacity to re-energise your-self'. Before I go further, it's perhaps worth exploring that notion and its development in a little more detail.

The concept of resilience originates in the natural world. It derives from ecological systems-thinking that focuses on how life withstands disruptions to habitat and how ecosystems absorb shocks and restore themselves to a state of equilibrium. It also exists as a concept in mathematics and physics, again referring to the ability of a system or material to return to a previous state after disturbance or displacement.[43] Both of these academic applications are consistent with the more popular uses of the term, which broadly refer to the ability (usually of humans) to bounce back from misfortune or adversity. The American Psychological Association, for example, defines the word as 'the process of adapting well in the face of adversity, trauma, tragedy, threats or even significant sources of threat'.[44]

As I have already noted, resilience as applied to humans has become something of a buzzword in recent years, but the basic phenomenon it describes is one that dates back to the beginning of our evolutionary history and is deep-rooted within us. Psychiatrist Professor Steven Southwick reminds us that 'Humans are remarkably resilient in the face of crises, traumas, disabilities, attachment losses, and ongoing adversities. In fact, resilience to stress and trauma may be the norm rather than the exception.[45] It's perhaps *because* humans tend by nature to be pretty resilient that their peers are unsympathetic when some who have been knocked down struggle to get to their feet again, or when others find it difficult to overcome obstacles in their way – even if these are obstacles that they themselves never had to negotiate. Martin Luther King, Jr rightly pointed out in 1964, when reviewing the issue of racial equality, 'It is obvious that if a man is entered at the starting line of a race three hundred years after another man, the first would have to perform some impossible feat in order to catch up with his fellow runner.[46]

At any rate, there's an implication in much of the conversation about resilience that the responsibility for achieving it lies at the door of the individual. Indeed, it's even possible to talk about a Resilience Orthodoxy on the subject. Its principal proponent and, arguably, initiator is the eminent psychologist Martin Seligman. Its cohorts include many of his research partners, notably his protégé Angela Duckworth, whose bestselling popular account, *Grit*, is a clarion call for the winning power of passion and perseverance over talent. And its allies number among their ranks Carol Dweck, who displays a similar philosophy to the Resilience Orthodoxy in her work on the Incremental Theory of Intelligence or, as it is more snappily known, Growth Mindset. Her view that individuals who believe in developing their talents (through hard work, determination, and so on) do better in life than those who see their talent as innate gifts similarly has a strong sense of individual resilience at its core.

Resilience Orthodoxy's influence now reaches everywhere. It is prevalent, for instance, in today's classrooms: a survey of British school teachers in 2021 revealed that they regarded resilience as the skill they most wanted to develop in their pupils.[47] And, as already mentioned, resilience has become a political football, evoked both positively as something to be emulated and negatively as a reproach to those – particularly younger people – who are deemed to lack it.

Perhaps the universal panacea-like nature of resilience is best encapsulated in a passage in Duckworth's TED Talk about 'Grit': 'My research team and I went to West Point Military Academy. We tried to predict which cadets would stay in military training and which would drop out. We went to the National Spelling Bee and tried to predict which children would advance farthest in competition. We studied rookie teachers working in really tough neighbourhoods, asking which teachers are still going to be here in teaching by the end of the school year, and of those, who will be the most effective at improving learning outcomes for their students? We partnered with private companies, asking, which of these salespeople is going to keep their jobs? And who's going to earn the most money? In all those very different contexts, one characteristic emerged as a significant predictor of success. And it wasn't social intelligence. It wasn't good looks, physical health, and it wasn't IQ. It was grit.[48]

It's not hard to see from this why the narrative of Resilience Orthodoxy should have become so compellingly attractive.

Before we get too swept away by it, however, it's worth delving into its underlying assumptions in some detail, because when it comes to the setbacks and trauma that are the yin to resilience's yang, things are not necessarily quite what they seem.

Chapter 2

What Doesn't Kill You (Almost Kills You)
The Toll of Trauma

15 July 1976: 4 p.m. on a scorchingly hot day in the small town of Chowchilla, Madera County, California. Bus driver Ed Ray, a barrel-chested man in his fifties, had picked up a group of twenty-six young kids from the Chowchilla fairgrounds pool and was taking them home. As he drove through the quiet, dusty roads of the town he came across a broken-down van, a white 1971 Dodge, that blocked the highway ahead of it. Ray pulled over to offer a hand, only to be confronted by three armed men, stockings pulled tight over their faces, who had leapt from the back of the seemingly stranded vehicle. They instructed Ray to open the bus doors and proceeded to board it.[1] Larry Park, then just six, recalled forty years later what happened next: 'The first man came on the bus. He had a gun. Ed Ray said, "What's going on?" He said, "Shut up and move to the back."'

As the younger children on the bus struggled to comprehend what was happening, their older peers tried to calm them by leading singalongs of playtime songs. Aware of just how conspicuous the bus was, the hostage-takers soon abandoned it by the side of the road, making a rudimentary attempt to camouflage it, before decanting their hostages into a couple of vans. Some eleven hours later they had reached Livermore, about 100 miles north-west of Chowchilla, where they marched the thirsty, motion-sick children to a hideaway in a disused quarry. Here, one by one, the young captives were forced to climb through a hatch in the roof of a removal lorry buried twelve feet beneath the rocks of the quarry and stow themselves in the body of the vehicle. The inside of the truck was unlit, sparsely furnished with a few dirty mattresses and stocked with a few sealed containers of food and drink. A handful of bags of bread lay strewn on the dirty floor. By now many of the children were sobbing.

As Ray and the children took stock of their new surroundings, the kidnappers closed the trapdoor in the roof and sealed it with a steel plate. They then weighed it down with two huge 100-pound tractor batteries and shovelled stones and earth on top. Ray later told reporters, 'There was a lot of crying and begging for mama. They kept hollering and saying, "Why did they do this to us."'[2] Michael Marshall, then a small child on board the bus, recalled years later how 'It would be silent, then somebody would burst out crying, and the whole group would just erupt.'

There were three men in the kidnapping gang: brothers James and Richard Schoenfeld and their friend Frederick Woods. Their plan was to demand $5 million (more than $25m today) for the children's safe return. However, when they tried to ring Chowchilla's police station that evening, the lines were so jammed with calls from parents and the media that they didn't manage to get through. In the meantime the roof of the truck had started to creak, and then to collapse, triggering another round of panic. 'I remember the children just screaming and crying,' Larry Park recalled. 'The sides of the van were bowing in. I knew that I was going to die.'

Eventually Ray and the oldest child on board managed to dig the group an escape tunnel, suffering cuts to their heads and hands in the process.[3] One child then crawled along it, reached the outside world and managed to find the quarry's night watchman. He in turn alerted the authorities. Under hypnosis, Ray was able to recall the registration number of the kidnappers' van. They were tracked down a few days later and arrested.

All the children were safely rescued. Physically, they were unharmed. But what long-term effect did the trauma of that event have on its young victims?

Psychiatrist Lenore Terr dedicated her professional life to answering questions such as this one. She knew that children as young as three, who might be unable to put a memory of a terrible event into words, nevertheless preserved memories of it in their play, often displayed fear and frequently had bad dreams: 'traumatic occurrences are first recorded as visualisations, or even, by the youngest infants, as feeling sensations,' she wrote. 'These perceptual registrations occur long before any remembrances can be recorded in words.[4] She also knew that short-term trauma can have a lasting effect. She now focused her attention on the children of Chowchilla.

It's perhaps unsurprising that many of the young victims of Chowchilla experienced panic attacks or nightmares about the kidnapping. But it was the lasting effects that were most striking and upsetting. Larry Park was still suffering fifteen years later. 'By the time I was twenty-one I was using meth, I was smoking crack,' he told a TV crew covering the anniversary of the crime. 'When you've got through something so traumatic, it's hard to be a normal kid again,' said Jennifer Hyde, another survivor. Even twenty-five years after the kidnapping the victims were reporting traumatic after-effects, often involving depression and substance abuse. The mental scars ran deep. There's some dark truth in the caustic remark of TV host Conan O'Brien: 'Nietzsche famously said, "Whatever doesn't kill you makes you stronger." But what he failed to stress is that it almost kills you.'[5]

Since the days of the Chowchilla kidnapping, considerable advances have been made in understanding both the nature of childhood trauma and the range of enduring impacts it can have on individuals. Arguably these have been most clearly articulated in the Adverse Childhood Experiences (ACE) methodology, masterminded by two practising clinicians, Centers for Disease Control epidemiologist Robert Anda and Vincent Felitti of the Kaiser Permanente Medical Care Program, who came together via a series of simultaneous but disconnected discoveries. Both men were curious to pinpoint what the impact of childhood experiences might have been on the adult patients they were seeing. Both found themselves identifying patterns they felt to be so apparent that they wondered why they had not been taught about them at medical school. Both men – one working with US veterans, the other running an obesity clinic – came independently to very similar conclusions before they encountered the other's work.

In the late seventies Robert Anda took up a practice working with veterans at a centre operated by the Veterans Health Administration (the single biggest provider of health services in the US) in Ashton, Wisconsin, a small town 150 miles north-west of Chicago. He was immediately struck by an incidence of particular types of ailments that seemed much higher than a general practitioner would expect to see on a day-to-day basis. In his examination of Second World War veterans he noted how 'I saw a lot of men dying from smoking-related illnesses, chronic lung disease, lung cancers, alcohol-related diseases and there was a lot of mental illness.'[6] Addiction and severe heart conditions were particularly prevalent. Anda later related the story of one patient called Ed who was virtually incapacitated by severe chronic obstructive pulmonary disease. 'For Ed to get up from his bed and go to the sink to brush his teeth was a near-death experience. It would take him five or ten minutes to recover.' Even so, he said, Ed would take his cigarettes and would wheel himself to the entrance of the hospital to regale his co-patients with war stories. He possessed an irrepressible energy to share the sagas of his time in service. He wanted to take his story to the world. Anda then went on to work as an epidemiologist at the US Centers for Disease Control (CDC) where, once again, he started to note clear correlations between early trauma and subsequent ill health – in this case, between depression that resulted from bad early experience and a subsequent smoking habit, which, since nicotine is a stimulant, appeared to be a harmful form of self-medicating designed to cope with depression and other deep-rooted maladies.

For his part, Dr Vincent Felitti was on his own journey of discovery, a journey that had begun in 1985 when he was working at a weight-loss clinic at Kaiser Permanente Hospital in San Diego – a 2,000-mile drive from Ashton. Here he felt a growing sense of pride in his clinic's initial success with the 1,500 patients it saw each year. But he also experienced a profound sense of frustration at the high subsequent dropout rate. His patient Donna was typical in this regard. A fifty-three-year-old with diabetes and a significant weight problem, she had lost more than 100 pounds when she had been at the clinic, but had then regained every last ounce over a six-month period beginning some eighteen months later. (In general terms, Felitti noticed that patients who gained weight did so abruptly and then remained stable for a while; if they lost weight, they regained all or most of it very quickly.)

Determined to find out why Donna, and so many others, should lapse in this way, he undertook surveys of prospective new admissions as though he were a social worker channelling his inner detective, intent on finding out the smallest details of a client's life. 'How much did you weigh at birth? How much did you weigh when you started school? How much did you weigh when you went to high school? How old were you when you became sexually active?'[7] And it was when running through these questions one day with one particular patient that Felitti made his breakthrough discovery. 'I misspoke,' he explains. 'Instead of asking, "How old were you when you were first sexually active", I asked, "How much did you weigh when you were first sexually active?" The patient, a woman, answered, "Forty pounds."' Baffled that the answer was so low – under three stone – Felitti repeated his 'incorrectly worded' question. The patient gave the same answer as before. Then she burst into tears. 'It was when I was four years old, with my father.'

A little while later, Patty, a woman weighing 408 pounds (more than twenty-nine stone or 185 kilograms) stepped in off the street and asked if Felitti and his colleagues could help her with her weight issues. 'Our first mistake was accepting her diagnosis of what the problem was,' he remarked in the course of a lecture where he discussed her case. Felitti had helped implement a programme – Supplemented Absolute Fasting – that could reliably (and safely) cut the weight of extremely obese patients by 300 pounds in one year.

Sure enough, within fifty-one weeks he had taken the cold caller from the street down to 132 pounds (just under nine and a half stone or sixty kilograms). He was thrilled.

But then, as with the patient to whom Felitti had misspoken, her weight went back on. 'She stayed [visiting the clinic] for several weeks and then did something I had not previously conceived to be physiologically possible – she regained thirty-seven pounds in three weeks.' He took the patient aside. 'I remember asking her "what's going on?" and she said "I think I'm sleep-eating."' She described how she would go to bed, leaving her kitchen neat and tidy, but 'When I wake up in the morning pots and dishes are dirty. Boxes and cans are open. Somebody's obviously been cooking and eating there. And I'm the only person [living there].'[8]

Patty revealed that she had sleepwalked as a child. But that still left the question 'Why now?' At first she resisted Felitti's attempts to dig for answers. Eventually, though, she mentioned a triggering moment. 'She finally acknowledged that it began the day someone at her job had spoken to her. Working as a nurse in a convalescent home, one of the patients, an older, married man, had complemented her on her weight loss. Now a few weeks on, he was sexually propositioning her every time he saw her, "Hey, you look pretty good! You lost all that weight, Patty, how about you and me *making it?*"'

'And that was the day the sleep-eating began,' she explained to Felitti. Clearly the proposition had been both inappropriate and deeply upsetting. Even so, Felitti couldn't help wondering why her response had been so extreme. It didn't take him long to uncover the truth. Patty revealed that she had suffered sexual abuse at the hands of her grandfather, which began when she was just ten years old.

Felitti had been fully aware that childhood sexual abuse took place. He had, however, always assumed that it was incredibly rare. Now he wasn't so sure.[9] He started to approach the issue more forensically. Soon he came to realise that, for a large number of his patients, obesity and sexual abuse were closely linked. For some, it was an adult experience: one rape victim who had gained more than 100 pounds in the year after her attack sorrowfully told him: 'overweight is overlooked, and that's the way it's got to be'. For 55 per cent of his patients the trauma stemmed back to childhood sexual abuse.

Felitti started to share his findings with the medical world, only to find that his colleagues were largely unconvinced.[10] The more cynical even suggested that allegations of childhood trauma were merely smokescreens for adult disappointment. 'You really need to understand, Dr Felitti,' barracked one fellow clinician at a national obesity meeting in Atlanta in 1990, 'that people who are more fluent in these matters recognise that these statements by patients are largely fabrications to provide a cover explanation for failed lives.'

Fortunately at dinner that night Felitti found himself seated next to someone from the CDC, who was rather more sympathetic to his thesis, pointing out to him, though, that if he was to be taken seriously he needed to collect much more evidence. Felitti had 286 cases on file; he would need thousands. Taking their advice, he embarked on a project to marshal more data. And it was while he was doing so that he first encountered Robert Anda – at a sparsely attended seminar ('I think about eight people showed up') hosted by the CDC, where Felitti presented the main thrust of what he'd discovered so far: 'I'd been practising internal medicine for twenty-five years and I'd never heard anyone tell me that they'd been sexually abused [but once I started asking patients about it] I heard it four times in a week.'[11]

For the next two years the pair reviewed the available literature, but realised that while existing medical texts did include some investigations of sexual abuse and violence in childhood, few looked at their long-term consequences. The two men therefore set about creating – virtually from scratch – what became the Adverse Childhood Experiences (ACE) test. Essentially it considered ten categories of childhood experience and, by allocating a score to each one, sought to come up with an aggregate ACE figure. The overall figure was a count for experiences in each category, not for each episode – so ten episodes of physical abuse on its own would only elicit an ACE score of one. The categories were as follows:

- Emotional abuse (Felitti clarifies this as 'substantial recurrent humiliation')
- Physical abuse
- Sexual abuse (as a rule, contact-based abuse, rather than, say, flashing)
- Emotional neglect
- Physical neglect
- Parents divorced or separated (the most common category, which was of huge relevance for 'child-onset obesity')
- Witnessed domestic violence
- Substance abuse in the household
- Mental illness in the household
- A family member in prison.

The questions that were asked were framed in the following terms: *Prior to your eighteenth birthday:*

- Did a parent or adult in your home ever swear at you, insult you or put you down?
- Did a parent or adult in your home ever hit, beat, kick or physically hurt you in any way?
- Did you experience unwanted sexual contact (such as fondling or oral/anal/vaginal intercourse/penetration)?
- Did you feel that no one in your family loved you or thought you were special?
- Did you feel that you didn't have enough to eat, had to wear dirty clothes or had no one to protect or take care of you?
- Did you lose a parent through divorce, abandonment, death or other reason?
- Did your parents or adults in your home ever hit, punch, beat or threaten to harm each other?

- Did you live with anyone who had a problem with drinking or using drugs, including prescription drugs?
- Did you live with anyone who was depressed, mentally ill or attempted suicide?
- Did you live with anyone who went to jail or prison?[12]

An answer in the affirmative to any of these questions would yield a score of one. The aggregate, out of ten, would become that respondent's ACE score. (One benefit of this approach was that it allowed people to declare a score to a doctor without having to go into intimate and distressing detail.)

With the framework in place, the two medics began their research in earnest, and between 1995 and 1997 were able to get 17,421 patients at Felitti's hospital, the Kaiser Permanente in San Diego, to complete the survey. The sample, admittedly, was not exactly representative of the population as a whole: the hospital's catchment area comprised largely white middle-class adults, 70 per cent of whom had been to college. But however relatively privileged they may have been, a significant proportion of patients – 67 per cent in fact – reported at least one adverse childhood experience. One in eight participants had an ACE score of more than four; 15 per cent of the sample reported having been emotionally abused, 20 per cent sexually abused and 28 per cent physically abused (of course in many cases these were the same people).[13] And what was so striking was that the higher the ACE score an individual was given, the worse their adult health. Someone with an ACE score of four or more, for example, was twice as likely to develop heart disease or cancer versus the population average. They were also three and a half times more likely to develop severe lung disease (chronic obstructive pulmonary disease).

Correlation, of course, is not the same as causation, and there were many who were sceptical about Felitti and Anda's findings. As Anda explains, 'There was a sense of disbelief, people actually said "Rob, this can't be true, if this were true somebody would have already known about it and it would have been studied and published, so there must have been something wrong with the way that you did the study." So we had to go back and check the way it was done – of course it was all correct.'[14] Those who were less sceptical, meanwhile, went to work to build on the pair's work, seeking to explore further relationships between the ACE score and life outcomes. Some found, for example, that there was a link between elevated ACE scores and poor academic performance, reflecting both increased hostility to schooling, arising from the individual's desire to assert what is technically known as a 'locus of control', and lower IQ levels (eight points lower, on average, than the mean). For her part, Dr Nadine Burke Harris, a clinician who now holds the role of Surgeon General of California, found that children with ACEs of four or more were thirty-three times more likely to have been diagnosed with learning and behavioural problems. Holding things together, these researchers found, takes a toll.

It might be objected that although the ten factors categorised in that initial ACE list all score the same, they are not of equal weight. Being sworn at, for example, is surely far less serious than being physically assaulted. The point, though, is that so many of the factors that go to form an overall ACE number involve humiliation – a condition that has been described as 'the nuclear bomb of the emotions'.[15] Criminal-violence expert Professor James Gilligan, who has spent decades studying the mental health of those in prisons and prison hospitals, has written of how 'one after another of the most violent men I have worked with over the years have described to me how they had been humiliated repeatedly throughout their childhoods', arguing that humiliation involves an 'annihilation of the self' that directly carries through to criminality.[16]

The ACE scoring methodology, therefore, has remained largely unchanged over the years since the system was first devised. What some practitioners have changed is the list itself. It was recognised, for example, that while growing up without one parent could potentially have a negative impact, being abandoned by one's mother was especially traumatic, and some argued that allowance had to be made for that. Researchers such as Nadine Burke Harris have therefore drawn on evidence from their own medical practices to expand the recognised risk factors for Toxic Stress (sometimes known as Toxic Childhood Stress). Harris herself (then at San Francisco's Center for Youth Wellness) added the following categories for children:

- Community violence
- Homelessness
- Discrimination
- Foster care
- Bullying
- Repeated medical procedures or life-threatening illness
- Death of caregiver
- Loss of caregiver through deportation or migration.

For teenagers, two additional categories were included:

- Verbal or physical abuse from a romantic partner
- Youth incarceration.[17]

By 2022 such organisations as the US National Scientific Council on the Developing Child had adopted expanded ACEs that included community, poverty and race-based factors. Of course no list that seeks to capture human experience can ever be exhaustive. ACE's value lies in its attempt to provide a checklist of some of the key traumas that occur in people's lives.

But however much the list of factors may have changed over the years, and whatever gaps there still might be, Felitti and Anda's initial finding has held and is constantly being reconfirmed. Essentially, a high ACE score and poor adult health are closely related. A high ACE score may have psychological consequences: depression, alcohol abuse, increased drug-taking, smoking, teenage pregnancy and even suicide. (Alec Roy, a psychiatrist working at the US Department for Veterans Affairs, notes that 'suicide attempters reported significantly more childhood trauma than non-attempters' and that

'Patients who had made three or more attempts had significantly higher childhood trauma scores than patients who had made two attempts, who had higher scores than patients who had made one attempt, who had higher scores than patients who had never attempted.')[18] And it is associated with physical illnesses that range from heart disease, stroke, cancer and lung disease, to diabetes and Alzheimer's.[19] Often it crosses these health categories. There's a clear link, for example, between addiction and suicide (up to 40 per cent of cocaine-dependent patients have attempted suicide at some time).

The figures are stark and shocking. A child with an ACE score of four or more is thirty-three times more likely to have behavioural problems in school than one with a lower or neutral score, and they are also three times as likely to be taking medication for ADHD.[20] When it comes to adult behaviour issues, according to Anda, 'For things like alcoholism we estimate that almost two-thirds of alcoholism has its origins in Adverse Childhood Experiences. About 80 per cent of shooting up drugs, half of depression, half of domestic violence, almost two-thirds of sexual assaults appear to have their origins and are the neurobiological consequences of adverse childhood experiences.'[21] (Gabor Maté, the Canadian-Hungarian former physician who has become well known for his campaigning work linking illness and addiction, says, 'in the life of every person who's ever been addicted, and ever will be addicted, there's always trauma' – something policymakers would do well to bear in mind.[22])

As for physical ailments, a person with an ACE score of four out of ten is twice as likely to develop heart disease in their lifetime, while someone with a score of seven or more has three times the chances of contracting lung cancer, and three and a half times the chance of suffering from heart disease.[23] Overall, in fact, research shows that life expectancy for individuals with ACE scores of six or more is twenty years lower than it is for people with no ACEs.[24] Here again, complex interweaving factors are in play. High ACE levels link with low life expectancy and with poverty; and poverty links in its own right with low life expectancy (in the US, children who live below the Federal Poverty Line are five times more likely to have an ACE score of four or higher than those who live above it).

Part of the reason for continued wariness on the part of the medical community is a sense that claims for the link between childhood trauma and subsequent mental and physical suffering may be – and, on occasion, have been – exaggerated. Gabor Maté believes that conditions such as addiction can always be traced back to trauma. Sceptics point out that such conditions can occur among people who have no memory of trauma, and who indeed may not actually have experienced it. The true picture, though, may well be rather more complicated. Bessel van der Kolk, whose book *The Body Keeps the Score* has become an international bestseller, argues that victims may indeed not recall episodes of their own trauma even when it can be demonstrated to have occurred. Critically, he goes on, their body records the toll nevertheless. He suggests that therapists may be able to deduce a history of suffering from flashbacks, sudden intense feelings, avoidant behaviours and dreams.[25] Furthermore, he claims, while particular incidents in a person's life may not always be sufficiently traumatic to be remembered individually, they can achieve an aggregate force that has an invisible impact on a victim.

In this context it's worth considering a study by Dr Mark Seery, an associate professor from the University of Buffalo, and his colleagues, which considered the psychological aftermath of the terrorist attacks of 9/11. The study concluded that the trauma induced by the event was indeed often the underlying cause of subsequent ill health, but that often later, more trivial events were the trigger for the physical or mental problem that then manifested itself. In other words, there is not always a straight line between cause and effect. Nor, of course, is all stress experienced equally. As a rule of thumb, however, it does appear to be the case that people who have, overall, experienced high levels of stress in their lives are more likely to find it more difficult to cope with subsequent stressful events than those whose lives have largely achieved some degree of happy equilibrium.

The path from trauma and stress to mental and physical illness is a multi-stranded one – a complex mix of social, psychological and physiological factors. At the social level, experts argue, trauma severs the sense of connectivity that is so vital to humans (the British psychiatrist John Bowlby postulated his Attachment Theory to describe this). We synchronise with those around us virtually from birth. Tiny babies mirror the smiles or tongue-poking of their carers. Older children share the explosive joy of collective laughter with those around them. But, as Bessel van der Kolk explains, when children experience trauma, 'Shame becomes the dominant emotion and hiding truth a central preoccupation.'[26] Stressed children may well come to feel estranged from those around them, fearing that if the truth of their suffering emerges they will be rejected by those who love them. The poet David Whyte says the power of friendship is to be understood by another: it is the 'privilege of having been seen by someone and the equal privilege of having been granted the sight of the essence of another'. Trauma closes us off from the experience of being seen or understood.[27] It causes us to build mental walls between ourselves and others. In other words, it unsynchronises us from the world around us.

The dominant experience of trauma is shame. When we experience a memory that could change our relationship with our family, our friends or the community around us our mind goes into battle with it. We tell ourselves it was our fault, or we submerge it in shame, telling ourselves it was down to our actions. The evidence suggests that for all of the mental manoeuvres our mind makes to deal with the trauma, our body is fully exposed to the harm of these traumas. This very much chimes with Freud's view that the human mind possesses a 'repetition compulsion' that traps victims in a recursive loop, constantly replaying their trauma in an attempt to overcome it, but, in the process, becoming estranged or unsynchronised from their tribe.

Such disconnection can have serious psychological repercussions. It is argued, for example, that the reason why Black people in Britain of African descent are six times more likely – and Black people of Caribbean descent nine times more likely – to develop schizophrenia than their white neighbours is that they suffer estrangement at a racial level. The aggression and hostility they encounter have a toxic effect.[28] Gabor Maté suggests that in the US there is evidence that such alienation has a physical manifestation. 'Black Americans are more likely to get prostate cancer and more likely to die of it and not because of lack of medical care,' he argues. 'Maybe there's something about being a minority in this particular culture that is so highly stressful that it deranges the immune system.'[29]

Critics of Maté and van der Kolk argue that their findings are based on insufficiently large samples, or that they oversimplify neuroscience to support their claims.[30] It's certainly the case that because many professionals are uncomfortable about asking patients to reveal possible sexual abuse in their past (even those comfortable with, and trained in, using the ACE questionnaire have only managed to screen around 40 per cent of their patients in a year), the evidence base is at best partial.[31] But the notion that certain conditions are not necessarily inherent in particular individuals, but are formed by external factors, is becoming increasingly accepted.

One researcher to espouse this view is Professor Richard Bentall, professor of clinical psychology at the University of Sheffield, who also has personal experience of the damaging effects of trauma and stress. 'One of the most important things which happened to me in my childhood,' he told BBC Radio, 'was something that in fact turned out not to be very pleasant, which was being sent away to boarding school when I was about fourteen years of age. I think my parents sent me to boarding school with the best of intentions. They were hoping it would be a gateway into what we might call the elite. But I found when I got there I didn't fit in at all. It was a single-sex school and the boys tended to come from a much richer background to me. I'm slightly ashamed to say I was always embarrassed when my dad turned up to collect me at the end of term in his beaten-up old Ford, which would lead to ridicule from the kids, and I kind of spent my adolescence not really having very many friends.'

Bentall reflected that his own childhood was characterised by 'some level of sub-clinical depression', which resulted in poor academic results. The experience of his older brother, however, was much worse. 'The story of my brother is the most distressing thing in my life. He went to the same school I did. He fitted in even worse than I did.' As he grappled to cope, 'He stole from the other boys as a sign of distress. He was caught. He was expelled.' After that his life went into a downward spiral. 'He got involved in drugs and his life disintegrated. He ended up without any qualifications, living at the top of a desolate tower block in Sheffield. Big council project. He chose to jump off the fourteenth floor of it.'[32]

Bentall himself was initially sceptical about the relationship that others claimed existed between childhood trauma and psychosis. But a friend operating in the field changed his mind. 'I was amazed, I started to go through the literature as it then was. It was very far from mainstream. Most people weren't interested in it, but where people had looked at it, it looked like early life experience had had a big effect. It was a shock to me. Even though I'd been practising CBT [Cognitive Behavioural Therapy], I often didn't talk to people about their early lives, it was all about how they were thinking in their current lives. I started to ask patients.'

He went on to describe the scepticism of his peers. 'The mainstream view was that psychotic disorders were largely the result of genetic determinants, and some people felt that the evidence for genetic determinants was so strong it excluded any possibility of childhood traumas playing a role.'[33] Bentall, however, was sure there was more to it than that. 'We looked at child sexual abuse, physical abuse, bullying by peers at school, death of a parent at an early age. We found a very clear picture. We looked at three different types of studies, epidemiological studies where large numbers of people had been questioned about psychiatric symptoms more or less at random; we looked at patient studies where patients had been compared to healthy people; and we also looked at a small number of prospective studies where children who had been known to have had traumatic experiences were followed up later in life. And what was striking was that the results were the same when you looked at each of these three studies.' Echoing the findings of Anda and Felitti, Bentall discovered that 'A child who experiences a significant traumatic event before the age of sixteen has a three-times increased risk of psychosis in adulthood … The other thing we found,' he says, 'was a dose-response relationship. The more severe the trauma, the greater the risk of psychosis.' Bentall's own experience with his brother emphasised the truth of this; indeed, his mother had said that he claimed to hear voices.[34]

Bentall's reference to a dose-response relationship suggests that trauma brings about a chemical change in our brains. Robert Anda explains the process in these terms: 'When we're stressed we have adrenaline and cortisol released from our adrenal glands. The cortisol that's released from our adrenal glands is toxic to developing neural networks. It makes it difficult for the nerves to make connections.' Since the brain develops sequentially, developmental abnormalities proceed to mount on top of each other.[35] Neural paths become disrupted and develop poorly. Children affected in this way may find regulating their emotions and calming themselves during stressful episodes difficult. Their emotional thermostat has, as it were, been set incorrectly. Trauma effectively puts them in a hyper-vigilant state. In technical terms, this is described as chronic dysregulation of the stress-response system, which in turn leads to an inhibition of the prefrontal cortex, and overstimulation of the amygdala. In lay person's terms, it's Toxic Stress.[36]

Such Toxic Stress brought about by abuse in childhood triggers internalising symptoms (intrusive negative thoughts), increasing the likelihood of anxiety disorders threefold, and depression 2.6-fold. It also triggers externalising symptoms, such as a propensity to lash out. One study in 2021 found that ACE accounted for a substantial variance in the tendency of individual adults to become angry (between 14 and 50 per cent of various measures of anger were attributed to an individual's childhood experiences).[37] This is not unique to humans. Scientists have observed, for example, that bees exposed to high-aggression environments when they are immature develop to be more aggressive than 'normal' bees. If their nest comes under threat – perhaps from a dog or bear disturbing them – then alerted watcher-bees will release high levels of pheromones to trigger a response. Bees that develop in a more stressful environment where these flashpoints occur frequently can end up unable to turn the thermostat of aggression down, even when those perilous threats disappear.[38]

Trauma and stress have a compounding effect. If the body activates the stress response too frequently (especially in the formative years of life), it loses the ability to adequately regulate a response in normal times. For children, who are especially sensitive to repeated stress activations, this has implications for the body's hormonal activations and for the immune system. So far as brain development is concerned, the effects are actually visible, as Dr Victor Carrión at Stanford University, who has studied the impact of trauma on the well-being of young people, has discovered. He scanned the brains of thirty young people who had all been exposed to trauma and were displaying post-traumatic symptoms and compared them to those of a control group.[39] Those with higher stress levels, he discovered, had a smaller hippocampus – the area of the brain associated with learning and memory – and this remained the case eighteen months later, even if the causes of stress had been removed.[40] The brains of traumatised children, in other words, don't look like the brains of non-traumatised ones.[41] In addition to scanning the children's brains, Dr Carrión also took saliva samples four times a day. He found that the more stress symptoms a child displayed, the higher the levels of cortisol in their saliva.

Trauma can also lead to a condition known as alexithymia – an inability to experience or express emotions in a 'normal' way or to assess how one is experiencing those emotions. Someone suffering from alexithymia can find relationships confusing and frustrating. They may therefore behave in the destructive manner that is typical of many with a high ACE score. They may also pursue high-adrenaline activities – such as dangerous sports – in an attempt to move from the experience of such non-specific negative emotions as anxiety to the specific intense emotions of excitement and fear.

Philippe Petit, a daredevil whose death-defying tightrope walks were turned into the award-winning documentary film *Man on Wire*, offers a fascinating case study in this regard. The Frenchman achieved global fame when, one August morning in 1974, he and his accomplices emerged from their hiding places at the top of New York's Twin Towers to install a steel cable 400 metres above the Manhattan pavement, which Petit proceeded to cross eight times. For most of us, this may sound like an act of sheer lunacy, but Petit was not only successful, he was unstressed ('No, no, I'm never nervous,' he later told *The Guardian*).[42] He has been open about his difficult early life. His parents were not 'really an existent entity' in his life, he recounts, and he was expelled from five schools. 'There is a child inside me,' he says, 'that wants to come out and do something to surprise all the adults.'[43] It's hard not to view his life and achievements from the vantage point of alexithymia. To that extent, his outlook chimes with that of obsessive base-jumper and free-climber Dean Potter, who fell to his death in 2015 while performing a wingsuit-jump in Yosemite Park. A few years previously he had told a TV interviewer: 'I want emotions rushing through me that normally aren't there in everyday life … the feeling totally overwhelms me … I wish I could find that without risking my life but right now it's the only way I know how to find it.'[44]

Childhood trauma can also manifest itself in a desire for control – a quality that is perhaps at the root of what makes our Super Elite athletes' sense of drive so extraordinary. Professor Kyle Ganson, a psychologist from the University of Toronto, explained to me the processes involved in these terms: 'People who experience trauma may feel some degradation of their identity and so seek out things like athletics. They set their mindset on "This is something I can control", "I can work really hard and push myself to an elite level." Let's say it's like a sexual assault or a physical assault,' he goes on; 'it's that *fight, flight or freeze* mode you kind of go into. You don't really have a lot of control in those moments and your survival brain kicks in. However, your response system and your brain tell you to respond – reacting to a total lack of control – just as a mechanism to try and survive. There's probably an aspect of it where people are trying to find ways to regain some of that control and likely overcompensate.'

Not only is success for the Super Elite athletes a form of control, but so are the strategies to get them there. As Ganson explains: 'You can just decide how many hours a day you work out or train, or how you eat, how much you sleep to make sure you're taking care of your body – a lot of control. Which then, of course, would potentially move people up the ladder of athletic performance and abilities. I think that can be a huge aspect of identity formation.'[45] Clinical psychologist Catherine Haslam and her co-authors frame it slightly differently: 'When trauma has an adverse psychological impact, this is because it fundamentally compromises a person's social sense of self and their relationship to the world at large ... trauma has the capacity to fundamentally undermine an individual's sense of self in ways that have profound consequences for their psychological and social functioning.'[46] In response to being unsynchronised by trauma, we seek, if possible, to forge a new identity that we can control.

If the psychological impact of stress is clearly apparent, so too do the physiological effects appear to be.[47] We understand that for life to be sustained, it is essential that various physiological variables – body temperature, blood composition and energy levels – are kept in a state of equilibrium, a delicate balance known as homeostasis (the process that the body goes through to maintain homeostasis is called allostasis). If chronic stress persists, it can cause sustained increases in inflammation levels, which in turn link to reduced immunity to infection. Researchers observe that increased allostatic loads and inflammation create bodily 'wear and tear', making people more susceptible to maladies that range from cardiovascular disease to cognitive decline. And they claim that our DNA can also sustain damage to the point where our bodies become aged. The process here involves damage to the telomeres, microscopic biological structures that sit at the end of each strand of DNA and look something like the cap at the end of a shoelace. Telomeres serve to protect our cells and help to determine how cells age. When they become shortened by wear and tear, they reduce a cell's ability to replicate itself healthily – a deterioration that has been associated with premature ageing and cancer.

Incidentally, it's not just childhood trauma that brings about these changes in our bodies. A 2019 survey on the impact of long hours and overwork on a group of junior doctors who were slaving through the most intense year of their apprenticeship, clocking up an average of 64.5 hours of work a week (in some cases they were working for more than eighty hours), revealed that the toll on their bodies was considerable. Researchers observed that the doctors' telomeres shrank in comparison to a cohort of students who were themselves enduring a stressful year of undergraduate study. In aggregate, one year of intense work was seen to age the trainee doctors' bodies by six years.[48] If you've ever watched a friend with an unrelenting job become older before your eyes, there is a physiological reason for this: stress really is ageing their body on fast-forward.

Such bodily transformations are not only observable in humans. The pioneering psychologist Hans Selye found that they occur in rats, too. Those submitted to high levels of stress, he discovered, had enlarged adrenal glands, shrunken lymph nodes and ulcerated intestines. Their bodies kept the score of their stress.[49] Selye, incidentally, was the man who 'stumbled upon the term stress, which had long been used in common English, and particularly in engineering, to denote the effects of a force acting against a resistance'.[50] He argued that excess stress occurs when the demands on an individual exceed that individual's reasonable capacity to fulfil them – that stress is our body's response when we feel out of control. These days, we tend to use the word 'stress' casually when we may only be feeling mildly annoyed or under pressure. True stress – Toxic Stress – is when people experience 'prolonged activation of stress response systems'.

Studies of animals have also revealed the impact that stress can have holistically on maturation and development. Dr Tyrone Hayes's experiments with toads are a case in point. His initial hypothesis was that inducing stress in tadpoles might cause them to mature more quickly, so that they could escape the watery environment that played host to their suffering. He therefore exposed them to corticosterone (a stress hormone whose human equivalent is cortisol). What he found was that such exposure late in the tadpoles' development did indeed speed up their development. However, early exposure had the opposite effect. It inhibited their growth. It also reduced their immune response and lung function, impaired their neurological development and raised their blood pressure.[51] It had a 'maladaptive' effect, causing irreversible consequences to build on top of one another, knocking out the hormones in the thyroid, stopping the development process. Dr Nadine Burke Harris noted a similar phenomenon in a child she once treated at her San Francisco surgery. Toxic Stress had stunted his growth to such an extent that at the age of seven he was the height of a four-year-old. Fortunately she was able to reverse some of the harm.[52]

For Gabor Maté, all forms of repressed stress can lead to a breakdown in the immune system, whether that breakdown manifests itself as dementia, Alzheimer's, addiction, ADHD, cancer, asthma, arthritis, motor-neurone disease or a host of other illnesses.[53] And the reason, he says, is a simple one. 'If you go to a dermatologist with inflamed skin, what kind of medicine are they going to give you? ... Steroid cream. If you go to a rheumatologist with an inflamed joint, what medication are they going to give you? Steroids. If you go to a lung specialist with asthma, what kind of inhaler are you going to get? Steroids. If you go to a gastroenterologist with inflamed intestines, what kind of medication are you going to get? Steroids. Now, what are steroids? They're copies of cortisol. What is cortisol? The stress hormone. We're treating everything with stress hormones. Maybe it should occur to us that stress has something to do with the onset of these conditions.'[54]

In support of this contention he cites a survey of 1,700 women that was carried out over a ten-year period: 'women who were unhappily married and didn't express their emotions,' he writes, 'were four times as likely to die as those women who were unhappily married [but] did express their feelings. In other words, the non-expression of emotion (and the repressed stress that is endured) was associated with a 400 per cent increase in the death rate'.[55] He has described these links between mind and body as the Bermuda Triangle for research – a Bermuda Triangle that, he fears, the medical establishment is unwilling to navigate.

Some of Maté's views have been contested, but his basic precept that aggravated emotions have an impact on our physical well-being is a well-established one. The notion, for example, that there is a link between cancer survival and personality type goes back a century. In 1926 a trainee clinician, Elida Evans, recognising that the 'medical profession has been rather reluctant to search for other than physical causes', published *A Psychological Study of Cancer* in which she used a Jungian categorisation of personality types to appraise 100 cancer sufferers whom she had treated at her practice.[56] Her conclusion was that cancer patients tended to avoid expressing negative emotions and instead exhibited 'gentleness and mildness, the lack of self-assertion'.

Half a century later Lydia Temoshok noted a marked difference in personality between those patients she had encountered with heart problems and those suffering from melanoma. Cardiovascular disease was principally found in competitive, tense, anxious individuals who were self-centred (Type A personalities). Cancer occurred most among cooperative, appeasing, self-sacrificing people who were free of negative feelings (Type C personalities).[57] Temoshok concluded that people who were cancer-prone had adopted a lifelong coping style that allowed for only occasional expressions of emotion, that their desire to control their emotions led to their inner needs being repressed, and that this repression ultimately created an unconscious suffering, a 'sort of quiet desperation – a form of hopelessness – [which] has been shown to damage the immune system'. It wasn't a cause of cancer, as such, but was a risk-factor that 'can cause a generalised deficiency in the cancer defence system'.

If this sounds a little vague and unspecific, it's worth noting the predictive powers of researchers in Germany who interviewed fifty-six women undergoing routine breast biopsies. Having assessed their personality types, they were able to predict a correct breast-cancer diagnosis in as many as 94 per cent of the cases involving patients with a positive diagnosis. What categorised these women was the lower level of fear they expressed, as compared with those who received a benign diagnosis.[58] Admittedly, the sample size here was small. But a meta-analysis in 1999, bundling together forty-six different studies representing many thousands of patients, produced very similar results. The authors of another study of cancer patients around that time wrote that they 'were surprised to find a virtual absence of anger in these patients [with a positive diagnosis]', while a further study reported on the associated increases in risk factors linked to 'separation/loss experiences' and 'stressful life events'.[59] Repressing emotion can literally make you ill.

Here, then, is a conundrum. On the one hand, we have experts effectively telling us that the more adversity we can overcome, the more successful we will be. On the other hand, we have other experts telling us that adversity can be debilitating in the short term and can harm our mental and physical health in the long term. Surely both can't be right. Or is there a Goldilocks area between the two extremes, a zone where not too much or too little adversity propels us to excel?

This is the question that Mark Seery, alongside Alison Holman and Roxane Cohen Silver from the University of California, set out to answer. Over the course of three years they surveyed several

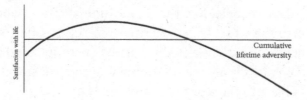

Figure 1: Lifetime adversity vs satisfaction with life. People at either extreme – those who have experienced no adversity and those who have experienced considerable adversity – report the lowest levels of satisfaction with their lives.

thousand people to ascertain what impact varying quantities of adversity had on their lives.[60] And what they discovered was, indeed, a sort of Goldilocks zone.

'People with *low* lifetime adversity reported *better* outcomes over time than did people who had experienced *no* adversity,' they concluded; while '*high* lifetime adversity predicted *worse* outcomes over time than did *low* adversity'. Seery suggested that there is something of an 'inverted U-shape' (perhaps, in fact, more an inverted J-curve) relationship between adversity and life satisfaction: 'More lifetime adversity was associated with higher global distress, functional impairment, and PTS symptoms, as well as lower life satisfaction.' Critically, though, the U-shape was not symmetrical: 'outcomes at the high end of adversity appear more negative than those at zero adversity.'[61] Seery says that those who had experienced a moderate degree of adversity in their past had much higher levels of emotional functioning – and life satisfaction – compared to people with very low levels, or levels that exceeded moderate amounts of adversity. Of course the challenge here is how to experience the upside of modest challenges without being scarred by ones that threaten to damage us.

The relationship between resilience and adversity, then, is a complicated one. It seems that the occasional knockback may help to strengthen us. But you don't have to move the dial that much before you experience the immense psychological and physical damage that adversity can cause. That still leaves us, though, with the outliers – those people, like the Super Elite athletes, who are able to transform the worst of experiences into the greatest of personal achievements. What enables them to be such outstanding exceptions to the rule? Or are we not being told the full story?

Let's go back to the story of Simone Biles.

Chapter 3

Her 'only competition is herself'
Seeking Resilience

If there was one thing that was certain about the Tokyo Olympics, it was that Simone Biles would return home with a clutch of medals to add to her existing treasure trove. Americans assumed a coronation for the tiny Texan, a curtain opener for a subsequent triumphant Golds Over America tour that would take the form of a thirty-five-night spectacular. Biles had returned from Rio with four golds and a bronze medal. It was thought she could produce an even better haul in Tokyo.[1]

The media were expectant. 'Biles could be the surest thing there is to a gold medal lock in years,' read one report.[2] You'd have to go back eight years to find an occasion when she had entered an all-round competition and not won gold. 'Unbeatable Simone Biles's only competition at the Olympics is herself,' read another headline. That headline turned out to be prescient in ways that no one had expected.

There were a few issues beforehand and in the early days of Tokyo, but, as an actor would put it, these seemed to be a case of 'bad rehearsal, good performance'. In pre-Games trials, Biles had sometimes had to take a few steadying steps on landing. During the qualifying round at Tokyo she had stumbled, stuttering out of bounds on the mat on a floor routine and serving up messy landings on the beam and the vault. But confidence was high as her first final – the team competition – loomed. The US hadn't lost at an international team meeting in more than a decade and, thanks to Biles, had been winning competitions by whole points in a sport normally decided by tenths. Earlier in the year the high-performance director of US sport, Tom Forster, had made what most considered to be a watertight prediction: 'I don't think it's going to come down to tenths of a point in Tokyo.'[3] In any case, Biles had recently achieved the impossible. She had been the first woman ever to perform a routine known as the Yurchenko double pike in competition.

Most gymnasts jump towards the vault arms-out and facing forwards. The Yurchenko refinement – named after the first female gymnast to achieve it – is to add an extra tumble, a round-off onto the springboard so that the gymnast gets the springy boost of the board on their feet, not their hands. Biles added an ambitious extra flourish: using the springboard to propel this back-handspring onto the vault, she then completed two pike back-flips (body folded, legs extended straight) before landing on her feet. The International Gymnastics Federation reacted cautiously, awarding Biles a modest score-card advantage – a move widely interpreted to discourage less gifted competitors from undertaking such a risky endeavour. But Biles knew the extent of her accomplishment, tweeting an ecstatic 'I'm sorry but I can't believe I completed a double pike on the vault'. As she had said two years before: 'I feel like you should never settle just because you are winning or you are at the top. You should always push yourself.'[4]

Four days into the Tokyo Games and Biles was preparing for the final of the women's team competition. She had posted on social media that she felt 'the weight of the world' on her shoulders, adding, 'I know I brush it off and make it seem like pressure doesn't affect me but damn sometimes it's hard hahaha! The Olympics is no joke!'[5] As she prepared to take her run-up to the vault she might have looked her normal composed self, but the routine that followed wasn't quite right: the landing involved an uncomfortable deep squat, followed by a huge stride as Biles sought to regain her balance. 'Who knows what has happened? She's either got lost or wasn't comfortable,' said one commentator.[6] Biles had seemingly changed her mind mid-air. Declaring her intention up front to complete a two-and-a-half-twisting

Yurchenko, she had ended up completing one and a half twists and then landing untidily.[7]

Biles was awarded a score of 13.766, the worst vault score in her entire career.[8] 'It's actually amazing that a gymnast with so much experience can feel the pressure,' said former gymnast Christine Still, commentating for the BBC. Biles then left the floor with one of the US team coaches, returning with a sweatshirt over her leotard. Within minutes, news outlets were reporting that Biles was pulling out of the competition 'due to a medical issue'. Team USA still performed outstandingly, fending off fierce Chinese competition, but ultimately had to settle for a silver medal as the Russians seized the gold.

Biles was very open about the reasons for the decision she had taken. 'I just think mental health is more prevalent in sports right now ...' she said at a press conference; 'we have to protect our minds and our bodies and not just go out and do what the world wants us to do'. She later added that she had also been worried in case mis-executed routines ended up injuring her: 'sometimes you just have to step back. I didn't want to go out and do something stupid and get hurt.'[9] On occasions, she explained, gymnasts fall victim to a condition called 'the twisties' – a mental block that causes a sense of spatial disconnection and can cause the athlete to fly out of control at great height and lightning-fast speed. In Tokyo, she said, she'd experienced the twisties 'more times than [I] would've wanted in practice'.[10] 'My perspective has never changed so quickly from wanting to be on a podium to wanting to be able to go home, by myself, without any crutches,' she told a journalist from *New York* magazine.[11] Interviewed on NBC, the swimmer Michael Phelps, a man-mountain – who, with twenty-eight medals, is the most successful Olympian of all time, and who has been candid about his own struggles with anxiety and depression – described how what had happened 'broke my heart'. He added, 'I hope this is an eye-opening experience ... an opportunity for us to jump on board, and to even blow this mental health thing even more wide open.'[12]

Phelps's sympathy and support were not always echoed elsewhere. News that Biles had told her teammates, 'I'm sorry, I love you guys, but you're gonna be just fine' provoked accusations that she'd abandoned her friends in their moment of greatest need.[13] In the UK the broadcaster Piers Morgan, perhaps seeking to court controversy but undoubtedly speaking for quite a few of his audience, asked, 'Are "mental health issues" now the go-to excuse for any poor performance in elite sport?'[14] He also – inevitably – evoked the R-word. 'You can either listen to snowflake Twitter, @Simone_Biles – or listen to me. You're a great champion, & great champions get back on their feet when they get knocked down. So, re-engage in these Games, win Gold, & inspire with the power of resilience not resignation. Go for it.'[15] Just a few months before, Morgan had stormed off the TV show he was co-presenting when challenged by the programme's part-time weatherman over views he had expressed. His lack of resilience then, and his call for it now, was an irony not lost on users of Twitter.

In the US, Matt Walsh bluntly stated, 'Simone Biles quit on her team because she wasn't having fun. This is called being a quitter. It's completely disgraceful and selfish.'[16] Fox Sport radio host Doug Gottlieb complained, 'For years, women have said, all we want is to be judged as equal. Generally, we don't have any sort of critique for our female sports teams. On one hand you want to be viewed, treated, and compensated the same as the men, but on the other hand whatever you do, just don't be critical of us.'[17] Conservative Radio host Charlie Kirk labelled Simone Biles a 'selfish sociopath' and told listeners, 'We are raising a generation of weak people like Simone Biles.' The gymnast, he said, 'just showed the rest of the nation that when things get tough, you shatter into a million pieces'.[18]

Not everyone agreed. Biles had more than her fair share of detractors, but there were also many who praised her for the way she had handled the situation. She went on to be featured as *Time* magazine's Athlete of the Year.[19]

★

Biles is, of course, far from being the only Super Elite athlete to stumble. Earlier that same year Naomi Osaka, the Japanese-American tennis superstar, first announced that, as she was suffering from depression, she planned to skip the usual obligatory news conferences at the French Open tournament; and then, when the inevitable backlash set in (not least from the organisers of the Roland-Garros event, who threatened her with expulsion), she decided to withdraw altogether. Meanwhile the cricketer Ben Stokes announced that he would be taking a break from the game to focus on his mental health (and to confront his stubbornly slow recovery from a finger injury).[20] Nor is the phenomenon a recent one. Back in the 1990s, for example, star footballer Stan Collymore talked openly and courageously about the impact on his life of clinical depression and anxiety.

What these various stories suggest is that even Super Elite athletes who, we're told, have achieved what they have *because* of trauma can still succumb to its toxic effects. It would be comforting to think that their tales of childhood suffering have a happy ending. A tough start in life made them resilient and determined. This resilience and determination was transmuted into athletic excellence, medals and glory. But this is far from being the case. Emily Kaier and a team of researchers in Tulsa, Oklahoma, who performed an ACE analysis on a group of 304 professional athletes, found that, typically, those who achieve greatness are not able to leave their early trauma behind. Athletes with an ACE score of one generally had good mental and physical health (it's possible, as some have suggested, that the physical activity in which they engaged actually helped them to cope with low levels of stress).[21] However those with a higher score were more likely to report issues with their health and had a greater dependency on alcohol and prescription medication. 'These findings indicated athletes may not be immune to the negative health effects of childhood adversity,' the researchers concluded.[22] Fame and success, it would appear, aren't a simple escape route from a difficult past.

The very pursuit of excellence, of course, can have adverse consequences. I vividly remember seeing a clip (though I haven't since managed to track it down on YouTube) of the nine-time gold medal-winner, American sprinter Carl Lewis winning a gold medal at, I think, the Los Angeles Olympics. After breaking through the tape, he kept running, pursued by breathless reporters and camera crews. Finally one group caught up with him. They caught him uttering over and over again a mantra that sounded close to self-hypnosis: 'I worked so hard! I worked so hard!' Such self-imposed pressure is bound to exact a toll.

When the Great British Medallist researchers looked at their cohort of competitors, they found that the Elite athletes often had moments of doubt or reflection that caused them to take a safer route. But, as Tim Rees has pointed out, 'That wasn't the case for the Super Elite athletes. They felt they had no choice. They had to keep going. They had to try to get into the squad. They had to try and get to the Olympics. And then had to try and win an Olympic Gold medal.'[23] Why? Perhaps such was the damage that trauma had done to their self-image that their identity was manifested in their accomplishment. For Rees, this was evident when he met the individuals concerned. *Whatever it takes, whatever it takes.* Such extreme behaviour can make life hard for those around the Super Elite. The GBM report cites instances of athletes who have dumped partners and friends. But, of course, it can also affect how they look after – or fail to look after – themselves.

It's interesting, in this context, to consider the vexed issue of drug abuse in sport – a recurrent problem over recent decades. One thinks, for example, of the ignominy experienced by Ben Johnson, the Canadian sprinter who beat Carl Lewis to the 1988 men's 100-metre title in Seoul, only to be stripped of the accolade less than seventy-two hours later. Carl Lewis, whose silver medal was elevated to gold on Johnson's disqualification, suffered his own humiliation when it emerged some years later that he had failed multiple drugs tests in US trials in the run-up to those very Seoul games. The question, though, from the vantage point of the psychological make-up of the Super Elite athlete is: do such people take such proscribed supplements purely to enhance their performance (the logical inference) or is there something more to it than that? Is it possible that, in at least some cases, drug-taking is part and parcel of the Super Elite personality type?

This picture is arguably even more complex than it initially appears. When Robert Anda and Vincent Felitti embarked on their pioneering work on ACE, they not only looked at the increased use of illicit drugs by those with high ACE scores, but also explored such people's use of prescription medication. What they found was that individuals with high ACE scores were significantly more likely to use prescribed medication than their lower-scoring peers. 'ACEs substantially increase the number of prescriptions and classes of drugs used for as long as seven or eight decades after their occurrence,' they concluded.[24] It's a finding that chimes with that of Professor Kyle Ganson from the University of Toronto, who believes strongly that 'trauma and life experiences are major drivers of the maladaptive behaviours we engage in ... Most of my work is focused on eating disorders in general,' he explained to me, 'but that includes things like performance-enhancing substance use and other muscularity-oriented sort of disordered eating patterns, like bulk-and-cut cycles or like targeted supplementation or restrictive dieting.' In other words, he is interested in how young adults adapt their consumption routines (of food, of drugs) to alter their appearance. They might, for example, elect to eat only carbohydrates or focus on consuming proteins and choose to restrict their fat and carbohydrate intake. But additionally he studies how they might also resort to various forms of drug-taking.

The research that Ganson and a group of colleagues have conducted on the use of performance-enhancing drugs among 14,322 adults with high ACE scores has yielded some eye-opening results. Those men 'whose basic needs hadn't been met' as a child were three and a half times more likely to take performance-enhancing drugs than those whose childhoods had been physically comfortable (the question asked here was 'How often had your adult care-givers not taken care of your basic needs, such as keeping you clean or providing food or clothing?'). The results for women were similar, if marginally lower. Men who had been physically abused as children were three times more likely to take performance-enhancing drugs than those with a low ACE score. As for men who had experienced sexual abuse in childhood, the team found that the likelihood of their taking anabolic steroids was nine times higher; for women, the ratio was six.[25] Ganson explained the phenomenon to me in these terms: 'In general, mechanisms like using substances as a means to increase muscle mass would potentially protect against future traumas – essentially using the substances as a means to protect oneself.'[26] In other words, people were enhancing and adapting themselves in adulthood to escape the trauma of their pasts.

Ganson went on to elaborate what he and his team had unearthed: 'If you've had an experience in adolescence, which we could argue runs from ten years old until twenty-five years old, we know the brain is still developing in that adolescent timeframe and is so significant for identity formation. If you have a trauma where you literally feel and experience your identity being shattered or displaced or disrupted in that developmental process, it's likely that you'll try to find ways to grab on to other identities that help formulate and build your sense of self again. Having a trauma happen during that major identity-formation period of one's life clearly has significant repercussions; it can lead to maladaptive behaviours, like drinking or anabolic steroid use, or other coping strategies that don't actually help someone in the future.' Put simply, the use of anabolic steroids is often down to some sort of trauma in childhood – sometimes physical, sometimes sexual, sometimes both.

Few athletes exemplify this tendency better than Marion Jones, one of the greatest all-rounders that US sport has produced in recent history. By the time of the Olympics Games in Sydney in 2000 her stellar performances in the 100 and 200 metres and long-jump had already earned her marquee sponsorships and magazine front covers. What was less known was the fact that these came on the back of a childhood that had been beset by setbacks and tragedy. Marion's natural father had left when she was very young. Her mother then married a retired postal worker, Ira Toler, who became a stay-at-home dad to Jones and whom she adored ('Ira was a wonderful figure in my life'),[27] but who died of a stroke just four years later. Jones wasn't yet twelve when she became fatherless for the second time.[28]

Attachment Theory teaches us that negative experiences in infancy create in us an unconscious need to avoid such trauma in the future. This unconscious need may be expressed in a variety of different ways – sometimes as guilt ('It's my fault, I should have stopped it'), sometimes as exceptional striving ('If I work hard enough, it won't happen again'), sometimes as a relentless desire for success ('I will earn the love and attention that I lost before'). Into the void that had opened up in Jones's life she poured her sporting determination and talent. Competing at first against her older brother and his friends, she found she could survive and thrive by toughening up and excelling. In time she became a Super Elite athlete.

As with many other Super Elites, a degree of uncompromising ruthlessness became part of Jones's make-up. When, for example, her husband, the shot-putter C. J. Hunter, failed a drugs test in the run-up to the Sydney Games, recording levels of nandrolone 1,000 times over the permitted limit, Jones first released a statement defending him, publicly kissed him in front of the world's press at a news conference and then, within a year, filed for divorce, citing irreconcilable differences.[29] It was a move that rebounded on her. Four years later, as Jones prepared to defend her five Sydney medals (three gold, two bronze) at the Athens games, Hunter informed FBI agents that Jones had taken a potent cocktail of illegal drugs in the build-up to Sydney, stating under oath that he had seen her inject herself – and indeed had injected her himself – with a range of chemicals that included human growth hormone, insulin, the steroid THG and the endurance-boosting drug EPO.[30]

For psychiatrist Ian Williamson, who teamed up with journalist Paul Gogarty to write about Jones, her lapse from grace was 'no more than a defence against feelings of helplessness and inadequacy'. As they explained: 'The losses and absences that characterised Marion Jones' early life were surely beyond her comprehension. But like all young children, she would have manufactured an explanation for these events ... most likely centred on her own part in the orchestration of proceedings. In other words, what have I done to make things unfold this way?' Her unconscious, they suggested, would have been constantly nagging her with insistent questions: 'Why do the people I love keep leaving (mother, father and brother), dying (Ira Toler) or show no interest in me (father)?'

'Her astonishing success as a sportswoman,' they concluded, 'provided the antidote to being unworthy, unwanted and uninteresting.' The trauma of Jones's upbringing demolished her sense of self, leaving her to construct a new identity based on being nourished by the applause of an adoring crowd. 'But it was a Faustian pact; without the winning, there was no applause. To be certain of winning, she needed to take drugs for, ultimately, she had no real belief in her own self-worth.'[31] I was reminded of the observation that Tim Rees, co-author of the Great British Medallists report, made to me about those who experience adversity or trauma and turn to sport as an outlet. They can become so obsessed with winning, he said, that they end up 'operating at the limits of what might be considered fair play'.

In seeking to create a new identity then, even the Super Elites – the over-achievers who can turn trauma into success – can end up paying a psychological price that is simply too high. Naomi Osaka, one of the best and most celebrated tennis players in the world, told a documentary film crew in 2021, 'For so long, I've tied winning to my worth as a person. Anyone that would know me, they know me for being a tennis player. So, like, what am I if I'm not a good tennis player?'[32] Her comment expresses a fear that so many Super Elites must experience.

To that extent, one of the tweets that Simone Biles put out after she withdrew from the Olympics team event in Tokyo suggests a breakthrough rather than a setback: 'the outpouring love & support I've received,' she wrote, 'has made me realise I'm more than my accomplishments and gymnastics which I never truly believed before'.[33]

Chapter 4

Crafting Stories of Self
Creating Layers of Personality

A thousand hopefuls line up for a singing audition, queuing from dawn in the rain. Each is praying that they will be the one to be plucked from obscurity and transformed into a star. At the end of a gruelling day, one is chosen to become a present-day Spice Girl. Asked by a group of disappointed and envious rivals what her secret is, she answers, 'At the end of the day, I just wanted it more.' So that must be the answer, they tell themselves. We didn't want it enough. She did. That's why she beat us.

It's a classic instance of what is known as *Survivor's Bias*. Presented with the stories of a whole range of different people who happened to be together at one particular moment, people are more interested in trying to draw lessons from the fates of the one or two who stand out than they are from the many who don't. They will speculate about what made those individuals special. They will assess what steps those individuals took to ensure their success. They won't stop to think that perhaps the winners were just lucky – that they happened to be in the right place at the right time. And they certainly won't consider that a study of those who weren't successful might shed a very different light on proceedings.

Here, in a nutshell, is the danger of the resilience story that we're constantly being told. We look at the miraculous few and we ignore the less fortunate many. Not only that, but we make inferences about those survivors that our study of the less fortunate would suggest rest on very unstable foundations. And so determined are we to stick with those inferences that we'll turn a blind eye to inconvenient facts about the fortunate few, if they happen not to fit the narrative that we've created for ourselves.

What I hope I've shown so far is that setback and trauma are not the simple triggers for achievement often claimed for them. The fact is that by the time a Super Elite athlete is reaching their peak, they will have been on the planet for more than 7,000 days. On any one of those days a whole raft of factors will have shaped their thinking, their attitudes and their feelings. And while it is clearly the case that an ability to overcome setbacks is very important, it cannot be claimed to be either the only consideration or some sort of magic ingredient X. In any case, the capacity to overcome early trauma and turn it into achievement is a double-edged weapon. It may help to drive excellence, but early adversity can also come at a very high price. As a lens through which to view the world, Survivors' Bias is a distorting one.

But there is one aspect of Survivors' Bias that is usefully revealing: its very existence offers us an interesting window on human psychology because it shows how important the creation of narratives is to us. We are constantly telling ourselves stories, and we do so to make sense of the complex world around us – a process that is sometimes called 'explanation hunger'. As the psychologist Robyn Dawes, who has dedicated his career to studying human judgement and decision-making, says: humans are 'the primates whose cognitive capacity shuts down in the absence of a story'. That compulsion to tell stories – about the world, about ourselves – can lead us astray, offering us seemingly convincing or comforting narratives that are at variance with the reality of the world around us. But since it is such a fundamental aspect of the way we tick, it has significant implications for the true nature of resilience.

The notion that the self is not a fixed entity, but a narrative creation that we assemble over time, isn't new. It stretches back at least a century to the American philosopher George Herbert Mead and his belief that 'the self is a social process'. A more recent iteration of the same idea comes from a colleague of Dr Robert Anda at the Centers for Disease Control: 'the self is built'. It doesn't magically appear. We construct it.

Dan McAdams, a psychologist from Northwestern University in Illinois, offers a simple model for understanding how experience translates into personality. It involves three layers. The first is made up of an individual's *dispositional traits,* the broad consistencies in behaviour that we might consider to be the nature side of the nature/ nurture debate. The second layer he terms *characteristic adaptations.* These are the goals and values we strive to achieve. The third layer is *narrative identity* – in other words, how we use the stories we tell about ourselves to help us make sense of our lives. Each individual, McAdams says, performs three roles: as an *actor* (dispositional), as an *agent* (adaptations) and – crucially – as an *author* (narrative identity).[1]

It's worth exploring these in a little more detail. First let's consider the individual as an *actor,* acting out their dispositional traits. The general consensus today is that individuality is built from identifiable blocks of personality traits, which can be gauged and measured. Often styled as the *Big Five,* or as the OCEAN model, these traits comprise openness (to experience), conscientiousness, extraversion, agreeableness and neuroticism.

Measuring someone's openness involves assessing to what extent they exhibit free-minded curiosity as opposed to close-minded caution. The extraversion scale runs from outgoing and energetic at one end to introverted and restrained at the other. Agreeableness, as the term suggests, denotes how accommodating and friendly an individual is, while neuroticism determines how nervous and sensitive they are. Conscientiousness is an individual's diligent commitment to delivering their goals. Recent research suggests that these categories are rather more fluid than their original proponents claimed, but they nevertheless offer a useful way to view and assess character traits that form the bedrock of individuality, and that can be identified and measured from childhood.[2] Some would argue that the Big Five can be as predictive as IQ and social class in determining outcomes in such areas of life as career achievement, lifespan and marital success.[3]

Dispositional traits, however, don't get us all the way if we're trying to understand the essence of individuality – and this is where the other two layers that McAdams talks about come in. The *characteristic adaptations* level, when we're acting as *an agent*, represents the things we do and think on a daily basis that reflect our motivations. They're the ambitions and values that propel us to take action. Yes, we might be extrovert by nature, but what precisely is it that we are striving for? What are our goals, our plans? What do we value? Dan McAdams and his writing partner Bradley Olson explain such adaptations in this way: 'Conceptions of personality that directly address questions like these tend to place human agency at the centre of personality inquiry.'[4] In other words, they involve the actions we are motivated to take that shape how others perceive us. In the sporting arena, for example, it is the relentless 'win at all costs' determination of the Super Elite athletes that differentiates them from their Elite rivals and displays their particular characteristic adaptations.

The third layer of personality involves the idea of the individual as the *author* of their life story – the lead player in their own narrative. We all tell stories about ourselves to ourselves to give our lives a sense of meaning and consistency and to enhance a sense of self-esteem. Of course we also broadcast those stories to others (these days, social media richly equips us to do this particularly effectively) as we seek to connect with them. As we do so, we invariably ensure that we're presenting a highly favourable version of ourselves: we are the heroes of our own stories. Curating who we are and what we stand for is a constant preoccupation. *New Yorker* writer Jia Tolentino articulated how the advent of social-media platforms represented an evolution in the way we maintain a public representation of ourselves: 'More than any other entity, Facebook has solidified the idea that selfhood exists in the shape of a well-performing public avatar.'[5] This projection of who we claim to be is critical to us as humans, especially as it is via this outward expression that we seek to forge connection with others. 'Our contention,' Mead once wrote, 'is that mind can never find expression, and could never have come into existence at all, except in terms of a social environment.'[6] We need to feel part of a group. Yes, a skateboarder might say, I wear baggy clothes because I like them, but it's also 'what we skaters do'. Someone sporting a Harry Styles tour T-shirt not only demonstrates a personal like, but makes a statement that enables affiliation with like-minded people: 'I was there! I saw him at Wembley!' it exclaims as it simultaneously reaches out and invites other Harry Styles fans to relate to it.

So how do these three layers of personality play out in the world of Super Elites and others who have scored great achievements? Well, first, of course, the athletes arrive on the scene with *dispositional advantages*: they possess a certain gift for sport, and they have a natural focus and discipline that help drive them forward. In the same way, great musicians often have a natural facility with a particular musical instrument. Some people find it 'easy' to paint or to write. Others have a natural affinity with numbers or abstract ideas or scientific concepts.

What arguably makes those individuals stand out are the *characteristic adaptations* they display: 'Whatever it takes, whatever it takes,' said the Super Elite athlete on the Ergo Trainer. And it's here that early hardship or trauma often plays such an important role. It arms people with a level of motivation that, to the less committed, may seem obsessive. It gives them a worldview that differs from the norm – one that involves the shaping of a fresh perspective. Trauma psychologists Rodica Ioana Damian and Dean Keith Simonton, talking about creative people, describe how to 'meet the criteria of originality and surprise one must be able to see things in unconventional ways and go against traditional ways of viewing the world. Thus, the person must learn to relax the constraints imposed by society on the thought process and imagine the impossible.'[7] They believe that trauma can create a sense of that necessary disconnection that will 'push people outside the realm of "normality"'. It's of a piece with the comment by Jean-Paul Sartre I mentioned earlier that the best thing a father can do for his son is to die young. It also ties up with the finding of one post-war study of creative writers that 55 per cent of those writers had lost a parent before the age of fifteen.[8]

Mihaly Csikszentmihalyi, the psychologist who coined the phrase *flow*, put it this way: 'Children growing up in difficult circumstances will try to escape from the painful situation by submerging themselves in some unusual, often solitary interest. This motivation in turn leads to a full investment of psychic energy in the area of talent, often accompanied by a strong desire to succeed. As Einstein noted, science and art are the highest forms of escape from reality.'[9]

For his part, Martin Lloyd-Elliott, a psychotherapist who studies the adaptations that highly successful adults often make, believes that high achievers are 'driven by both a conscious and unconscious desire to compensate for an ego that has been wounded by trauma'.[10] And two British-based sports scientists, David Collins and Áine MacNamara, who were given space to respond to the Great British Medallists survey in the pages of the same volume in which it was first published, acknowledge that 'there is growing recognition that facing and overcoming a degree of challenge is desirable for aspiring elites and, as such, should be recognised and employed'.[11] '[We] proposed,' they say, 'that talent *needs* some degree of challenge to develop optimally, and thus talent pathways have to optimise challenge rather than merely providing unremitting support.' (It's important to point out, though, that they add a very significant qualification. Their work on what they style the *Almosts* – the performers who were successful as youngsters but never made it to the top – showed that this non-Elite group actually demonstrated more trauma than the top achievers: the fact that they never made it suggested they were perhaps defeated by it, trapped in the danger zone of Mark Seery's inverted J-curve, see p.49.)[12]

Those who aspire to meet extreme challenges may well behave in ways regarded by others as antisocial. 'We are synchronous human beings,' says Bessel van der Kolk. 'The source of pleasure in our lives is to be in sync with each other.' If we don't feel ourselves to be in sync – if the 'shame' that is 'the dominant experience of trauma', as van der Kolk puts it, comes to the fore – then we may choose to revitalise our identity in ways that break accepted social norms (because we regard being in sync as of secondary import- ance) or we may adopt such maladaptive behaviours as drinking or drug-taking to mask the sense of shame. This preoccupation with identity revitalisation is the reason why Super Elite athletes often come across as selfish and self-obsessed and why, for their own part, they are – unlike Elite athletes – willing to acknowledge selfishness and ruthlessness on their part.

It's perhaps the final layer of personality – narrative identity – that has the greatest capacity to wrong-foot people who are exploring the nature of outstanding achievement. Here, as I have just described, individuals create the stories that explain their lives and give them meaning, not only to themselves, but to others. They tell stories that make sense of their experiences.

The potent stories we tell ourselves about ourselves are what the researchers Tilmann Habermas and Susan Bluck call 'Autobiographical reasoning', which they describe as 'a process of self-reflective thinking or talking about the personal past that involves forming links between elements of one's life and the self in an attempt to relate one's personal past and present'. They explain how vital this is for us when we're trying to make sense of seem- ingly unrelated experiences that occur throughout our lifetime. 'Autobiographical reasoning indicates the evolution of a biograph- ical perspective that frames one's individuality in terms of a specific developmental history. It relies on autobiographical remembering but goes beyond it by enhancing understanding through actively creating coherence between events and the self.' As Habermas puts it, 'Both philosophers and linguists have suggested that causal or explanatory coherence is central to life narratives since without it the narrator cannot present herself or himself as having lived a rea- sonable life.' Stories are immensely persuasive – to others, to ourselves. As the American novelist Richard Powers puts it, 'The best arguments in the world won't change a single person's mind. The only thing that can do that is a good story.'[13]

As we tell stories we edit out what doesn't 'fit', removing inconsistences and contrary narratives. Young adults might seek to explain historical actions by mentioning the lessons they learned in adolescence. Older adults tend to refer to critical events that they believe formed turning points in their own stories. Habermas and Bluck observe that so subconsciously familiar are we with narrative structure that we mimic it when explaining our own experiences. Certain memories may be returned to because they 'substantiate family myths, reveal the narrator's present character, or are assumed to have determined the narrator's later life-course'. Psychologist Daniel Stern, who was the first person to talk of the idea of a 'narrated self', talked of weaving together 'an array of past and present lived experiences … into a coherent narrative'.[14] It may be a process most apparent from late adolescence onwards, but it's interesting to note that children as young as four exposed to a fire alarm could recall the event seven years later if they had formed a story around it.[15]

Because what is involved here are *stories*, rather than sets of objective facts, it's easy for them to be misinterpreted, both by the person telling them and by those listening to them. An outstanding athlete, in their own recounting of their life story, may well pick on a moment that they regarded as transformational. Of course it may indeed have been a turning point, but it's also entirely possible that it has been made so by subsequent retellings. The competitor may tell themselves that extreme, perhaps unreasonable behaviour on their part has been their pathway to success and adulation, reinterpreting events to fit a story that makes sense to them.[16] 'This internalised narrative,' the authors of the GBM report say, 'allows the Super Elite athletes to justify their behaviours (like self-absorption, obsessive preparation) and commit to high performance and mastery in sport to compulsive levels.'[17]

Key to such narratives is an inner consistency. Jennifer Pals, a psychologist who specialises in the understanding of narrative identity, talks in terms of 'the construction of a positive, resolved ending so that the event did not continue to disturb the self'. She also emphasises the importance of coherence in the narratives that we create. 'Indeed,' she argues, 'if a story is incoherent and consisting of a collection of seemingly random, disconnected, or completely contradictory pieces of information about the past, then it is not a story at all, and a meaningful sense of identity will fail to emerge from it.'[18] In certain circumstances, being unable to fully reconcile the discordant elements of our internal narrative causes a confused sense of identity. Pals explains that sometimes we seek to bring the trauma that we have experienced into the stories we tell, but are then challenged when we feel unable to contemplate the shame generated by misfortune. As Bessel van der Kolk explains, this is how trauma can lead us to disconnection: 'shame becomes the dominant emotion and hiding the truth the central preoccupation.'[19]

The Super Elite will often obsess about their narrative identity – about the aura they project, the way they assemble their story into an arc towards triumph. The very top competitors frequently speak in impassioned terms about being compelled to leave certain experiences in the past, to ensure they are no longer defined by them. But this is highly subjective territory, as David Collins and Áine MacNamara point out. Those Super Elites who publish their autobiographies, for example, can all too easily be prone to confuse what was genuinely formative with what was subsequently helpful justification. Collins and MacNamara cite one Super Elite athlete who complained of 'Fucking sports books ... people telling their stories to make themselves look good'[20] (or, as one analysis of sporting memoirs less emotively puts it, 'autobiographies emphasise not facts, but personal experiences and personal lives as cultural constructions').[21] Collins and MacNamara go on to cite another Super Elite who said caustically of some of their peers, 'I've lived through the competitions they are writing about and I certainly didn't see what they saw!' The fact that a highly successful individual may point to a particular moment as transformative in their lives is significant by very virtue of the fact that they said it was. But that's not quite the same as saying that, judged objectively, indeed it was.

The stories we all tell ourselves are, in other words, slippery entities. They're not inventions, but they're not statements made on oath, either. They are the fuel in our tanks – the motivations, justifications and explanations for what we've done and what we aim to do in the future. They don't constitute objectively verifiable cases of cause and effect. They are after-the-fact interpretations that help us comprehend the noise and confusion of a life unfolding. In our retellings, we invariably cast ourselves as the justified protagonist; in our own stories, we're invariably *the goody*.

There's another dimension to story-telling, too, that needs to be taken into account, and it involves what is technically termed our 'explanatory style': our tendency to apply an optimistic or pessimistic filter when interpreting what may be a wholly disparate range of events. Professor Martin Seligman, who runs the Positive Psychology Center at the University of Pennsylvania, has spent his thirty-five-year career exploring this area of the human psyche. His findings have become widely renowned.[22]

In order to measure what impact a pessimistic or optimistic outlook might have on the life of an individual, Seligman first sought to categorise how people frame misfortune. Initially this involved creating three axes. Over time these axes became the *Three Ps* of emotional resilience, each one representing a 'cognitive trap' that we fall into when confronted by misfortune:

- *Permanence* – our brain's fear mode tells us that whatever misfortune we may have experienced is irreversible and enduring. We can't imagine a time when we ever get beyond it. Our colleagues will never forget our drunken lapse into dancing at the formal office drinks.
- *Pervasiveness* – our instinct is to believe that our misfortune will permeate every corner of our lives. The badly worded tweet that we sent will become known to everyone and will bring us societal disgrace. Pensioners will boo us on the bus.

72

- *Personal* – we assume that whatever misfortune has befallen us is our fault. 'All of this was down to me, I'm the problem here.'

Seligman and his fellow researchers applied these metrics to ninety-nine physically healthy members of a Harvard University year group, to arrive at a measure of the nature of their explanatory style. When confronted by a setback or an adverse event, did they regard it as being permanent, pervasive and their fault? Or were they able to take a more measured, stoical stance, blaming circumstance and bad luck? The research team then followed those volunteers as they progressed through life. What they found was that those who regarded bad events as being permanent, pervasive or personal were invariably less physically healthy in later years. 'We believe,' they wrote, 'that we have shown unambiguously that a psychological variable – pessimistic explanatory style – predicts physical illness two and three decades later.'[23] The more helpless someone felt in the face of a setback, the more they felt they were responsible, and the more their well-being suffered. Conversely, those who adopted a more optimistic outlook enjoyed better health overall; they could 'somehow reach inside and strengthen the body'.[24]

Of course it is possible that we are pessimistic about some aspects of our lives and optimistic about others. But as a rule, a pessimist will regard a negative event as just that – a negative event – while an optimist may view it as a turning point, a 'springboard' moment that explains a subsequent transformation. Daniel McAdams refers to such moments as 'redemption sequences'.[25] Our inclination towards optimism or pessimism, then, has a material effect on our lives. And it adds another complicating layer to our narrative identity, further shaping our interpretation of events from our past to explain our present and look into our future.

So where does that leave us in our search for the true nature of resilience? Well, in the first place, it should make us wary of the view that a setback should simply be viewed as an inflection point that directs us towards success. As Jennifer Pals has observed, we can be immensely selective in what we choose to identify as key turning points in our lives – she cites as evidence of this a patient who described her divorce as a key moment of transformation in her life, but failed to mention the death of her child in that story of personal development.[26] Stories can be a form of self-deception. They have a hallucinatory quality to them, inviting us to imagine scenarios, construct alternate avatars of individuals, spin one-off episodes into seemingly logical extrapolations. The lessons of simple fables can be helpful to us, but they are by nature reductive.

But our obsession with story-telling also provides an important resilience clue. If, as Bessel van der Kolk has put it, trauma 'interrupts the plot', what is required to overcome it is – in Pals's words – 'the construction of a positive, resolved ending so that the end [does] not continue to disturb the self'.[27] In other words, we should avoid focusing on the fact of a setback or the experience of trauma, but instead focus on the precise nature of the techniques we can use to build a positive story for ourselves. The experiences of Super Elite athletes who have overcome adverse events provide some useful pointers (though, as we've seen, they may still pay a high price for this), but these are only one part of the equation.

It's time, therefore, to leave behind the myths that have accumulated about the heroic figures who have used their adversity to catapult themselves to success, and to look in more depth at what the work that has been done on individual resilience has to teach us.

PART TWO

The Origins of Inner Strength

Chapter 5

The Billion-Dollar Resilience Industry
Exploring the Resilience Orthodoxy

If there's one walk of life where resilience is repeatedly put to the test, it's the military. The average soldier may not engage in combat every day or even frequently, but he or she knows they have signed up for a career where, at some point, they may well be called on both to put their own lives on the line and to kill other people. The stress that soldiers are put under is well documented, whether in the form of the shell shock experienced by troops during the First World War or the more recent reframing of such pressures as Post-Traumatic Stress Disorder (PTSD). It's also apparent that while the act of breaking the ultimate human taboo – killing another person – may be sanctioned by society when that society is at war, it nevertheless exacts a huge toll on the individual.

Studies of armies over the past couple of centuries or so have revealed that, in large-scale wars, those soldiers who have been conscripted to swell the ranks of regular troops can find it very difficult even to open fire. As the Dutch historian Rutger Bregman explained to me, 'We have got a lot of evidence from historical wars that if you draft soldiers and you send them to the front, most of them just can't do it. They just can't shoot to kill.' He cites the pioneering work undertaken by the American military man and historian S. L. A. Marshall, which concluded that 'only around 15 to 25 per cent' of American soldiers who fought in the Pacific and Europe during the Second World War 'were actually shooting at the enemy'.[1] He also describes how earlier generations of soldiers would often avoid firing, or would shoot in the air, or would reload their weapon only when they knew they were being observed. After the Battle of Gettysburg in 1863 during the American Civil War, it was found that many of the muskets collected from the battlefield had not been loaded once, as was correct for single-shot armaments, but twice. 'These soldiers were very well trained,' says Bregman. 'They knew you don't put two bullets in the musket.' What was going on? 'Back then,' Bregman explains, 'it took a lot of time to actually load the gun: that was like 95 per cent of all of the work – loading the gun. So what do you do? You just load it again and you load it again and you load it again. And that way you can sort of get away with not shooting at the enemy without your superiors actually noticing.'

Today, wars tend to be fought by smaller, tighter bands of career soldiers. But that doesn't mean the mental agonies that clearly afflicted conscript armies ('Do I shoot, or merely try to look as though I'm shooting?') no longer exist. If anything, they may well have got worse. In the past, those looking at the psychological toll of war tended to focus on the impact of exposure to violence. Nowadays, experts increasingly believe it is the acts that soldiers *commit*, rather than the violence that they are *exposed to*, that have the greatest potential to create trauma.[2] With their precision high-tech weaponry, modern soldiers are far more likely to hit their targets than was previously the case – and, given what we know about the mental suffering of earlier generations, it is also highly likely that they will suffer more as a consequence. Taking another person's life, even the life of an adversary, can trigger powerful feelings of guilt and can inflict what is often referred to as 'moral injury'. Witnessing the death of a friend in combat can also exact a huge toll: one study that explored the lingering grief that soldiers experience at the loss of a comrade found that the death of a fellow combatant thirty years earlier weighed more heavily with them than, say, the recent death of their spouse.[3] The impact of being responsible for another human's death can be long-term and debilitating. The post-war experience of one recent veteran stands for many: 'All I knew is I hurt inside and I didn't know why, you know? I didn't know why I should feel so bad if I didn't do anything wrong. I was not a baby killer. I was not – I did my job.

I did what everybody else did. But always that nagging question, why do I hurt like this?'[4]

It's no doubt for this reason that soldiers will often avoid talking about death altogether. 'We recruit people to kill,' says Pete Kilner, a retired lieutenant colonel in the US Army who lectured at West Point Military Academy. 'We train people to kill … Yet after the fact, we don't talk about killing. We talk about destroying, engaging, dropping, bagging – you don't hear the word killing.'[5]

There's another dimension to modern warfare that can serve to compound such trauma. In the past, when soldiers went away to war, their contact with their old life was reduced to the occasional letter. Today, thanks to such digital technology as email, social media and FaceTime, the complexities of the two worlds constantly collide. Once there was a protective insulation between two starkly divided realities. Now soldiers may be physically on the battlefield, but they can simultaneously and virtually be at home. As Colonel Darryl Williams put it to psychologist Martin Seligman, 'This is the first war that you have a cellphone and can call your wife from the front line.' The mental dislocation that such a bifurcated life can cause is considerable. 'Much of the depression and anxiety our soldiers have is about what is going on at home,' said Colonel Williams.[6] It should therefore come as no surprise that the mental health of combatants (both past and present) is often very poor. According to one survey in 2010, the occurrence of PTSD among veterans of the US military was more than twice the level of that of the population at large – 16 per cent as against 6.8 per cent.[7] A British study found that on returning from active duty, one in eight soldiers was responsible for a physical assault.[8] In extreme cases, violence turns to killing. At Thousand Oaks in California, in November 2018, for example, thirteen people were shot and killed by a former US Marine, who then turned the gun on himself. Commenting on the tragedy, President Trump said that the Marine 'saw some pretty bad things, and a lot of people say he had PTSD', adding that service people who returned from active duty were 'never the same'.[9]

*

Such has been the epidemic of mental ill health among US service personnel and veterans that the military have called in psychologists to help. And in particular they have turned to Professor Martin Seligman. 'We do not want our legacy to be the streets of Washington full of begging veterans, post-traumatic stress disorder, depression, addiction, divorce, and suicide,' senior personnel told him.[10] They accordingly commissioned him to tailor a programme that might forestall such misfortune.

As a scholar who has dedicated his career to researching mental health and well-being, Seligman was an adroit choice for the military. He established his reputation back in the 1960s with his work on 'learned helplessness': a state of passivity that he argues individuals assume when they come to expect that they have no control over the world around them. (Seligman demonstrated this proposition by showing that if dogs are administered unpredictable, inescapable electric shocks they will eventually give up trying to avoid them.) From there he broadened out into what is (rather loosely) known as 'positive psychology', a discipline that seeks to improve the well-being of everyone, and not only that subset of the population suffering illness and maladaptive afflictions. He also studied the explanatory styles discussed in Chapter 4.[11] Elected to the post of president of the American Psychological Association by the biggest margin in its history, Seligman also professes to be a keen bridge player, once declaring that his philosophy in the game is: 'At matchpoints, underbid and overplay.'[12] In the interest of balance, it's only right to point out that there are some who are sceptical about aspects of his work. The science writer Jesse Singal, for example, while describing Seligman as 'iconic', also says that he is 'divisive'.[13]

It was Seligman's work on the Penn Resilience Program (PRP) that caught the eye of the military. This is essentially an intervention that, like Cognitive Behavioural Therapy (CBT), is designed to help people manage their problems by assisting them in changing the way they think and behave. Seligman says that his insights have been forged by his personal experiences as 'a depressive and a pessimist', and that he road-tests interventions on himself before trying them on others.[14]

Over time, the PRP has evolved to include a series of his approved exercises – delivered in a group setting that usually involves between five and fifteen participants – by an instructor who isn't necessarily required to have a formal grounding in the discipline. The programme typically extends over a series of sessions that total around twenty hours. In that time the participants will be introduced to techniques to help them enhance personal qualities that include self-awareness, strength of character, the ability to connect with others and the power to focus on those areas of their lives over which they actually have control and then take appropriate 'purposeful' action. They will also have the opportunity to practise those techniques. They might, for example, be invited to document 'three good things' each day, or to identify how to use their 'signature strengths in a new way'. The programme's website claims that people will end up with a 'set of practical skills that can be applied in everyday life to navigate adversity and thrive in challenging environments'. It also claims that the programme is 'demonstrated to build resilience, well-being, and optimism'.[15]

Such was – and continues to be – the popularity of his resilience programme that in 2003 Seligman founded the Positive Psychology Center at the University of Pennsylvania. Five years later he and his team were given a lavish $2.8 million grant to run a controlled evaluation of a new Positive Psychology Curriculum intervention targeted at school children, named after Strath Haven, the Philadelphia school that was used to pilot it. And it was in that year that the US Army engaged the Center to create a resilience programme that would help them overcome soaring levels of PTSD and suicides amongst service personnel. 'We have read your books, and we want to know what you suggest for the army,' they told him.[16] Seligman believed that, even in soldiers, post-traumatic *growth* was 'a lot more common than post-traumatic stress disorder' and he proposed to military leaders that he would simply 'move the whole distribution toward growth'.[17]

The original PRP had been constructed to help school students cope with the stresses of adolescent development, and it would require adaption for it to reduce depression and trauma in service personnel. Seligman's team therefore duly set about creating the Comprehensive Soldier Fitness programme (CSF), a scheme that has so far trained more than a million military personnel and thus represents the biggest resilience programme in history. Its ambition was reflected in its budget. The original contract with Seligman's Positive Psychology Center was announced as being worth $31 million, but the investigative journalist Jesse Singal suggests that in the end the contract with the military has 'probably cost taxpayers north of $500 million'.[18]

Seligman's brief was to train all military personnel to be resilience-ready – and not only those who had already experienced trauma. He describes the programme's contents in simple terms under the umbrella goal 'we teach people mental toughness', and the fundamental view that 'emotions don't just fall on you – there's always an activating thought'. Those who undergo the training are given tips on how to avoid 'thinking traps', how to 'detect icebergs', how to put 'bad events in perspective' and how to develop problem-solving skills under stress. Effectively they are invited to make sense of negative events and achieve post-traumatic growth as a result. Jesse Singal has described some of the materials used in the course. '"Resilient people bounce, not break," reads one slide from a CSF session. Under that, two images: "You" over a tennis ball, "Not you" over a cracked egg with yolk oozing out.' Troops, he says, are exhorted to 'hunt the good stuff' in life in order to become stronger.[19] Seligman is very positive about the programme's achievements, while an official army document concluded that 'significant positive effects are sustained and performance of participants is generally improved'.[20]

Seligman is far from being the only figure to be toiling in the field of individual resilience. Two other key figures need to be mentioned here, along with the proprietary concepts that they have coined: Grit, and Growth Mindset. Grit is the brainchild of Seligman's one-time research assistant Angela Duckworth. Growth Mindset is a concept developed by Stanford psychology professor Carol Dweck. They differ from one another in their emphases and details but, like Seligman's resilience programme, are driven by a common central notion: that the way we frame challenges is critical to achieving greater mental toughness and that the framing strategy can be taught and learned. It's the interconnectedness of their ideas that has prompted me to refer to them collectively as the Resilience Orthodoxy. If you're ever given resilience training, the chances are that it will be based on a strand or an aggregation of the work that comes from the Resilience Orthodoxy camp.

Duckworth's insights reached an international audience with the publication in 2016 of her book *Grit*. Subtitled 'Why passion and resilience are the secrets to success', it builds on research that she undertook with Seligman into the academic performance of school pupils to suggest that when it comes to achievement, natural talent counts for considerably less than an ability to display steely resolve in the face of setbacks (Duckworth and Seligman's original paper was titled 'Self-Discipline Outdoes IQ in Predicting Academic Performance of Adolescents').[21] Couple resilience with a passion for what you do, Duckworth argues, and you will far exceed the achievements of those who are merely 'talented'. She illustrates this assertion with studies of children who have excelled in areas as diverse as music and spelling bees (that uniquely American tradition that straddles a line between performatively precocious nerdiness and child traumatisation), arguing that such children achieve elite performance not because they are natural geniuses, but because they display a disciplined attitude. Grit, Duckworth concludes, 'beats the pants off' other predictors of success.[22]

Some argue that Duckworth's 'Grit' is essentially the same as the quality of conscientiousness that makes up one of psychology's Big Five (the others being openness, extraversion, agreeableness and neuroticism). But for Duckworth there is a difference between the two. 'Grit overlaps with achievement aspects of conscientiousness,' she argues, 'but differs in its emphasis on long-term stamina rather than short-term intensity.'[23]

The parallel concept of Growth Mindset bloomed in the wake of the huge commercial success of Carol Dweck's 2006 book *Mindset*. As with Duckworth, the Dweck hypothesis is that it's attitude rather than raw ability that shapes the academic success or failure of children. Conscious intention is everything: it is resolve in the face of setbacks that distinguishes those who succeed from those who fall behind. As Dweck later explained, she was fascinated to find out 'why some children wilt and shrink back from challenges and give up in the face of obstacles, while others avidly seek challenges and become ever more invested in the face of obstacles'.[24]

To explain this, Dweck essentially makes a distinction between two types of mindset. The first is *fixed*: it operates on the assumption that our intelligence and ability do not, and cannot, change. The second is a *growth mindset*: unlike the fixed mindset, this is fuelled by a belief that intelligence and personality are in fact malleable, that they can be cultivated, and that development and adaptation bring achievement in their wake. There's more than an element of the Seligman notion of explanatory styles here. Fixed and growth mindsets offer another way in which we can make sense of the complexity of the world around us. There's also a powerful element of resilience thinking: a belief that it's what you do and how you respond to challenges and setbacks that matters, not what you intrinsically are.

Dweck's early work with her research partner Claudia Mueller shows the two mental approaches in action.[25] The pair's 1998 study describes how they asked a group of fifth-grade pupils (aged ten to twelve) to perform ten non-verbal cognitive problems, many of them involving identifying a pattern in a matrix of geometric designs, and all characterised to the pupils as being of 'moderate difficulty'. Those children who performed well were either praised for their intelligence ('You must be smart') or for their effort ('You must have worked hard'). All were then given a far more difficult challenge that was designed to end in failure, after which they were given negative feedback about their performance. They were then told to complete a questionnaire that asked them whether they wanted to continue with similarly challenging questions or whether they would prefer the next set of problems to be less testing. They were also asked to suggest to what they attributed their failure. To round things off, the children were given a third and final set of ten questions.

What Dweck and Mueller reported was that those children who were praised for effort after the first task went on to choose more challenging problems, displayed greater persistence in attempting to solve them and recorded better results than those who were initially praised for their intelligence. The contrast in attitude and attainment between the two groups was stark. Of those children praised for effort, 67 per cent chose to do the more challenging problems; of those praised for their intelligence, only 8 per cent did.[26] For Dweck, the lesson was a clear one: 'In a fixed mindset,' she wrote, 'students believe their basic abilities, their intelligence, their talents, are just fixed traits. They have a certain amount and that's that … In a growth mindset, students understand that their talents and abilities can be developed through effort, good teaching, and persistence.'[27] Fixed-mindset people have a fatalistic view that you play the cards you are dealt. Growth-mindset people believe you can strive to get better cards. Essentially it's about fostering a sense of self-esteem and, of course, resilience. When you encounter a challenge or a setback, you don't allow it to define you. You strive to overcome it. And you reap the rewards accordingly.

Such seemingly self-empowering messages have been widely welcomed. Resilience and growth-mindset training and courses are now ubiquitous. The Grit model has even been described as 'a national obsession' in the US,[28] praised to the skies in, among other publications, a ninety-page 2013 US Department of Education report entitled 'Promoting Grit, Tenacity, and Perseverance: Critical Factors for Success in the 21st Century'.[29] In 2013 the White House hosted an international meeting to celebrate the importance of 'Academic Mindsets' in the US education system, part of a declared effort to make mindset research a 'national education priority'.[30] In the UK the education system has become awash with growth-mindset thinking. Eleanor Palmer Primary School in Kentish Town credits the concept's creators with shaping their ethos: 'Rather than simply praising success we praise effort and persistence.'[31] Highgate Wood Comprehensive, a few miles away, states that 'growth mindset is the cornerstone of our learning ethos'. Eton College boasts a course that teaches resilience through growth mindset.[32] From Inverness in Scotland (where the High School's handbook boasts that the school teaches growth mindset 'to enable pupils to understand more about their ability to learn'[33]), to Swansea in Wales (where growth mindset is mentioned on the ethos page of St Joseph's Catholic Primary School's website),[34] to Northern Ireland (where 4 per cent of the common curriculum lays out the foundation of growth mindset for learning),[35] forms of resilience philosophy have taken centre stage.

The Resilience Orthodoxy has established a beachhead in business, too. Many organisations consider evidence for Growth Mindset or Grit when interviewing job applicants. The UK government's innovation department advises that British business should hire for Growth Mindset. Google's leadership team have said that they look for evidence of Growth Mindset in candidates. Textio, a firm that designs software to reformulate job postings in more inclusive language, advises firms that vacancy ads that refer to Growth Mindset fill eight days faster than those that don't.[36]

It is pretty clear, then, that Resilience Orthodoxy is everywhere. The question its ubiquity begs is: does it work?

Let's start with the experience of the US military programme. Quietly, Seligman's resilience training has had its share of critics. Some have understandably raised objections as to the wisdom of taking a methodology designed for school children and applying it to the armed forces.[37] Others have pointed out that the lavishly funded programme was introduced without the usual control group that one would expect to see in such undertakings. ('We urge the

Army to conduct randomised controlled trials testing the efficacy of the program prior to its implementation,' wrote two psychologists in the 2011 issue of *American Psychologist* in which Seligman described the programme.[38] In fairness, Seligman has said that he 'advocated explicitly for controlled pilot studies before going ahead' but was 'overruled'.)[39] And the fact is that in the decade or so since the initiative was launched, the take-up has been poor. It was supposed to cover a workforce of more than a million individuals. But by 2011 – two years into the programme – almost one-third of those service personnel who had received training to help run courses for their fellow soldiers reported not having conducted a single class.[40] Seligman has extensively promoted the programme, but has scarcely commented on how effective it has been since his 2011 book *Flourish*. All these factors have to be taken into account in any attempt to interpret such data as has been released by the military. Even so, it is possible to reach one or two tentative conclusions from what is known.

The declared ambition of the Comprehensive Soldier Fitness programme was not explicitly to help military personnel overcome spiralling rates of PTSD and to reduce suicide rates in veterans (though these problems figure heavily in Seligman's accounts of the challenges he was brought in to resolve[41]), but to 'create an Army that is just as psychologically fit as it is physically fit'.[42] Seligman's own research persuaded him that around 75 per cent of those who undergo terrible experiences are able to channel the accompanying stress into what is known as Post Traumatic Growth (PTG) – that is to say, that they are able to turn moments of sadness and fear into a greater appreciation of life, increased empathy, or perhaps a renewed sense of purpose. 25 per cent of subjects, however, find themselves struggling and succumbing to the debilitating effects of trauma. Like Seligman, eminent psychotherapist Donald Meichenbaum suggests that one factor that determines which side of the divide individuals fall is the nature of the personal narrative they create after the event. 'The stories patients tell,' he argues, 'hold a powerful sway over their memories, feelings, behaviour, identity, and shape their future. Patients don't just tell stories, their stories tell them.'[43] So far, so good – in theory. However when it came to measuring the real-world impact of the Comprehensive Soldier Fitness program, there has been limited evidence to suggest that the reframing exercises of the scheme help mitigate the extreme flashpoints of combat experience.

Army data isn't routinely published, and Seligman says the program's results 'were not peer-reviewed, because the Army chooses instead to use independent evaluators', but such data as has been shared has been met with scepticism in many quarters.[44] One doubting piece in *American Psychologist* concluded after a review of the program's results, 'it is unclear whether training occurring before, during, or after deployment can foster post-traumatic growth among military personnel'.[45] Even those working on the programme have expressed concerns, one summary by those implementing the initiative concluding in 2013, 'Comprehensive Soldier Fitness is not a panacea for anything … The program,' the authors wrote, 'will not bring about an end to low base rate behavioural problems, such as suicide and violent crime within the Army. It will not cure PTSD. It will not solve the Army's alarmingly high number of soldiers who are prescribed psychotropic medication for behavioural health problems. It will not cure addiction of any kind … It will not prevent a divorce from happening or make a soldier a great parent.[46]

Certainly, such statistics as are available are not encouraging – and the military themselves seem to be aware of this. An analysis completed by six senior military leaders and published in *Military Psychology* in 2013 reported that when the Comprehensive Soldier Fitness course was made voluntary, no one at all signed up to attend.[47] Clearly, serving military personnel did not believe it would help them. In the same report, a study of personnel currently serving in Afghanistan who had undertaken Seligman resilience training concluded: 'despite the training, both resilient thinking and morale were observed to decline across the deployment period'. Simultaneously, it was noted, during the period when training was mandated, the use of prescription medicines to help people sleep rose 84 per cent.[48] Soldiers might have been exhorted to 'hunt the good stuff', but they preferred to track down sleeping tablets. *We hunted it, it wasn't there, sir.*

Suicide rates among veterans remain stubbornly high. According to a 2019 article in the *New York Times*: 'More than 45,000 veterans and active-duty service members have killed themselves [in the six years between 2013 and 2019] ... That is more than 20 deaths a day – in other words, more suicides each year than the total American military deaths in Afghanistan and Iraq.[49] Indeed, among active-duty service personnel the suicide rate actually rose by one-third between 2013 and 2018, while among veterans it went up by 80 per cent between 2005 and 2016. By 2016 a military retiree was one and a half times more likely to kill himself or herself than someone who hadn't served in the armed forces. Nick Brown, a British psychologist who has taken issue with what he regards as overclaimed research findings, has openly challenged Seligman's work in the pages of *American Psychologist*. 'The idea,' he wrote, 'that techniques that have demonstrated, at best, marginal effects in reducing depressive symptoms in school-age children could also prevent the onset of a condition that is associated with some of the most extreme situations with which humans can be confronted is a remarkable one that does not seem to be backed up by empirical evidence.'[50] In the same vein, Jesse Singal pithily concluded after an exhaustive examination that the Seligman intervention was 'a mess' and that 'there's zero evidence that CSF, a mandatory Army program for over a decade, does *anything* to help soldiers'.[51]

If peer-reviewed studies suggest that resilience training hasn't helped soldiers, has it had any impact on school children? There is reason to be similarly cautious about such claims for it as have been made. The co-creator of Penn Resiliency Program (PRP), Jane Gillham, who undertook a meta-analysis of seventeen implementations of the course, concluded that it did have an impact in reducing depressive symptoms in children, though she acknowledged that the effects were small. However, even that qualified assertion is open to objection. It was based on a compari-son with control groups who were offered no intervention at all. When some form of intervention did take place, no measurable difference could be observed between the control group and the experimental one. As Gillham's own paper ultimately acknowl-edges, 'data show no evidence that PRP is superior to active control conditions'.[52]

A 2001 Australian study came to much the same conclusion, stating that 'There was no evidence that the Penn Prevention Program had any impact on the variables measured at the end of the program or at the eight-month follow-up assessment.'[53] Similarly a meta-analysis of nine trials across Australia, the Netherlands and the US fifteen years later, which involved 4,744 adolescents, found 'No evidence of PRP in reducing depression or anxiety and improving explanatory style ... The large-scale roll-out of PRP cannot be recommended,' it stated.[54] Resilience interventions may be taking place in schools all around the world. It doesn't mean that they work.

Seligman himself appears uncertain. The website that publicly promotes his work asserts that the school resilience programme 'builds character strengths, relationships and meaning, as well as raises positive emotion and reduces negative emotion'.[55] But a peer-reviewed article that he contributed to a journal in 2009 strikes a much more cautious note: 'The positive psychology programme did not improve other outcomes we measured, such as students' reports of their depression and anxiety symptoms, character strengths, and participation in extracurricular activities.'[56] The qualified phrases 'small but statistically significant' and 'small but significant effects' have cropped up a couple of times in his recent work. The former appears in his comments on a finding that his army programme reduces cases of depression, panic disorder or PTSD from afflicting 5.07 per cent of soldiers to affecting 4.44 per cent. The latter can be found in his assessment of a meta-analysis of his school programme, where he adds that when the effects were re-measured some time after the interventions, they were found to be 'larger than zero for depressive (but not anxiety) symptoms'.[57]

So much for Seligman's contribution to the Resilience Orthodoxy. What about Grit? Again, there are some ambiguities in the data and how it should be interpreted. A 2020 study whose title rather gives its conclusion away – 'In a Representative Sample Grit Has a Negligible Effect on Educational and Economic Success Compared to Intelligence' – the authors took issue with those who had previously supported the claims of Grit, arguing that the samples they drew upon were unrepresentative. Others have poured cold water on the figures that the advocates of Grit have come up with. Shortly after Duckworth's book first appeared, Marcus Credé, a researcher at Iowa State University, published a rigorous analysis of all the data used in the book, immersing himself in almost ninety studies of the subject. His conclusion was that, when it came to raw numbers, the Grit effect either appeared to be overstated or insufficient attention was paid to the specifics of how the results were expressed. For example, Duckworth claimed that among cadets at the West Point military training centre, those who scored highly for Grit were '99 percent more likely to complete summer training'. The problem with that figure, Credé pointed out, is that it neglected to take account of the fact that the overall completion rate for the 'Beast Barracks' course is 94 per cent. While it is impressive that 98 per cent of the grittiest candidates made it through, and a four-point lift in success is certainly not negligible, it is also somewhat misleading to present the results in such an eye-watering fashion.[58]

For his part, Jesse Singal has pointed to the dangers of looking at concentrated clusters of data rather than its entire range (an issue known in research circles as 'range restriction'): it would, he says, be unwise, for example, to extrapolate general height statistics from 'a random sample of NBA players'.[59] Singal's own interpretation of Duckworth's data (stripping out other standard predictors of performance, such as educational grades and military performance scores) led him to conclude that 'grit accounts for, at best, just 0.8 percent of the variance'. 'This suggests,' he argues, 'that grit is not a particularly useful instrument for measuring academic achievement at West Point.'

Disputes over data and interpretation are hardly unusual in academic research. Indeed, the rigours of peer review are a crucial part of the research process – the system is designed to invite challenge, scrutiny and disagreement. But given the ubiquity of the Resilience Orthodoxy ethos, the very real reservations expressed about it should be a matter of concern – not only because they suggest it may be less effective than advertised, but also because in expending energy pursuing it, people may be distracted from seeking out interventions that might well prove to be more helpful. It's also just possible that it's all causing more harm than good.

Certainly there are aspects of resilience, Grit and Growth Mindset that are troubling. Take Duckworth's spelling-bees phenomenon, for example. She asserts that the route into this rather peculiar world of achievement is 'solitary deliberate practice'. Pleasure and enjoyment, she says, have no place. But if these are absent, is there so much to be said for encouraging a child to seek a joyless life adorned by a somewhat bizarre accomplishment, rather than suggesting that they should, say, develop their powers of curiosity in learning for its own sake? In any case, don't we now have Spellcheck?

Duckworth is emphatic that Grit means doing 'a particular thing in life and choos[ing] to give up a lot of other things in order to do it ... The kid who sticks with one instrument is demonstrating grit.' Her own background gave her some experience of this approach in action, though she has written about it somewhat ambivalently. Her father, Ying Kao Lee, worked for thirty-five years at the DuPont Company, inventing a lacquer that prevented car paint from fading in sunlight.[60] 'My father would literally say things like "you're no genius," to me,' his daughter recalls. 'But he would also say things to my mother, who was an amateur painter, like "you're no Picasso." He would say to my sister and me, "you're never going to win a beauty pageant."'[61] She told a journalist how when she told her father that the meaning of life was to strive to be happy, 'He looked at me surprised and puzzled. He said, "Why would you want to be happy? I want to be accomplished."' Her own words seem to owe a debt to her father's ethos: 'Maybe it's more fun to try something new,' she told a reporter, 'but high levels of achievement require a certain single-mindedness.'[62] As educator Alfie Kohn points out, Duckworth explicitly has no time for music scholars whose exploratory curiosity sees them frivolously flitting from instrument to instrument.[63] It's hard not to concur with the view of Harvard professor of education Jal Mehta that Grit is built on 'a heavily impoverished view of human motivation; in the long run, most people do not persevere at things because they are good at persevering, they persevere because they find things that are worth investing in'.[64]

An additional issue with Duckworth's contribution to the Resilience Orthodoxy is that it is, arguably, unsuited for the times in which we live. The late educationalist Sir Ken Robinson famously campaigned against the prevailing consensus in schooling. 'We have a system of education that is modelled on the interest of industrialism and in the image of it,' he said. 'Schools are still pretty much organised on factory lines – ringing bells, separate facilities, specialised into separate subjects. We still educate children by batches.'[65] Is that the best way to meet the demands of a rapidly changing world, he asked, where the capacity for problem-solving is going to be far more valuable than the ability to work robotically and learn things by rote? One report Duckworth cites to further her view that academic performance is a function of self-discipline found that pupils who thrived in one study 'were not particularly interested in ideas or in cultural or aesthetic pursuits'.[66] Another she mentions argues that self-control (which affords the gritty resilience) is significantly correlated with high grades – but also with conformity and an aversion to risk-taking. Such qualities might have been well suited to the factory age. As Robinson argued, though, it's questionable whether they are particularly desirable today.

There is also a physiological aspect to Grit that needs to be considered. When an injury or infection is detected by the body, our immune system is primed to launch an inflammatory response to eliminate the pathogens responsible and to repair any tissue damage. This response can be measured by assessing the level of an inflammatory molecule known as C-reactive protein (CRP) in our bodies. Evidence suggests that while inflammation is a vital and healthy response to a threat, excessive inflammation can have a negative effect, contributing to serious diseases such as heart disease, diabetes and osteoporosis. It has even been associated with certain forms of cancer.[67] And it appears to be linked with our longevity: those who reach the ripe age of 100 generally have inflammation levels consistent with those of people in their sixties.[68] Such inflammation isn't generally observed until middle age. Its underlying pathology, however, begins in childhood.[69]

With that early impact in mind, two Canadian researchers, Gregory Miller and Carsten Wrosch, measured inflammation levels among a group of teenage girls over the course of a year. They discovered that those students who were unable to 'disengage' from – that is to say, turn away from – goals they had set themselves whose pursuit might impair their mental or physical health, experienced markedly increased inflammation levels. As the researchers put it: 'The rate of CRP increase was twice as rapid among women with poor disengagement tendencies as it was among women at the sample average.' Obviously, Miller and Wrosch didn't advocate that the girls should therefore go to the opposite extreme and take a laid-back, casual attitude to attainment. But they did argue for 'a more balanced perspective on persistence'. Working hard for something that is within our reach or just beyond it offers potentially rich rewards. Striving to achieve excessively ambitious or unattainable goals makes us unwell. The researchers referenced Kenny Rogers' refrain: 'You've got to know when to hold 'em / Know when to fold 'em / Know when to walk away / And know when to run.'[70] Showing Grit in the face of likely failure is advice that may damage your health. Persistence in what you enjoy, and what you're good at, is a much healthier mantra.

*

As for grittiness among school children, there's a pretty big question mark hanging over a claim that Duckworth made in a TED Talk about high-school children in Chicago. She said that gritty kids were more likely to graduate 'even when I matched them on every characteristic I could measure'. Her own paper on the subject suggested a 0.5 per cent variance and did not measure other traits, such as conscientiousness. Meanwhile a large-scale British study that looked at the predicted academic achievement of sixteen-year-old pupils came to the conclusion that it was conscientiousness that mattered (it accounted for 6 per cent of the variance in GCSE grades) and that Grit added nothing.[71] Duckworth herself has acknowledged that the influence of Grit on academic success may be in the 'small to medium' range.[72] Others have sought to rebalance the education debate by pointing out that we can't ignore the role of intelligence in academic achievement. The authors of 'In a Representative Sample Grit Has a Negligible Effect on Educational and Economic Success Compared to Intelligence' believe that 'intelligence contributes 48–90 times more than grit to educational success and 13 times more to job-market success'.[73]

Placed under a critical microscope, Growth Mindset, too, would appear to be rather less than its advocates crack it up to be. The notion that swapping the words 'you have tried hard' for 'you are smart' has a transformative effect on performance is a very arresting one. But Dweck's impressive findings have not been replicated by the researchers who have followed in her wake. Alfie Kohn also raises a concern that approaches making reward or praise conditional on children impressing us are eventually 'construed by the recipient as manipulation'. Ultimately, Kohn tells us, children become wise to the manipulation: 'substantial research literature has shown that the kids typically end up less interested in whatever they were rewarded or praised for doing, because now their goal is just to get the reward or praise'.[74] The fact that Dweck's interventions took place in the lab rather than the classroom may have something to do with this. At any rate, when Yue Li and Professor

Timothy Bates from the University of Edinburgh tried multiple times to reproduce Dweck's results with ten- to twelve-year-olds, they found that 'praise for intelligence had no significant effect on cognitive performance ... Children's own mindsets,' they went on, 'showed no relationship to IQ, school grades, or change in grades across the school year.' Their conclusion was that there was 'little or no support for the idea that growth mindsets are beneficial for children's responses to failure or school attainment[75] ... We're running a third study in China now, with two hundred twelve-year olds,' Bates told the science writer Tom Chivers. 'And the results are just null. People with a growth mindset don't cope any better with failure ... Kids with the growth mindset aren't getting better grades, either before or after our intervention study.'[76]

Meanwhile, a 2018 study with a vast sample size of 365,915 participants found 'that the overall correlation between growth mindset and academic achievement is weak ... Furthermore,' the researchers said, 'this [already low] correlation was moderated by age ... the relationship between mindset and academic achievement was stronger for children and adolescents than for adults.'[77] Brooke MacNamara, who was involved in two analyses that in total covered the academic development of in excess of 400,000 pupils, observed, 'The evidence for growth mindset interventions improving academic achievement is not strong.'[78] Dweck's startling numbers – 67 per cent of children praised for effort choosing to do the more challenging problems compared with only 8 per cent of those praised for their intelligence – have come in for some critical attention, too. The highly influential science blog *Slate Star Codex* described the defining growth-mindset study as 'really weird', adding, 'Everything is like 100% in one group versus 0% in another ... Either something is really wrong here,' it went on, 'or this one little test that separates mastery-oriented from helpless children constantly produces the strongest effects in all of psychology and is never wrong.'[79] 'Normally I would assume these results are falsified,' the blogger concluded, 'but I have looked for all of the usual ways of falsifying results and I can't find any.'

There has been something of a digging-in on both sides of the debate. For her part, Dweck has suggested that those seeking to replicate her findings have failed to implement correctly the interventions she proposed. In the opposite trench, Russell Warne, a doctor of educational psychology and a member of the editorial board of several journals in the field, who has looked closely at the claims and counterclaims made, has written: 'I discovered the one characteristic that the studies that support mindset theory share and that all the studies that contradict the theory lack: *Carol Dweck*. Dweck is a co-author on all three studies that show that teaching a growth mindset can improve students' school performance. She is also not a co-author on all of the studies that cast serious doubt on mindset theory.'[80] Countering Dweck's claim that the problem was that people were mismanaging the interventions, researchers in the Netherlands repeated what she advocated, to the letter. They reported that 'even when the original procedure used in Mueller and Dweck's experiment was followed, [students] were not influenced by the type of praise (i.e. mindset) to which they were exposed'.[81]

One other major debate needs to be taken into account when weighing the pros and cons of the Resilience Orthodoxy approach. Its clear implication is that resilience, Grit – whatever you want to call it – is essentially a personal choice. Either you overcome what life throws at you or you submit to it. It's up to you. Seligman in particular has been highly critical of the tendency over the past century or so to look beyond the individual when seeking to explain individual behaviour. For him, the great dividing line came in 1886. In that year a riot took place in Haymarket Square in Chicago, during which a pipe-bomb was thrown into a crowd, prompting the police to open fire. Within five minutes seven policemen and at least four civilians lay dead. At the time the disaster was blamed on the supposedly bad moral character of the immigrants involved in the demonstration. Four of them, all 'lower-class' workers barely surviving on starvation wages, were hanged. But a sea-change then swept across

American society. There was a dawning realisation that the perpetrators were also, in their way, victims. 'The big idea claimed that it was not bad character but a malignant environment that produced crime,' Seligman has argued. 'Theologians and philosophers took up this cry, and the end result was "social science": a discipline that would demonstrate that environment, rather than character or heredity, is a better explanation of what people do.'[82]

Seligman's own work on resilience offers a very different narrative. 'In general,' he told one interviewer, 'when things go wrong we now have a culture which supports the belief that this was done to you by some larger force, as opposed to, you brought it on yourself by your character or decisions.' It is, he says, 'a recipe for passivity and giving up and helplessness'. He believes that we live in a climate of 'pervasive victimology'.[83] He sees in Duckworth an intellectual soulmate: 'Angela's proposal that school failure might stem in part from the character of the failing students, not just the system that victimises them, appealed to the positive psychologist in me. Here was just the right sort of maverick, someone with very high intellectual credentials and a sterling education but not housebroken enough by politics to prevent her doing serious research on the character strengths of students who succeed and the character deficits of students who fail.'[84]

Seligman and Duckworth say their first research was conducted at a 'socioeconomically and ethnically diverse magnet public school in a city in the Northeast'. Since they are based at the University of Pennsylvania in Philadelphia, and Seligman has created other interventions in schools in the city, it seems fair to assume that that's where they undertook their study. So, since Duckworth mentions the school's socioeconomic diversity, let's examine what that actually involves.

Philadelphia is incredibly poor. With a quarter of its residents reported in 2020 to be living in poverty, it is, statistically, the poorest large city in the United States.[85] Across the US as a whole, 12 per cent of the population are regarded as being 'food insecure' – that is, lacking sufficient food to live a healthy life. In North Philadelphia the figure is more than 30 per cent. We've already encountered the notion of an ACE score (see Chapter 2) and the finding that children with an ACE score of more than four are thirty-three times more likely to experience educational or behavioural problems than those with a lower score. In 2013 a Philadelphia Expanded ACE study found that 40 per cent of the people of the city had a score of four or higher. 'Underachievement among American youth is often blamed on inadequate teachers, boring textbooks, and large class sizes,' Duckworth and Seligman concluded in their first paper. 'We suggest another reason for students falling short of their intellectual potential: their failure to exercise self-discipline.' Given Philadelphia's very real social problems, is it not just possible that other factors might be in play, too?[86]

Across the Atlantic, back in 2012, Chris Cook, a data analyst from the *Financial Times*, took all the national GCSE results for Year 11

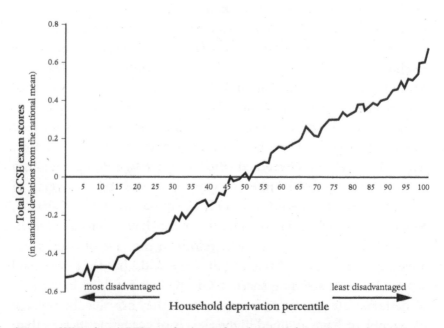

Figure 2: UK students' GCSE results (2012) plotted against their socio-economic backgrounds. There is a clear correlation between social disadvantage and low exam scores.

schoolchildren in 2010 and plotted them against the relative poverty of the pupils' neighbourhoods.[87] I'm not a statistician, but I believe the graph that he came up with offers what scholars might call *a correlation*.

The Grit model assumes a harmonious classroom where it's all about learning. It makes no attempt to engage with the challenges of poverty, domestic issues, adolescent angst and status anxiety that beset those sitting at their desks. As one leading educational researcher put it, 'Schools form a spaghetti junction of overlapping and interconnected relationships' that defy neat categorisation and make it hard to spot trends.[88] To ignore them is to ignore so much of what teachers and pupils face every day.

As with the Super Elite athletes that we encountered in Part One, even those who are held up as poster children for the Grit movement are not necessarily all they seem. Gene Brody from the University of Georgia, who has been involved in a number of studies of Black adolescents, has taken a close look at those African American children with low socioeconomic status who have demonstrated high degrees of self-control and self-regulation. 'The resilience literature,' he says, 'is characterised by a widespread assumption that, if children and youth are doing well in terms of external behaviours – for example, if they excel academically and evince high levels of self-esteem – they have successfully negotiated major adversities.'[89] Unfortunately, he argues, it's not that simple. Those Black youths he studied who were able to demonstrate high levels of self-control despite growing up in the abject poverty of what he calls the *Black Belt* (South Carolina, Georgia, Alabama, Mississippi, and Louisiana) – 'children [who] have been called *resilient* because their competence develops in the face of contextual adversity' – may have thrived against the odds, but they have paid a price for their seeming success. On the one hand, by being able to demonstrate greater personal control, they are able, by the age of twenty, to have attained higher levels of academic success than their peers and to be less prone to alcohol and drug abuse. But by the same age they are also showing more obesity, and suffer from higher blood pressure and higher stress hormone levels. Epigenetic ageing analysis suggests that their bodies are also showing more signs of wear and tear. They may have suppressed the pain they have grown up with, but it has still made its mark.

Orthodox education policy makes no allowance for the implications of Brody's study, and of others that make similar claims. David Johnson, a clinical psychologist working at the Post Traumatic Stress Center at Yale University, observes that 'Many strict school reform programs have this "No Excuses" policy. Yes you might be living in poverty, yes you might be subject to racism, yes you might be being beaten every night but that's not an excuse not to perform in school.'[90] But for such experts as Brody and Jack Shonkoff, the director of Harvard's Center on the Developing Child, this is a woefully inadequate response. Shonkoff explains his objection in these terms: 'We don't say to the people who got cancer, why don't you suck it up and be like the person who didn't get cancer. But when we see problems in school, problems in behaviour, we say to people "why don't you suck it up and be like that other guy who is doing well in school and who isn't doing drugs?"' Shonkoff believes that we are wrongly 'captivated by the self-made person', and that this focus on individual success causes us to ignore the burdens that crowd in on so many people. 'Can you learn how to deal with conflict constructively when you grow up hearing your parents screaming at each other every night? Can you learn how to focus your attention when you live in a neighbourhood where you hear sirens and gunshots? Can you control your impulses when you never know if your father with a drinking problem is going to strike out in a rage? Can you delay gratification when all of your friends around you are doing drugs? Can you plan for the future when it's hard to get through even a single day?[91] ... Resilience is not something that is just a matter of grit and determination,' he concludes.

Diane Ravitch, a lifelong historian of education who served as Assistant Secretary of Education under President Barack Obama, puts it this way: 'The notion that kids in poverty can overcome hunger, lack of medical care, homelessness, and trauma by buckling down and persisting was always stupid and heartless,' adding that it appears to come not from academia, but is rather 'exactly what you would expect to hear from Scrooge or the Koch brothers or Betsy DeVos'.[92] (In fairness, Ravitch is doing a great disservice to Ebenezer Scrooge who, after all, changed his ways and became a second father to Tiny Tim. Her basic point, though, still stands.) Jal Mehta, education professor at Harvard, is similarly concerned by the finger-pointing that appears to be going on here. 'The most prominent critique,' he says, 'is that an emphasis on grit is a way of "blaming the victim" – rather than take up larger questions of social, economic, and racial justice, if only the most disadvantaged kids were a little "grittier" they could make it in life.'[93]

Perhaps the last word on this particular subject should go to Hazim Hardeman, a high performer who was contacted by his local paper after he became the first student from his deprived 'North Philly' background to join the ranks of Bill Clinton, Susan Rice and Senator Cory Booker as a Rhodes scholar. His was seemingly a classic Grit story. He had grown up in a neighbourhood riven with gun violence and poverty. Yet now he was studying at Oxford. But Hardeman took issue with his local newspaper when they chose to profile his achievements. 'Don't be happy for me that I overcame these barriers,' he told them. 'Be mad as hell that they exist in the first place.'[94]

We should be sceptical of the grand claims of the Resilience Orthodoxy then, but I'd caution against throwing the baby out with the bath water altogether. There is, after all, a lot to be said for telling people – children, in particular – that they have agency over their life and that their attitude can have a positive impact. What's more, recent research suggests that it can work at a modest level. In 2019 *Nature* published a report by twenty-five researchers, including both Carol Dweck and Angela Duckworth, based on a representative sample of 12,490 American teenagers. All of them had been told 'that the brain is like a muscle that grows strong and smarter when it undergoes rigorous learning experiences' and had been asked to reflect on how they might strengthen their own brains through work, and how they would use their knowledge to help a struggling peer. The conclusion the researchers came to was that a fifty-minute intervention 'reduced by 3 percentage points the rate at which adolescents in the US were off-track for graduation at the end of the year'. There was acknowledgement that the school environment was an important factor here ('unsupportive peer climates risked paying a social price for taking on intellectual challenges in front of peers', the researchers hypothesised) and higher-performing students tended not to be particularly affected by the programme. Nevertheless, over the whole cohort of pupils there was a 0.1-point improvement on the four-point GPA school grading system.

That may sound a small number, but if a fifty-minute exercise can enhance performance even by a fraction, that could represent the difference between success and failure for some pupils. For their part, the small group of students at risk of not completing school might see some benefit in this brief life lesson. Even so, it's important not to kid ourselves. This relatively small effect (which hasn't been consistently observed by others) is a bit like the benefits that come from learning a different style of revising, taking notes or being encouraged to be a bit more constructive. It's not the transformation of a youth into a resilience-charged warrior.[95]

Arguably what all this comes down to is the distinction that psychologists make between a trait and a state. A trait is a long-term characteristic; it's part of an individual's personality. A state, by contrast, is something more temporary. Proponents of the resilience school of thinking appear to regard the training they offer as the means to develop a new character trait. Perhaps what they're actually doing is fostering a state – helpful, perhaps, but not something that automatically becomes inextricably locked up with someone's outlook and personality.

One of the most measured arguments I have heard comes from Adrian Bethune, a thought-leading teacher in Hertfordshire who is a strong advocate for finding progressive, pupil-led approaches to learning. I asked him what he thought of such strategies as Growth Mindset. 'There is good research behind it,' he responded. 'The problem is that in education people look for quick fixes and implement things poorly so they don't get the desired effects.' He directed me to the more positive reports that suggested that growth mindset had achieved small but measurable effects in children's learning. Bethune's conclusion was a pragmatic one: 'Nuance is the key and that is often lacking in education. It's such an extrinsic, results-focused, busy arena that schools want quick fixes and don't dig down into the detail.'[96]

As I considered the claims and counterclaims made for resilience, I wondered what Seligman now makes of it all. His work may have been widely praised and his suggestions just as widely taken up, but it has also come in for a lot of criticism, which he seems to have taken to heart. I therefore contacted him, explained what I was doing and asked him where I should turn next. As I pushed the Send button I felt I was being rather presumptuous. To my delight, an answer popped back within six minutes – a nine-word response in twenty-point font:

15:16 Wed, 27 May
Seligman, Martin E. P.
****@****.edu
Google Kubzansky for the last ten years of research.

Professor Laura Kubzansky teaches Social and Behavioural Sciences at Harvard and, as I quickly discovered, her take on resilience is rather different from that of Seligman. For her, resilience is not a trait we are born with or that can be inculcated (in this she concurs with resilience expert Dr Ann Masten, who says that 'Resilience – potential or manifested – should not be construed as a trait, although many traits could influence resilience'[97] and that resilience is a type of 'ordinary magic').[98] Kubzansky is also highly sceptical of the individualistic ethos that runs through the Resilience Orthodoxy: 'If it becomes all about the individual and the individual not somehow rising above things and heroically achieving,' she writes, 'that becomes a really easy discussion point and perhaps even a distraction. Because, with a focus on the individual, larger entities and social structures do not have to take responsibility. This results in the thinking that it is not the government's job, it is not an organisation's job, it is not a community's job, to think about why people are not doing better.'[99]

Kubzansky goes on to point out that even those people who are able to meet adversity with resilience pay a price in terms of their physical health (our Super Elite athletes and the Black Belt students come to mind here): 'we have consistently found a residual effect of exposure to adversity on physical health,' she says, 'so that the psychologically resilient individuals do not have quite as good subsequent health outcomes as the individuals who did not confront adversity.' Adversity hurts, in other words – whether there's a bounce-back or not. 'It suggests to us that you cannot fully undo or unroll or reverse the potentially harmful effects of adversity exposure; you may be able to mitigate them, but you may not be able to make them go away.'[100]

What Kubzansky's work suggests to me is that we should not be thinking of resilience either as some kind of natural personal trait or as an injunction to toughen up a bit. And we certainly shouldn't regard it as a permanent mental state. Indeed, it's a term we should really be treating very gingerly indeed. As Professor Haslam, whom I mentioned earlier, has highlighted, we seem to have moved from a discussion of stress and how to deal with it, which came to the fore in the early years of this century, to a belief that 'the real problem here is that people just aren't resilient enough'. That in turn has triggered the notion that there are people around who can, as Haslam puts it, be 'fixed with some handy intervention, like either a bit of cognitive restructuring or some help with reappraisal framing', or told 'maybe go and have a massage' if those techniques don't work.[101] To that extent, the Resilience Orthodoxy has become a distraction from the very real mental issues that confront people every day.

Given that current models of resilience have so clearly been weighed and found wanting, let's leave them behind and instead explore a very different model of human behaviour in general and of resilience in particular – a far more convincing model, to my mind, that takes account of the many objections that have been expressed about resilience, Grit and Growth Mindset.

Back in 1966 the psychologist David Bakan observed that human motivation (and therefore our ability to respond to adversity) was founded on principles of 'agency and communion'[102] ... Agency,' he wrote, 'manifests itself in the formation of separations; communion in the lack of separations. Agency manifests itself in isolation, alienation, and aloneness; communion in contact, openness, and union. Agency manifests itself in the urge to master; communion in non-contractual cooperation.' In other words, our existence has a yin-and-yang quality: we operate as individuals when we show individual agency, but we also rely on others to give us a sense of communion and contact.

A decade or so later came the beginnings of what, in its fully fledged form, would be known as Self-Determination Theory. From the 1970s through to the 1990s psychologists Richard Ryan and Edward Deci set themselves the task of unravelling the secrets of human motivation and why, when presented with the same situation, different people will behave so differently from one another. In a social situation, for example, some will bound eagerly and effervescently into a room; others will sidle in, radiating diffidence or even hostility. When it comes to work, some will approach a task with drive and a desire to learn; others will undertake it reluctantly, their motivation virtually imperceptible. Some children are eager to learn; others can't wait to get out of the classroom.

Ryan and Deci's conclusion was that the qualities 'essential for facilitating optimal functioning of the natural propensities for growth and integration, as well as for constructive social development and personal well-being' were threefold: autonomy, competence and relatedness.[103] Autonomy is the ability to exercise a locus of control.[104] It's the sort of thing that Daniel Pink talks about in his bestselling book *Drive* when he suggests that motivation is down to autonomy, mastery and purpose; or that David McClelland, a psychologist from Yale and the author of *Need Theory*, refers to in his model of the levers of motivation, which he defines as power, achievement and affiliation. Competence involves feeling 'confidence and effective in relation to whatever it is that you are doing'. Relatedness describes the need to feel cared for by others, to feel that you belong to the groups that are important to you. As the following table shows, the differences between McClelland in the 1950s and Deci and Ryan in the 1990s are largely ones of terminology.

Three Needs – David McClelland (1950s)	Self-Determination Theory – Deci and Ryan (1990s)
Power	Autonomy
Achievement	Competence
Affiliation	Relatedness

What these models suggest is that to look at resilience as a personal trait is dangerously reductive. We are motivated by a range of factors and forces, both internal and external. To focus narrowly on one or two, to the exclusion of the third, is to mislead ourselves about what really makes humans tick.

In this context it's worth considering briefly a seminal study that Dr Emmy Werner undertook on the Hawaiian island of Kauai for a period of forty years from 1955 to 1995. Over those four decades she tracked the lives and experiences of a full cohort of locals from birth, following the lives of every islander born in 1955. Her ambition was to understand how the complex mosaic of their life experiences affected their long-term well-being. Reflecting the nature of the Kauai population as a whole, two-thirds of the participants were drawn from families regarded as stable, and one-third from backgrounds categorised as being 'higher-risk'. Some, Werner noted, were able to transcend life's inevitable setbacks; others found them difficult to negotiate. In extreme cases the outcome of adversity manifested in the form of challenges such as learning difficulties, delinquency, teenage pregnancy or mental-health problems, or a combination of a number of these factors.

Werner's conclusion was that those who were able to overcome adversity had certain qualities in common. They had a clear sense of identity and control or, as she put it, 'By the time they graduated from high school the resilient youths had developed a positive self-concept and an internal locus of control.' In addition, they were able to draw on others for help and support: 'The resilient children also found emotional support outside of their own families. They tended to have at least one and usually several close friends, especially the girls. They relied on informal networks of kin and neighbours, peers and elders.'[105] Real-world validation, then, for that tripartite approach to human behaviour advocated by McClelland and Deci and Ryan. And particular validation for the factor that conventional resilience thinking wholly ignores: community. As Alex Haslam explains, 'Resilience is something that when you look at it in the world, it isn't a manifestation of individuals as individuals. It's a manifestation of groups and of individuals as group members. Resilience is something that only occurs in and to groups.' Indeed, it's this emphasis on collective strength that is key. To give him his due over the years, Martin Seligman himself has acknowledged the vital importance of *relatedness* in shaping the well-being of individuals, but it's something that is underplayed when it comes to the tenets of the Resilience Orthodoxy. Social connection is crucial to all our welfares.

So let's leave resilience, Grit and Growth Mindset behind and explore the true origins of personal strength. In order to avoid confusion with the current associations of the word 'resilience', I am going to term the phenomenon *fortitude*, and in the chapters that follow I want to advance a social-identity approach to explaining how it functions. First I want to look at the personal qualities involved. Then I want to consider the social aspects of fortitude. The terms I have elected to use for fortitude's three pillars are drawn from previous researchers, but are also subtly different, as the following table shows.

Fortitude (a social-identity explanation of resilience)	Self-Determination Theory – Deci and Ryan (1990s)	Three Needs – David McClelland (1950s)
Control	Autonomy	Power
Identity	Competence	Achievement
Community	Relatedness	Affiliation

Let's start with control.

Chapter 6

Control

The Cornerstone of Fortitude

A diner on the outskirts of Brooklyn, New York. Twenty-something Christine Miserandino and her best friend were eating a late supper of French fries, dipping them in gravy as they gossiped about various topics of interest: their day, study, boys. As they ate, Miserandino took out some pills and, as was her evening routine, started laying them out on the table in front of her. Her friend eyed her. Then she asked her a question: 'Christine, what's it like to have lupus?'

Lupus is an autoimmune condition that Miserandino had suffered from since childhood. Left unchecked, it leads to the body's defence system mistakenly attacking healthy tissue. Miserandino was largely able to keep it at bay, its only visible sign for most people who met her being the walking stick that she sometimes used, but it exerted a severe toll nevertheless. Her friend had accompanied her to doctors' appointments, had seen Christine doubled over and vomiting from the pain that lupus can inflict; she'd grown familiar with doctors and strangers saying to her, 'But you don't look sick.' The fact, though, that even now she had to ask what lupus was like was baffling and frustrating. 'If I can't explain this to my best friend,' Miserandino thought, 'how could I explain my world to anyone else?' She decided that 'I had to at least try.'

Christine proceeded to grab every spoon on the table, plus several from the empty tables around them. Then she pressed all twelve spoons into her companion's palms. 'Here you go, you have lupus,' she said.[1] As the cold metal clanked in her friend's hands, she explained that what distinguishes sick people from healthy ones is that sick people have to make decisions about resources and scarcity that their healthy peers rarely stop to consider. 'The healthy have the luxury of a life without choices,' she later explained, 'a gift most people take for granted.' A healthy person has a virtually limitless supply of 'spoons'. When you have lupus, however, you have a sparse and finite supply, and you have to decide very carefully each day how to allocate each spoon. Even then, that 'doesn't guarantee that you might not lose some along the way'.

Miserandino asked her friend to outline a typical day. First, her friend said, she would get up and have breakfast. Miserandino briefly interrupted her to take a spoon, and then continued to keep a tally: 'Showering cost her a spoon ... Reaching high and low that early in the morning would actually cost more than one spoon, but I figured I would give her a break; I didn't want to scare her right away.' Getting dressed would be another spoon. Before her friend knew it, she'd spent six spoons – and she hadn't even yet made it to work. Christine explained that coping with lupus demands that level of conscious attention because, once the spoons are gone, they're gone. Sometimes, she said, you can borrow against tomorrow's spoons, but it's always possible that tomorrow brings challenges you hadn't anticipated, in which case you face a dangerous deficit. What would happen, for example, if you caught a cold or felt unwell? Being prepared for any eventuality is a key element of managing lupus.

'Christine, how do you do it? Do you really do this every day?' her friend asked, welling up. Miserandino explained that there were good days and bad days. But she could never escape having to count her spoons. She handed over one that she had been concealing. 'I have learned to live life with an extra spoon in my pocket, in reserve. You need to always be prepared.'

In the two decades since Christine Miserandino first articulated her Spoon Theory, it's become a globally employed metaphor. It helps those suffering or recovering from illness to express their feelings and explain the challenges they face every day. My energy is finite and limited – I have to use it carefully. Those fortunate enough to be healthy and able-bodied might appear to have endless energy in comparison to people like Christine, but the metaphor has relevance for them, too. They may believe that they have an infinite number of spoons at their disposal. The fact is, though, that negotiating everyday life and exercising the constant control that demands both extort a price, whether that is conscious or unconscious.

The price has to be paid because a sense of personal control is the cornerstone of fortitude. In fact it is an integral part of what it is to be human. A sense of control over our own destinies ensures a sense of self-esteem and a feeling of empowerment. It safeguards us against depression. It helps ward off physical illness. It even makes us better parents.

It also reduces stress levels – and not only in humans. In one experiment rats were deprived of a sense of control via an injection of Botox that froze their muscles and limited their mobility. A measure of control, however, was returned to some of them in the form of pieces of wood on which they could chew. The researchers found that the stress levels of those rats able to exert some control over their lives through chewing did not go above the previous baseline. Among those denied that degree of control, by contrast, stress levels rose to seven times their previous level.[2] Chewing is, of course, a well-known panacea for stress – in humans as well as rodents (the technical explanation for this, according to the researchers, is that 'it prevents both the pressor response and the stress-induced secretion of adrenocorticotropic hormone'). Next time you find yourself powering through a couple of packs of Wrigley's Extra in the course of the day you might want to consider that it's not the fresh minty taste you should be thinking about, but any stresses you might be experiencing.[3] Rats are not the only members of the animal kingdom that respond to the presence or absence of control. Monkeys similarly given or denied power over aspects of their lives (such as when their food and water is delivered to them) later show either more or less confidence accordingly.[4]

When it comes to the physiological impact of control, it was actually Martin Seligman who was among the first to demonstrate its crucial importance. I've already mentioned his experiment with dogs that led to his theory of learned helplessness. In another experiment, he and his team injected rats with a cancerous tumour with a 50 per cent lethality rate (in other words, half of the animals injected in this way wouldn't survive). The researchers then placed the rats at random in one of three environments. In the first, sixty-four mildly painful shocks were administered over a period of time, which the rats could avoid if they learned to press a bar. In the second, the same series of shocks were given, but the rats had no means by which they could avoid them. The first group of rats, then, could learn how to control their environment; the second had to endure what Seligman described as a state of helplessness. The third group – to which electric shocks were not given – was the control group.

As predicted, half of the rats in the control group died of the cancer with which they had been injected. But the fates of the two groups that had received electric shocks followed very different paths. Among the rats that had no control of the electric punishment meted out to them, 63 per cent perished. Among those that learned to exercise control over their environment, the mortality rate was 25 per cent. Seligman explained the outcome in the following terms: 'The low rate of tumour rejection was not a function of shock *per se*, but resulted from the animals' lack of control over shock. The lack of control in other aspects of their life directly impacted their bodies' holistic response to threat.' He and his researchers concluded that the body's immune system plays a role in preventing the spread of cancer 'and there is evidence that the immune system is suppressed after uncontrollable aversive events'. Administering electric shocks to rodents might seem an extreme way to test helplessness, and to have no parallels in normal life. It's interesting to note, though, that noise stress has been shown to adversely affect the immune system of mice, disrupting their production of T and B cells.[5] Control has many manifestations, but lack of control leads to the same result.

As with lab rats, so with humans, as various studies from the 1950s onwards have shown.[6] It's been observed, for example, how

Zen meditators and yogic masters – individuals who are able to exert astonishing powers of control, to the point where they are able to manipulate their heart rates – can withstand extraordinary levels of pain without registering a measurable response. In one series of experiments in the 1960s that might raise ethical qualms today, yogis were sealed in airtight boxes for ten hours and had their hands plunged into freezing-cold water. All demonstrated extra-ordinary mastery of their bodies' response to the shocks, suggesting a high level of control over what had previously been regarded as automatic responses to stimuli.[7] A similar picture emerges – at a less superhuman level – from an experiment run by James Averill and Miriam Rosenn at the University of Berkeley in the 1970s. Here volunteers were told to prepare themselves for an electric shock, but were given a choice of audio streams to listen to as they waited: one was a constant flow of background music, the other was a dreary monotone that gave way to a warning signal five seconds before the electric shock was administered.[8] While what they heard had no impact on the discomfort they experienced, 'skin conductiv-ity' measurements revealed that those who had aural warning of the shock about to come experienced less psychological stress. As Averill observed, 'The provision of personal control, even if only illusory, is one such intervention; and its beneficial effects are some-times dramatic.'[9] Similar findings emerged from an electric-shock experiment conducted by Ernest Haggard in 1943. Volunteers who administered a shock themselves experienced less stress than those who received it from a third party.

So strong is our desire to feel in control that when we think we lack it, our minds will perform tricks on us to suggest that perhaps we do indeed possess it.[10] It's been shown, for example, that people who have been deprived of a sense of control will perform all sorts of mental gymnastics to persuade themselves that in fact they do have control.[11] They'll invent or believe conspiracy stories that offer the false comfort that there is an explanation for events that may, in reality, simply be random. One study found that they'll believe they can detect patterns in the random, snowy, static images you see on a television that has not been tuned to a particular channel.[12] Another study established that people placed in an initial situation where they felt they lacked control then showed a greater pre- paredness to drive a long way to reach an ice-cream store that offered a selection of fifteen flavours than to drive the short dis- tance to one offering only three.[13] It's not even as though the control at stake in such scenarios is a matter of life and death. Even the simple act of telling someone that the answer they've just given to a question is incorrect, when it is in fact correct, is sufficient to disorientate them and make them feel they lack the control they thought they had.[14]

If these various experiments show the impact of control in the short term, there are plenty of others that reveal its longer-term effects. The findings of Professor Snehlata Jaswal and Anita Dewan are an interesting case in point. The two researchers evaluated 139 girls who were studying at a Chandigarh college. Those girls who felt they lacked a sense of personal control became locked in a vicious cycle of depression: the less control they felt they had, the more depressed they became.[15] Not only that: the less control they believed they had, the more likely it was that they believed that their lives were controlled by the whims of chance and fate.[16] Ultimately such people become locked in a condition sometimes called the 'depressive paradox': they feel both that events are beyond their control and that they are to blame for their misfortune.[17] Put in rather more technical terms, if individuals with a high internal locus believe that they have autonomous control over their lives (and can therefore also have more impact on their environment), additionally there are people who have an external locus of control that causes them to feel a degree of powerlessness over the circum- stances and outcome of their life.

In this context, it's troubling to note that in the US, for example, there is a growing tendency among teenagers to believe in an exter- nal locus of control – in other words, to believe that their fate is beyond their control. Jean Twenge, a psychologist based at San Diego University, who has become one of the foremost experts in youth development, has looked closely at the long-running Monitoring the Future (MTF) survey conducted by the University of Michigan that, since 1975, has tracked the attitudes and lifestyles of American teenagers nationwide. Back in 1977, she notes, around 54 per cent of twelfth-graders (aged seventeen or eighteen) agreed that 'people who accept their condition in life are happier than those who try to change things'. By 2015 the proportion of twelfth-graders accepting this fatalistic proposition had risen to more than 68 per cent. In 1977, 44 per cent of twelfth-graders agreed with the statement 'every time I try to get ahead, something or somebody stops me'. By 2015, 56 per cent of the youngsters believed this – an increase of more than a quarter.

The academic Jonathan Haidt has interpreted this data as reflecting the consequences of a new, more restrictive style of parenting, whereby children are so tightly managed and constrained in their

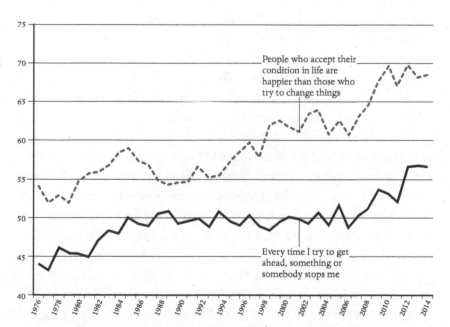

Figure 3: The rising fatalism of 12ᵗʰ-graders, as charted in the long-running Monitoring the Future survey conducted by the University of Michigan.

play that they feel no sense of control over independent decision-making. For his part, New York Stern Professor Scott Galloway believes such a decline in a sense of personal control has led to something of a pushback on free speech on college campuses. 'I'm sure there are studies of the people who overcome injustice, who are resilient, who bust out of the hand that's been dealt them; one of the key components of that type of resilience is them believing they have a locus of control.' It's Galloway's contention that when students sense that their thoughts are being policed, they don't feel they have the agency – the control – to express what they believe.[18]

If an absence of control has psychological repercussions, so, as with lab rats, it has physiological ones, too. The repressed stress that comes from not feeling fully in control can slow recovery times for everything from injuries to ailments. Dental students who were administered puncture wounds in the hard palate at the top of their mouths took 40 per cent longer to heal during the stressful exam season than they did during their carefree summer break.[19] Cancer victims with a low sense of control have been shown to be more likely to suffer a recurrence of the disease or to die from it.[20] For Gabor Maté, the man who so strongly believes that mind and body are closely interrelated systems, the list of physical health problems that can be associated with a lack of control is almost endless. 'When we have been prevented from learning how to say no, our bodies may end up saying it for us,' he writes. 'In my private family practice, I observed these same patterns in people I treated for multiple sclerosis, inflammatory ailments of the bowel such as ulcerative colitis and Crohn's disease, chronic fatigue syndrome, autoimmune disorders, fibromyalgia, migraine, skin disorders, endometriosis and many other conditions. In important areas of their lives, almost none of my patients with serious disease had ever learned to say no.'[21] His list could also have included cardiovascular disease. It should come as no surprise that the 'freedom to control one's life' is one of the six 'predictors' that the *World Happiness Report* uses to help determine the levels of happiness ('subjective well-being') in countries around the world (the others are GDP per capita, healthy life expectancy, corruption, social support and giving to charity).[22] As many researchers have shown 'freedom to control one's life' has health implications, too.

Control might superficially sound like one of the pillars of a standard resilience model. It's about agency, about empowerment, about people taking command of their own destinies. But, actually, it has another dimension to it – one that the resilience way of thinking does not allow for. The Resilience Orthodoxy, as we've seen, focuses on the individual. Control is certainly an internal, personal force, but it also has a significant external, interpersonal aspect to it. We seek control of our own destinies, but the extent to which we are successful or unsuccessful is shaped by factors outside us and often beyond our immediate grasp.

One of these factors is status. Essentially, the higher your status, the more control you feel; the lower your status, the greater your sense of powerlessness. The clinician Nancy Adler has shown how these states play out in terms of physical health in a study of female residents of San Francisco. She asked each one to consider which of the ten rungs they felt they occupied on a ten-step ladder, the MacArthur Scale of Subjective Social Status. She then used their self-assessment, alongside other measures of stress and health, to form judgements of her patients' relative vitality. What she found was that where these women placed themselves on the social-status ladder proved a better predictor of their health than their income, their education and other more objective measures of social standing. The higher a woman placed herself on the status ladder, the smaller would be her waist–hip ratio (a measure of obesity, amongst other elements of well-being); the lower would be her base level of that key chemical indicator of stress, cortisol; and the less sensitive she would be to the effect of cortisol.[23] Because she was less stressed and *felt* less stressed, she was therefore less likely to resort to stress-mitigating or escapist habits, such as drinking or binge-watching movies, than women who regarded themselves as being of lower status. The higher Adler's women placed themselves on the ladder, the more likely they were to say they felt in control of their lives, and the more likely they were to say they dealt with problems by tackling them head-on.

This is no isolated study. We often assume that it's those in high-status positions who experience the most stress and the various ills that attend it. In fact research finding after research finding shows precisely the opposite. One such is that of Professor Michael Marmot, one of the founding intellects of social epidemiology – the discipline that examines how our position in society impacts on our health – who showed in his study of the UK Civil Service that, among male civil servants aged forty to sixty-four, 'the higher the rank in the civil service, the lower the risk of death'. Let's be clear: none of the civil servants that the study looked at could claim to be experiencing real material deprivation – they had good jobs; they weren't going short of meals. Even so, by virtue of the fact that they had less control over their work and so felt more stress, those lower down in the pecking order fared less well in terms of health than those higher up.[24]

Marmot concluded that the jaded notion that 'it's tough at the top' is false: 'No, the key to the status syndrome lies in the brain. It is stress arising from the inability to control our lives, to turn to others when we lose control or to participate fully in all that society has to offer. The myth that it is more stressful to be at the top of the pile than at the bottom should long ago have given way to facts. A way to stress an animal, of the human or non-human variety, is to remove control. This is true whether the animal or person is high status or low status, but low control is more common the lower down the pile you find yourself.'[25]

In terms of the health impact of relative status and the sense of control that comes with it, Marmot had this to say: 'Low grade chronic stress, acting through the brain, mobilises hormones – cortisol and adrenaline and noradrenaline – that lead to profound biological changes. Among these is likely to be the metabolic syndrome, linked to insulin resistance that increases risk of diabetes and heart disease.' The higher an individual's status, the longer they will enjoy good health; the lower it is, the more likely it is that their health will be undermined by ulcers, loss of muscle weight and the suppression of the immune system.[26]

And while wealth and status aren't quite the same thing, the fact remains that richer people live longer than poorer people. In the UK the gap in life expectancy between the wealthy and the poor is nine years.[27] In Australia, one report suggests, it could be as much as nineteen years.[28] In between those two extremes lies a gradient. Catherine Haslam and her colleagues argue that 'the health of people in the top 5% income bracket is better than that of those in the income bracket just below them', and the same effect is observed stepwise down the income distribution of society. They observe that 'even for those groups for whom all basic economic or financial needs are well met and where it is unlikely that there are substantial differences in education or key health services, we find that differences in wealth and income matter for health and well-being'. Obviously there's a practical factor here, at least at the extremes: poor people may have to settle for unhealthy housing, for example. But it's the psychological factor that is really key.

It's not hard to see why economically disadvantaged people should feel a lack of control, or that there should be a correlation between being at the wrong end of income inequality and experiencing depression.[29] Critical to a sense of control is having the resources available that allow us to act on the decisions we make. Without them, we lack the necessary leverage and experience a sense of powerlessness. Two Canadian researchers who talked to new mothers in Ontario a few weeks after they had given birth found that those from higher up the social hierarchy found it easier to cope with the stresses of motherhood ('new-baby blues') than those from lower-class, poorer families.[30] They concluded that because lower-status women have fewer resources, they have less of a sense of control, which in turn heightens the stresses and strains they experience. Effectively, money buys you control. Not having money deprives you of it.

As Catherine Ross and John Mirowsky put it: 'People in lower socioeconomic positions have a triple burden: They have more problems to deal with; their personal histories are likely to have left them with a deep sense of powerlessness; and that sense of powerlessness discourages them from marshalling whatever energy and resources they do have in order to solve their problems.'[31] We've already established that people born into poverty are statistically more likely to have high ACE scores, to have more problems to deal with and to have the fewest resources to marshal in order to deal with them. Ross describes how deprived communities can become locked into 'perceptions of powerlessness' – perceptions that are exacerbated by 'Exposure to uncontrollable, negative events and conditions in the neighbourhood in the form of crime, noise, vandalism, graffiti, garbage, fights, and danger ... [N]eighbourhood disorder,' she argues, 'produces more mistrust among those who feel powerless to control their lives than among those with a strong sense of personal control.'[32] It's not that low-income, low-status lives and social problems go step-in-step. It's that the lack of control that low-income, low-status lives involve can create challenges that simply don't trouble those at the other end of the spectrum.

No doubt some would argue that cause and effect are being muddled here. The model I've described assumes that someone has control, and the mental and physical advantages that go with it, because they have status and/or money. Might it not be the case, sceptics may argue, that the opposite is true: people have status because they are able to exert control? In other words, however you dress it up, it's all still down to the individual – external factors don't play a role?

That may be true in individual cases. But it's worth bearing in mind that status and comparative social advantage can be, and frequently are, passed down the generations in a way that isn't a simple matter of heredity (after all, just because one generation of a family is talented and successful, it doesn't automatically follow that the next one will be, but it *is* likely that they will benefit directly from their forebears' talent and success). It's also worth considering that researchers who have looked both at humans and animals have often found it very difficult to isolate biological reasons for an individual's dominant or subordinate role.[33] Indeed, one study found that the physiological effects of status and control could be created merely by telling volunteers at random that they belonged to either a high- or a low-status group: those informed that they were high-status were found to have healthier blood pressure than those who thought they were low-status; interestingly, when the members of that higher-status group were then informed that they were about to play a game that might well redefine where they stood relative to the others, their blood pressure went up.[34] It's less that control gives us status than that status gives us control.

If status and wealth affect our sense of control, so, too, does a closely associated factor: the work we do. It's something that the psychologist Melvin Kohn – in frequent partnership with Carmi Schooler – was among the first to observe and describe back in the 1970s and 1980s. 'In all cases, job affects man more than man affects job,' the pair observed, adding, 'We find that the job has a substantially greater impact on [workers'] psychological function than the reverse.'[35]

For people in higher-status jobs this has historically been good news. Kohn and Schooler's research, which took the form of longitudinal studies of male workers in various walks of life – from drivers to accountants, and from builders to teachers – found that 'higher positions in the supervisory hierarchy results in substantially more complex, less routine, less closely supervised, and physically lighter work [and] higher levels of pay.'[36] Such a sense of control had a positive knock-on effect in other areas of their lives. 'Men who are self-directed in their work are consistently more likely to become [less obsessed with rules], self-confident and not self-deprecatory, to become less fatalistic, less anxious, and less conformist in their ideas.'[37] By contrast, men in low-status jobs, who simultaneously had less control, suffered from low levels of self-confidence and high levels of self-deprecation. These played themselves out in a belief in a strict adherence to rules and a resistance to change, and also manifested themselves in the way the next generation was brought up. Middle-class parents tended to encourage creative expression. Those with little or no autonomy at work were observed to grant little of it at home.[38] Kohn and Schooler's conclusion was that work is the 'principal mechanism by which class exerts its psychological impact'.[39]

If Kohn and Schooler are to be believed, it's not difficult to see how the poor treatment of one generation can have grim implications for the next. Research has found that parents deprived of control at work and determined to exercise it at home will have children who, because they in turn are deprived of control, are more inclined to depression, more likely to demonstrate hostility and aggression towards their peers and more likely to exhibit low self-esteem.[40] An authoritarian adult is also significantly more likely to have children who are bullies – a phenomenon that one set of researchers has called 'shame displacement'.[41] Another study back in 2013 suggested that almost half of all adolescents who engaged in bullying had authoritarian fathers.[42] If we have no control over ourselves, we pay it forward. Subsequent research has refined and elaborated on Kohn and Schooler's work. Some suggest that how parents behave at home is more a question of their experiences than of their status at work – indeed, poor treatment at work can have a greater negative psychological impact than unemployment. But the essentials remain the same. Lack of control at work can manifest itself in stricter, less permissive parenting.[43]

It can also impact on our well-being in other ways. A social-media post by Daphne K. Lee that went viral in 2020 outlined a phenomenon that Chinese workers label *bàofù xìng áoyè*: 'revenge bedtime procrastination'. '[P]eople who don't have much control over their daytime life,' she explained, 'refuse to sleep early in order to regain some sense of freedom during late night hours.'[44] In response to her post, one Twitter user, Kenneth Kwok, outlined what *bàofù xìng áoyè* meant for him: 'Typical[ly I work] 8 to 8 in office, [by the time I] arrive home after dinner and shower it's 10pm, probably won't just go to sleep and repeat the same routine. A few hours of "own time" is necessary to survive.' It's not an experience that is unique to the Chinese, either. Psychologists suggest that this tendency is univer-sal: people 'may be less likely to stick to their intended bedtime after a particularly taxing day', they conclude.[45] Denied control in our jobs, we find ways to rebel. Unfortunately, as I show in Chapter 12, depriving oneself of sleep happens to be a particularly self-destruc-tive form of rebellion.

If all this implies that there's a simple divide between higher-status jobs that offer control and lower-status ones that don't, it's not quite as straightforward as that. Over recent years there has been a trend apparent across a wide range of jobs and careers for workers to feel that the autonomy allowed them at work is slipping away (a 2017 survey funded by the UK's Department for Education and the Welsh government suggests that – in Britain, at least – this is an issue that stretches back to the 1990s[46]). Nearly two-thirds of workers sounded out for a 2011 UK government survey said that their management didn't allow them a say in the decisions it made, while half said they weren't even consulted.[47] (Interestingly, the same survey showed that 90 per cent of those who said that their employers *did* allow them a voice stated that they felt a sense of loyalty to their organ-isation, compared with 35 per cent of those who felt they were denied a say.) Team-working, which accounts for the way most of us earn a living, all too often doesn't really seem to provide a rewarding sense of agency to those within the team. Many of us – probably the majority of the workforce – work within a team (a 2017 survey of UK employees reported that six out of ten employees did so in that year), but the trend is for us to feel that we have little or no influence over what the group actually does (the same survey showed that 86 per cent of team members felt that way).[48]

Lack of personal control seems to be baked into so much of the modern work environment. James Bloodworth, a journalist who went undercover as a worker in one of Amazon's warehouses, described to me how tightly controlled the workers there are, in order to maximise their productivity. You're handed a scanning device, he said, after which 'You pick up an item off the shelves, you scan it and as soon as you scan it a timer starts. You need to get to the next item before the time runs down. You do this for ten and a half hours a day.' A dystopian Catch-22 quickly envelops the order-pickers. You can't run, because that would breach safety guidelines, but speed is vital to stay on track with the bosses: 'If you run you'd get a disciplinary. And if you didn't make your targets you'd get a disciplinary.'[49]

Health professionals are another group feeling the strain. A 2017 survey undertaken in the UK showed that the average duration of an appointment at a doctors' surgery was 9.22 minutes.[50] That's barely ten minutes for the doctor to talk to the patient, establish rapport, gently probe, examine, diagnose, prescribe and make follow-up notes. It's scarcely surprising that the Royal College of General Practitioners should have called this sub-ten-minute target for doctors' appointments 'unfit for purpose'.[51]

Or consider the teaching profession. Thanks to demands from politicians and interest groups internationally, the classroom has been invaded by a phenomenon known as 'curriculum crowding', whereby the list of subjects mandated to be taught has become ever longer and ever more prescriptive.[52] In the UK, for example, the Cambridge Primary Review of schoolchildren under the age of eleven reported as long ago as 2009 that, over the course of time, the 'list of subjects has simply become longer and longer, and nothing has been removed to accommodate the newcomers'.[53] In the process, policymakers have managed to lose sight of the interests of both teachers and pupils. One teacher, discussing their decision to retire after eighteen years in the job, described the joylessness of the new-style classroom: 'We were basically regurgitating the curriculum script. It was awful. I hated going to work that last two years with all the stress of academic achievement expectations … All administrators want to hear is the exact same stuff from one room to another from school to school.' Another stated that 'Teachers have been complaining about more testing every year. And every year we hear, "We'll look into that," and every year someone higher up decides, "We need more data." That, in turn, means more testing, more seatwork, and less play. I personally couldn't take it any more and took early retirement.[54] For children, the lack of autonomy, the lack of a sense of personal control, the relentless burden of testing, grading and ranking leaves them oscillating between stress and the boredom generated by joyless teaching.

Office work (or as it is often called, in these remote-working days, 'knowledge work') displays the same worrying pattern, fuelled by an exponential increase in digital communication that has caused workers to become increasingly yoked to their laptops and struggling to cope with endless video calls, emails, Teams notifications and chat pings. A handful of recent statistics reveal just how bad things are getting. When coronavirus struck in March 2020 and lockdowns were imposed, Microsoft reported that the number of video calls made globally on their Teams technology surged by 1,000 per cent in the first month. On 31 March alone 2.7 billion separate meetings were held.[55] Over the following year (again, according to Microsoft) Teams meetings rose by a further 150 per cent.[56] Employees' working weeks increased accordingly: the tech giant found that among its own staff the working week had increased by four hours – about an additional forty-five minutes a day.[57] One senior executive working in the marketing profession told me, 'I have over forty hours of video calls per week, they usually start before nine and end after seven p.m.' A manager in the technology sector concurred: 'I spend most of my day on Zoom calls, it's definitely exhausting but it's become an important part of the job.' It's not difficult to see why so many people in so many walks of life feel they have no control over the way they conduct their working days. Their hours are getting longer. Their independence is being reduced. It's no wonder so many people report burnout and stress.

Lack of employee control, then, is clearly bad for the employees themselves. But it's also bad for their bosses. It's terrible for morale. It leads to high rates of sickness and absence. It can also have a serious impact on the way in which employees approach their work.

Put in the baldest of terms: people from whom control is removed will do stupid things.

   This uncomfortable truth was vividly demonstrated by one of the social-media sensations of 2017: video footage of a middle-aged Vietnamese American passenger being dragged from a plane sitting on the tarmac at Chicago's O'Hare Airport. United Express flight 3411 had been scheduled to leave for Louisville at 5.40 p.m. Problems arose shortly after boarding, however, when the crew were instructed to find seats for four additional cabin staff who needed to be taken to Louisville to work another scheduled service the following morning. The crew asked the passengers whether any of them would be prepared to help out by giving up their seats. Three volunteered, and were given $800 travel vouchers and free overnight hotel accommodation by way of compensation. No one else, however, was prepared to put up their hand. The United employees therefore made their own selection, lighting upon one Dr David Dao Duy Anh. He, as he later stated, had commitments in Kentucky the following day, so he refused to disembark. An argument ensued. The airline then instructed three reluctant security officers from the Chicago Department of Aviation to physically remove the sixty-nine-year old. They proceeded to haul him from his seat, drag him along the gangway (in the course of which his head banged against an armrest) and remove him from the plane. He emerged with glasses knocked askew on his bloodied face, having lost two teeth, and suffered concussion that landed him in hospital. Filmed by several passengers on board, the incident made for grim viewing on social media and was immediately picked up by news outlets. United Airlines paid a heavy price for the conduct of its staff, both in terms of the compensation they had to offer and the hit to their reputation that they suffered. The *Washington Post* reported that Dao settled for a sum in the region of $140 million. The reputational cost is harder to calculate, but it can hardly have helped the company that the film footage garnered millions of views across Facebook feeds, and that the incident was covered and endlessly discussed in Twitter streams and across newspapers and television.

United subsequently commissioned a detailed internal report. Its findings make for fascinating reading. The agents, the report stated, 'did not have the authority to act independently and authorise higher levels of compensation or provide other modes of transportation'. They had to stick rigidly to the rules set out for them by the company – rules that did not empower them to resolve disputes.[58] They had no control. The consequences spoke for themselves.

United flight 3411 may be an extreme instance of what happens when people have denied control, but it's not a unique one. Across the contemporary world of work, a lack of leeway is becoming normalised. It is constricting, leaving employees metaphorically gasping for air. It is also counterproductive. Now, more than perhaps at any other time, people are being presented with challenging situations that they are given no scope to resolve intelligently or imaginatively.

If this is what lack of control looks like, what does the world hold for those able to achieve at least a measure of control?

As already suggested, the evidence shows that those blessed with more control over their lives, and over themselves, generally have better health than others. They are less prone to stress. They also experience lower levels of fatigue and exhaustion: electing to undertake a task – or at least feeling that you have had a role in deciding whether and how to perform it – exacts less of a toll than would be the case if you were simply instructed to perform it. It's an aspect of the benefits of individual control that was convincingly demonstrated by Dr Derek Johnston and his research team. They recruited 100 nurses in a Scottish teaching hospital, kitted them out with heart monitors and then observed how well they bore the daily demands of their jobs. Every ninety minutes the nurses were also prompted to say how they rated their feelings at that particular moment – about the demands placed on them, their sense of control, their feelings of tiredness – so that these could be plotted against the data gleaned from the monitors.[59] As was only to be expected, the nurses demonstrated increased fatigue as their shifts progressed, and this increase was marginally higher for those working night shifts over day shifts. But the critical finding that the researchers made was that tiredness was not related to levels of physical activity: 'some individuals show increasing fatigue as physical energy increases,' they reported, 'while others show the opposite.' The reason? A feeling of tiredness, the researchers suggested, is 'related to perceived control over work and perceived reward associated with work'. If we feel that we're in the driving seat as we perform a task, we feel energised. If we don't, then energy levels drop and we feel exhausted accordingly.

Tiredness is more than a matter of immediate physical well-being and comfort. As Christine Miserandino so well demonstrated with her Spoon Theory (see p.112), we all have finite levels of energy. It therefore follows that how we expend that energy has implications for everything else we do. Miserandino had to channel all the vigour she possessed into the everyday tasks that most people take for granted. Those with low levels of control have less energy, when it comes to coping with the stresses and strains of everyday life, and feel debilitated accordingly.

This sapping of energy is a phenomenon observed in a more empirical way by the social scientist Roy Baumeister, who evolved the theory of *ego depletion* to expound it, and who carried out various wonderful and ingenious laboratory experiments to demonstrate it. In one famous trial he gathered sixty or so participants in a room that was pungent with the sweet aroma of freshly baked chocolate cookies. Some were presented with and allowed to eat the sweet snacks; the others were offered only radishes to snack on. All were then asked to solve a difficult, frustrating puzzle (it was, in fact, by design a puzzle to which there was no solution). Those who had had to switch their minds off from the aroma of chocolate and settle for radish made far fewer attempts to solve the impossible conundrum than those who had been given the cookies. In fact they spent half as long as the cookie-consuming volunteers on the task. 'Resisting temptation seems to have produced a psychic cost,' Baumeister suggested, 'in the sense that afterward participants were more inclined to give up easily in the face of frustration.'[60] Further research has shown that expending energy on tasks that demand self-control leads to poorer performance in subsequent tasks.[61] Baumeister himself (frequently working with his wife, Dianne Tice) showed how, among other things, people shown emotionally taxing films, or given unsolvable anagrams, or told to suppress amusement at comical movie clips, all performed the next task they were given with much less conviction. Interestingly, in such cases there was a physical as well as a psychic debt to be paid. Moments of 'depleted ego' coincided with lower levels of glucose in the blood: the mind was starving the body of energy to prepare for future demands.[62] Self-control saps our energy – as anyone who finds themselves exhausted after a seemingly sedentary day staring at video calls will be able to attest.[63]

Obviously the converse holds true as well: greater control serves as a buffer against strain and tiredness and, in the workplace, results in greater job satisfaction. A useful theoretical framework for this insight was created in the 1970s by the sociologist Robert Karasek and his *Job Demand-Control* model. It was later reframed by others as the *Demand-Control-Support* model, to take account of how important the support that an employee feels they are receiving is to their well-being. Mark Seery has described how a sense of control gives us the 'reserve capacity' to respond to such challenges that come our way. Control is both a vicious and a virtuous circle. Those who don't have it fall prey to levels of stress and exhaustion that further undermine their sense of control. They are also twice as likely to suffer from the commonest cause of death among humans, coronary heart disease (CHD).[64]

Julie and John Gottman, who have explored the mental health of US combat soldiers, have found that the sense of helplessness that often accompanies a breakdown in a personal relationship can have fatal consequences: 'Combat-stress clinics in theatre have found that the one major critical incident that precedes suicidal and homicidal ideation in Iraq and Afghanistan is a stressful [domestic] relationship emotional event,' they write, giving bad phone calls home ('communications that leave both partners feeling abandoned'), threats to leave the relationship, and 'fights over control and power at home' as examples of what can tip people over the edge.[65] Martin Seligman records that the majority of suicides among soldiers who served in Iraq resulted from failed relationships.[66] Those who have control, by contrast, have the reserve energy to deal with any setbacks that come their way. In the process they build a sense of capability and confidence that enhances their feeling of control.

Control offers other benefits, too. If it's true, as Dutch researchers have suggested, that because people with low levels of self-control can be unpredictable, they may appear untrustworthy,[67] it follows that people with high levels appear accordingly more predictable and therefore more trustworthy. A sense of control also makes it less likely that they will suffer from loneliness – a state that is quite often associated with those who are low in extraversion or agreeableness (two of the Big Five personality traits mentioned in Chapter 4). And it is a powerful weapon against depression and suicide. As we saw earlier, it makes us happier and more optimistic. For Professor Deane Shapiro, who has spent much of his career studying the impact of control on our experience of life, there is 'increasing agreement among both clinicians and researchers that control is one of the most critical variables involved in an individual's health and wellbeing'. His own conclusion is that there is 'a linear relationship between control and health'.[68] (Interestingly, in the experiment mentioned at the beginning of this chapter involving dental students and puncture wounds to their palates, it was found that students who were lonely took longer to recover.)

The optimism that stems from control can literally be a lifesaver. A 1990s survey of 999 people aged between sixty-five and eighty-five showed that optimism and longevity are closely correlated. Participants in the study supplied details about such aspects of their lives as their family situation, their educational background and their consumption of alcohol and cigarettes. They also filled in a questionnaire that sought to measure how optimistic they were by nature. Over the course of the decade that the study ran for, and reflecting the natural passage of life, around 40 per cent of the sample passed away. However, it became apparent that the optimists tended to outlive the pessimists. Indeed, the data suggested that they were only 55 per cent as likely to die as their less sanguine peers.[69] They didn't have healthier diets or lower body-fat index, but they were less likely to suffer from heart disease.

A study of cancer survivors demonstrates this relationship even more starkly. In one study a group of women diagnosed with early breast cancer were interviewed shortly after undergoing a mastectomy, to establish how they perceived 'the nature and seriousness of the disease and how their lives had been affected by it'. Their responses were put in one of four categories: denial – characterised as a belief that the operation was merely preventative and a refusal to believe that the diagnosis was bad; fighting spirit – a sense that the disease could be conquered; stoic acceptance – 'I know it's cancer, but I've just got to carry on as normal'; and helplessness/hopelessness – an overwhelming sense that nothing could be done. When the researchers then revisited the women five years later they found that there was a strong relationship between those early reactions to diagnosis and the current situation. Three-quarters of those who had responded with the high degrees of control (demonstrating either denial or fighting spirit) were still alive and currently cancer-free. Only 35 per cent of those who had shown low degrees of control (stoic acceptance or helplessness/hopelessness) were in the same position.[70] Of the women who had died in the interim, 88 per cent had initially reacted with either helplessness or stoic acceptance. Only 12 per cent of those who had died had reacted with denial or fighting spirit.

Given my loathing of the victim blaming that I feel too often accompanies the Resilience Orthodoxy, I must confess that I felt a certain unease when I first came across such findings. 'You didn't show sufficient optimism or inner toughness,' the implication seemed to be; 'so it's your fault that your health suffered.' But actually that's simply not the case. As I've pointed out throughout this chapter, control is not that easily won and it isn't readily within the grasp of great swathes of the population. It's no simple matter, for example, to persuade a bureaucratically minded employer that everyone might be better served if they were permitted a more autonomous culture, or for us to free an individual from their financial woes, or to magic away any of a whole range of personal hardships that leave someone feeling helpless.

Nevertheless, there are things we can do at a personal level to enhance our measure of control. Many interventions targeted at sufferers of such conditions as panic attacks, depression and anxiety can help provide them with greater leverage over their personal situation: for example, nursing-home residents who are taught such self-control strategies as mindfulness and meditation tend to live longer than those who aren't. If you can explore ways to find the positives in life, then your mental – and your physical – health will benefit accordingly. Even being aware of the danger areas can help. Hans Selye, the scientist we encountered earlier who coined the word 'stress', has described how the body's equilibrium, or homeostasis, is under constant threat from stressors that may take the form of either physical threats or – more potently – such emotional ones as fear of the withdrawal of love: 'It may be said without hesitation that for man the most important stressors are emotional,' he observed.[71] Gabor Maté directs us where to look for these threats: 'The research literature has identified three factors that universally lead to stress: uncertainty, the lack of information and the loss of control.'[72]

Chapter 7

Identity

Building a Robust Sense of Self

'Grabbing the snips, I run to the roadside IED and start frantically chopping wires. Then I attach a line to the charge, trail it back to the Warrior, and give it a tug. Nothing ... The whole task has taken less than five minutes.'[1]

A snapshot view of an incident in the life of a bomb-disposal expert. Major Chris Hunter earned the Queen's Gallantry Medal for his service in Iraq.[2] His memoir *Eight Lives Down* is a fascinating account of dozens of encounters with lethal bombs, which Hunter describes with the casual elan of a postal worker despatching a parcel. Punctuating these life-and-death moments, however, are incidents that Hunter regards as rather more adrenalising: tearing around in tanks and jeeps while being fired at, and trying to avoid ambushes.

Why would anyone want to do such a job? It's something that Hunter reflects on in his memoir. 'It's certainly not because I have a fetish for taking things apart or understanding how they work,' he writes. 'I never had any deep fascination with electronics or model airplanes when I was at school, and I was crap at engineering and the sciences. I know some do it for the adrenaline rush, others to seek atonement for darker episodes in their lives. But I think most do it out of a good old-fashioned sense of duty – just because they want to make a difference ... Not a single day goes by now when somebody isn't killed by an IED. Every device I can neutralise takes me one step closer to tracing and bringing down the groups responsible.'[3] Even allowing for the possibility of memoir bias ('Me, a hero? I was just doing my job'), the strong impression that the book creates is of a man who is not an adrenaline junkie, as one might assume a bomb-disposal expert to be, but a dedicated, calm professional.

It's interesting to compare Hunter with another bomb-disposal expert, this time an American, as he shares with a journalist his experience of getting trapped underwater while trying to defuse an undischarged torpedo. 'If you can wiggle your fingers, the line that's wrapped around you or whatever situation you're in, if you can do one little thing to make it a little bit better, then do that. If you can do another thing and then another thing, and then you can have cascading positivity as opposed to spiralling negativity. You get to know the technical parameters of whatever job you're doing and then you go, "Is this really an emergency? Yeah, but it's really only an emergency if I can't find a solution. What is my next step to make this situation just slightly better?"[4] ... The only time I ever really felt crippling fear,' he goes on, 'was the moment that I lost sight of what my next step was. We were in a situation where there was a device and it was way more dangerous than what we expected. I had not done a good job because I had not prepared myself for the worst-case scenario. For the first time as an officer, I was like, "I don't know what to do." I was scared for my team. I was scared for myself.' A moment of fear, but again not an underlying adrenaline rush. As with Chris Hunter, this bomb-disposal expert has a job to do and he's getting on with it.

If these explosives experts are exerting a very strong sense of control ('I know what I'm doing here'), there's something else going on, too. They have an equally strong sense of their identity ('I am a person who makes bombs safe'). They know who they are and what they do – and therefore they do it, in the process normalising what for anyone else would be an overwhelmingly stressful task. Their self-assurance is reminiscent of the comment muttered to herself by Laurie Hernandez, gymnastic teammate of Simone Biles, at the Rio Olympics shortly before her balance-beam display helped propel the US team into the gold-medal position. 'I got this,' she said.[5]

As Professor Alex Haslam and his team have shown, it's this strong sense of identity that allows those who share it to cope with situations that to others might seem intimidating or even impossible to cope with. Because bomb-disposal experts identify as bomb experts – just as, say, bar staff identify as bar staff – they are able to assess the very different challenges that come their way in much the same manner and make calls as to whether they can cope with them. Indeed, Haslam found, when he talked to representatives from both groups, that the bomb-disposal experts believed their job to be less stressful than that of bar staff. They had 'got this', and that knowledge made it possible for them to cope with the demands of their job.

Back in the 1930s the philosopher George Herbert Mead said, 'the self is something which has a development; it is not initially there, at birth, but arises in the process of social experience and activity'.[6] Building on the idea a couple of decades later, the psychologist Erik Erikson traced the steps by which this occurs. The first steps in the creation of our identity, he said, involve 'introjection' – a process whereby we unconsciously take on the ideas, attitudes and personality of others (typically a parent or carer). As studies since Erikson's time have shown, parents will almost certainly reminisce with their children and tell them stories that shape their children's perceptions of themselves. Fathers typically create narratives that emphasise autonomy and achievement ('You've always been the fastest runner in the family'). Mothers typically play up notions of affiliation ('You're creative, like your Aunt Sarah').[7] Children enjoy these stories and, it has been observed, will ask to hear examples from the family archive over and over again. In so doing they are reaffirming an agreed recollection of a shared biography.

By the time we reach adolescence we are tentatively reaching beyond our childhood identity towards a more independent adult one. Studies of university students have shown that first-year undergraduates tend to decorate their room in a similar way to their bedroom at homes – for example, displaying cherished possessions that offer comfort and a sense of continuity. At the same time, however, they are starting to evolve into the adults they will become away from the family nest, not least in the new focus they will bring to bear on relationships.[8] The answer to the question 'Who am I?' will evolve throughout all our lives. At the same time, though, we seek an overall consistency in the story of who that 'I' is.[9] As Erikson put it, 'The sense of identity provides the ability to experience one's self as something that has continuity and sameness, and to act accordingly.'[10]

A strong sense of identity is powerfully enabling. Erikson argued that it was this quality that gave Mahatma Gandhi his commanding presence and powerful ability to sway minds. Others have shown how adolescents who have developed a coherent life story and who exhibit a more mature identity exhibit a higher level of self-esteem as well.[11] A study of women tracked from the ages of twenty-one to sixty-one found that those most able to turn challenging experiences into a coherent identity-strengthening narrative were more satisfied with their lives as they entered their seventh decade.

On the other side of the coin are the former Second World War soldiers with post-traumatic stress that Erikson worked with, whose experiences, he believed, had effectively caused them to lose their sense of identity.[12] Then there are the ex-combatants of the more recent wars in Vietnam and Iraq whose disrupted personalities, according to a 2016 study by Natalie Purcell and her colleagues, have made it very difficult for them to make peace with themselves. 'I think you feel ashamed of what you did,' one vet recalled many years after returning home. 'You know you're trained to do that and it just stays with you. I guess I feel very sad sometimes. I feel proud to be a soldier who tried to do something that I thought was right for the country. But it's hard to be a soldier. It tears away from your moral fibre. It changes your life.'[13] 'I'm now uncomfortable because it might change the ways he looks at his son,' said another ex-combatant, explaining how awkward he felt when his father asked him whether he had killed anyone in action. Another former soldier, asked what he feared his wife might find out about his service forty years previously, replied simply, 'That I'm a killer.'[14]

Likewise struggling to give cogent accounts of their lives are the depressive adults described in one study, who offered autobiographical 'ruminations' rather than curated tales, and who displayed a tendency to obsessively overthink negative (often generalised) aspects of their lives in a repetitive, circular fashion.[15] Their 'ruminations' were not dissimilar to the 'repetition compulsion' that has been observed in trauma patients, whereby people replay their terrible experiences in an attempt to come to terms with them.

Former president Barack Obama's first memoir, *Dreams from My Father*, offers a fascinating insight into the mental agonies of a young man who was confused about his identity and struggling to connect with his peers. Though he was mixed-race, Obama's Kenyan father was almost wholly absent from his life (Obama met him once, briefly, at the age of ten), and Obama was brought up in Hawaii by his white mother and grandparents. It wasn't until he went to college that he fully encountered Black culture, and at first he found it difficult to identify with. He confesses that he felt confused, directionless and uncertain, recognising fifteen years later that he had 'had no idea who my own self was'.[16] It was only as Obama engaged with politically active Black students, took to referring to himself as Barack to signpost his connection with his father and his African origins, and gradually came to terms with the news he received in his final year at college that his father had died in a car crash that a new, more stable identity was forged. As he later explained to a journalist, 'somehow I emerge on the other side of that ready and eager to take a chance in what is a pretty unlikely venture: moving to Chicago and becoming an organiser ... a moment in which I gain a seriousness of purpose that I had lacked before'.[17]

Common to all these experiences and narratives is a fear on the part of the individuals concerned that if the people they love knew 'the real them', they would withdraw their affection. It's part and parcel of what psychologist Bessel van der Kolk talks about in his exploration of the impact of trauma on children where, as he puts it, 'Shame becomes the dominant emotion and hiding truth a central preoccupation.'[18] When one is uncomfortable with one's identity, the temptation is to conceal aspects of it, to disconnect from others. In the words of clinical psychologist Catherine Haslam and her colleagues, 'When trauma has an adverse psychological impact, this is because it fundamentally compromises a person's social sense of self and their relationship to the world at large.'[19] A Gandhi confident about his identity was equally confident about the demands of leadership. A young Obama unsure of his identity was left anxious and depressed.

A sense of identity can have implications for people's physical health, too. During the 1980s, when HIV/AIDS first crept into the world (the first mention of it in the *New York Times* was on page 20, where it was described as a 'Rare cancer seen in 41 homosexuals'),[20] the mortality rate among its victims proved distressingly high. However, as Steve Cole, Margaret Kemeny and Shelley Taylor from the University of California found, when they conducted a nine-year study into seventy-two initially healthy HIV-positive gay men, the pattern and progress of the illness were not consistent across all those who suffered from it. Those who, in an era when homophobia was prevalent, were sensitive to the prejudices of others and therefore anxious to conceal their sexuality – in other words, men who concealed their true identities – suffered physically as a result. As the researchers put it, they 'experienced a significant acceleration in times to critically low CD4 T lymphocyte level, times to AIDS diagnosis, and times to HIV-related mortality'.[21] It's a pattern sadly all too common among those who experience racism, sexism, homophobia and other forms of discrimination, manifesting itself in higher incidences of psychiatric and physical health illnesses among those who struggle most to cope.[22]

It's found, for example, among those who believe that their physical appearance is the object of criticism. Diane Quinn and Jennifer Crocker, who studied the impact of prejudice on the lives of obese adults, observed that because overweight people are often regarded as personally responsible for how much they weigh, they can be the victims of others' hostility.[23] Some respond by bonding more closely with other members of the spurned group – an approach styled 'rejection-identification' – but while such a 'body positive' celebration is laudable, it is often not sufficient in itself to fully overcome the toxicity of social stigma and can still leave people suffering from low self-esteem.[24] In much the same way, the experience of racism can exact an appallingly high toll. One study in the US, which found that 'Racist discrimination is rampant in the lives of African Americans', observed that it 'is strongly related to psychiatric symptoms and to cigarette smoking' (a habit that we've previously seen Robert Anda describe as 'self-medicating' against trauma).[25] Another study showed how victims of prejudice were often reluctant to blame discrimination for negative outcomes in their life, instead turning in on themselves to ascribe their misfortune to their own perceived shortcomings.[26]

Many people with a stigmatised identity engage in what is often called 'identity management'. I can recall a gay friend telling me how, when a taxi driver casually asked him whether he was 'off to meet his girlfriend', he replied that he was: he had no idea whether the taxi driver was homophobic or not, but didn't want to run the risk of hearing something that might ruin his evening. Tom Daley, who has described how his homosexuality left him 'feeling *less than*', has said that it was also a spur to build an identity as a successful diver. He was determined that he was 'not going to disappoint everyone when they discover[ed] my truth'.[27]

Is damage to a sense of identity irreversible? Not according to Jack Shonkoff, the director of Harvard's Center on the Developing Child, who has worked with people with high ACE scores. 'If I had to boil this down to one thing for people to learn from this science,' he says, 'it's to totally put to bed forever the sense that children who are born under disadvantaged circumstances are doomed to poor life outcomes. The scientists say that's just not true.'[28] ACE interventions have proved effective in helping people to stop defining themselves in terms of the trauma they have experienced and to start building a more positive narrative. Once you understand why you feel the pain you do, where it comes from and why it is not your fault – why, in other words, your pain is your experience, not your identity – you can start to turn your back on the damaging narrative that you have created for yourself. Physician Nadine Burke Harris argues that such interventions with her patients with Adverse Childhood Experiences 'soothe their disrupted stress-response systems and manage their symptoms more effectively'.[29]

It also helps, as Robert Anda explains, for those with high ACE scores to know that they are not alone: 'what I've found,' he says, 'is that if people understand, when they're asked about these ten categories of Adverse Childhood Experiences, if they already know that these experiences are common they're more likely to be relieved than frightened. There's something that is kind of a miracle, that they don't feel alone anymore, that I'm not the only person who experiences these things.'[30] Comforted by the knowledge that they are not 'less than' (in Tom Daley's words), those struggling to come to terms with trauma and bad experiences can then set about reframing their story, so that it is no longer shaped or defined by the ordeals they have suffered. If they can do that, they will become more accepting of themselves – and will feel they are more deserving of the acceptance of others.[31] The interventions involved can include learning such techniques as mindfulness and meditation. Dr Nadine Burke Harris also advocates healthier sleep patterns. 'Regular exercise has also been shown to help regulate the stress response,' she adds, because it seems to be able to 'help the body better decide which fights to pick and which ones to walk away from'.[32]

And just as learning that others too have suffered can lighten the burden, so spending time with similar people can prove very beneficial. Pride festivals aren't simply fun – they literally give life to those participating in them. Celebrations such as Black History Month are not important only in themselves. The affirmation they embody will have physical and mental benefits for those who are involved in them. Self-help groups are invaluable, too, whether they take the form of organisations such as Alcoholics Anonymous or more informal assemblings of ex-service people.

And this leads me to the final, key piece of the fortitude jigsaw puzzle. We can set out individually to improve our sense of control and our sense of identity. But for those qualities truly to take root, we have to go beyond our individual selves and connect with others. Our sense of 'me-ness' has to be overlain by an awareness of 'we-ness'.

Another story from the 1980s AIDS crisis illustrates the point very powerfully. Even when both the health risks of the virus and the necessary preventative measures required to combat it were understood, Albert Bandura, one of the greatest twentieth-century psychologists, noticed that some members of high-risk groups continued to put themselves in jeopardy – engaging in unprotected sex, for example, or, among intravenous drug users, sharing needles. His conclusion was that the reason often lay in a desire to conform to social norms. When placed in intimate situations, some individuals felt reluctant or embarrassed to ask others to adopt a precautionary approach.

However, Bandura also found that those with a more confident sense of self-identity took a more health-conscious approach with those around them[33] – a finding very much in line with that of another study, which concluded that gay men or intraveneous drug users who had 'lapsed' from safe behaviours did so because they felt coerced by their partners, while those who didn't had a strong image of who they wanted to be.[34] Bandura's conclusion was that people's behaviour was shaped by what they felt their own group would regard as right or wrong. Individual identity, in other words, was overlaid by a broader sense of social identity.

As Bessel van der Kolk has described, 'our systems are made to move in synchrony with the people around us'.[35] It's time, therefore, to move beyond the place of individual control and identity in creating a sense of fortitude, to consider the role played by those around us.

PART THREE
Finding Fortitude

Chapter 8

Community

The Power of Us

When the plane hit the North Tower of New York's World Trade Center on Tuesday 11 September 2001, Marcy Borders, a twenty-eight-year-old legal assistant employed at the Bank of America offices was on the eighty-first floor. At first, as those around her assumed that a light aircraft had accidentally struck the tower, Borders' manager urged her to stay calm. But it soon became clear to her that something catastrophic had occurred. 'The way the building was shaking, I couldn't sit there,' she later recalled. 'You actually saw chairs coming out of the windows, office supplies and what I now know were people.'[1]

Along with her colleagues, Borders made her way down one of the packed stairwells, catching sight of 'people with objects in them, burned skulls' as she did so. At the bottom, a firefighter yelled an instruction to 'Run and don't look back'. In the dusty confusion, Borders briefly tumbled to her hands and knees. 'I couldn't see my hand in front of my face … Every time I inhaled my mouth just filled up with [dust], I was choking.' As she got to her feet again, photographer Stan Honda snapped a photo of her. It captures her standing statue-like, her whole body coated in dust, her arms extended and her hands held out as though she had been holding a delicate china teacup and saucer just a moment before. The 'Dust Lady' photograph soon became one of the defining images of that appalling day.[2]

Meanwhile, the emergency services were pouring in, guiding people to safety, taking in for themselves the enormity of what had just occurred. Many were to perish within hours as the South Tower was attacked and both towers then collapsed. Those who got through that day witnessed scenes of appalling devastation, suffering and death. Police officers later described how they saw people jumping from the burning buildings; how they had to create makeshift morgues in the street; and how they themselves had to run for their lives when the final cataclysms occurred.

In the wake of 9/11 came the investigations and studies – into the causes, the response, the lessons to be learned. Among them was one that examined how the 2,943 police officers who had been present that day had subsequently coped with what they had seen and what they had had to do – how they had dealt psychologically with the disaster, both at the time and afterwards.

One key central finding came as no great revelation: the more exposed an individual had been to the traumatic events of that day, the greater the stress he or she tended to feel afterwards. Indeed, a significant number were diagnosed with post-traumatic stress. What came as a surprise, though, was the discovery that four to five years later the vast majority of police officers exposed to that day's horrors – 85 per cent in fact – had either recovered from PTSD or were recorded as being 'resilient': that is, they exhibited few (if any) mental scars from 9/11.

Marcy Borders, by contrast, never got over 9/11. 'It haunted me every day,' she told one journalist. She became depressed. 'I drank a lot and never went out.' Gradually a dependency on alcohol morphed into a dependency on drugs. 'My life spiralled out of control. I didn't do a day's work in nearly ten years, and by 2011, I was a complete mess.'[3] As she battled with addiction, she split up with her partner and lost custody of her children. Then, at the age of forty-one, she was diagnosed with stomach cancer, an illness that she was convinced was caused by the vast amount of dusty, noxious material she had inhaled (similar maladies have afflicted others present on that day). Unable to pay her medical bills, she died the following summer at the age of forty-two.[4]

Why should Marcy Borders have struggled to cope mentally after 9/11 when so many of the police present on that day seem to have been able to come to terms with the disaster they witnessed? It's impossible to offer a single hard-and-fast answer. But a key finding of the survey of the mental health of those police officers certainly points to one key factor. Essentially, the researchers concluded, the roots of the officers' recovery were social. Not only could they call on the support of family and friends in the aftermath of the disaster, but they could also draw on their network of fellow officers to talk about shared experiences and feelings. The more they were able to do this, the lower the stress levels they exhibited a few years later.[5] Marcy Borders had family and friends, too, but denied the camaraderie of fellow workers with whom she could feel sufficiently unguarded to talk about what she had gone through, she started to feel isolated. She retreated further and further from others, and she suffered terribly as a consequence.

Her tragic experience of a traumatic event is, sadly, not unique. An aggregated meta-analysis covering 90,480 individuals across 268 different studies concluded that a lack of social support is twice as good a predictor of PTSD as the level of the severity of the trauma experienced.[6] In the words of Alex Haslam, 'Resilience is something that only occurs in and to groups.'[7] The support of others helps us.

If the police who attended 9/11 are evidence of this, then so too is another group who live their lives under constant threat and stress: the military. As we've seen, former service men and women suffer a toll on their physical and mental health of which those in civilian life can have little or no conception. But the fact remains that many ex-military personnel are nevertheless able to make relatively swift and easy transitions between active service and home life. Not only that, but some find that the calm of civilian life even leaves them missing their military existence. Losing the adrenaline rush that life in uniform can offer no doubt plays a part in this. However, in the view of the journalist Sebastian Junger, who has made a particular study of combat troops, the camaraderie of military life plays a far more crucial role in shaping how they feel.

Junger spent twenty years reporting from battlefields around the world. He experienced being under fire. Indeed, he witnessed the deaths of fellow reporters in combat zones. And yet, time and again, he was struck by the fact that former personnel carried a sense of loss when they left military service. 'How is it someone can go through the worst experience imaginable, and come home, back to their home, and their family, their country, and miss the war?' he asked himself.[8] He described, for example, the lives of a group of twenty soldiers that he spent time with in 2007 at an outpost in eastern Afghanistan. 'There was no running water, there was no way to bathe and these guys were up there for a month at a time. They never even got out of their clothes. They fought, they worked. They slept in the same clothes, they never took them off, and at the end of the month, they went back down to the company headquarters, and by then their clothes were unwearable, they burned them and got a new set.' And yet, even though the soldiers had to endure these squalid conditions, although they saw friends being killed and ran almost daily risks themselves, they wanted to be there. The euphoria of war was certainly a factor. Junger recounted one young soldier, faced with the boredom of a day when there was no combat, saying, 'Oh God, please someone attack us today!' However, Junger became convinced there was more to it than that.

This other factor came sharply into relief for him at a dinner party back home where Brendan, a newly decommissioned soldier, was describing the bleakness of the situation in Afghanistan to a fellow guest. 'Brendan, is there anything at all that you miss about being out in Afghanistan, about the war?' she asked. He paused for a long while before answering, 'Ma'am I miss almost all of it.'

'I think what he missed,' Junger said, 'was brotherhood. He missed connection ... [If] you think about Brendan,' he went on, 'you think about all these soldiers having a bond like that, in a small group, where they loved twenty other people in some ways more than they loved themselves. They are blessed with that experience for a year, and then they come home, and they are just back in society like the rest of us are, not knowing who they can count on, not knowing who loves them, who they can love, not knowing exactly what anyone they know would do for them if it came down to it. That is terrifying. Compared to that, war, psychologically, in some ways, is easy, compared to that kind of alienation ... That's why they miss it,' he concluded. War offered comradeship. By the same token, civilian life involved an end to that comradeship. It's something that needs to be borne in mind when seeking to explain why so many former military personnel struggle to make the adjustment from war to peace.

The bonding power of camaraderie can be found in the very worst of places, as researchers who studied liberated US Air Force prisoners after the Vietnam War discovered. The answers to the questionnaires they sent out described a world of abuse, torture, disease, malnutrition and all manner of sensory deprivation. But they also revealed how the service men benefited mentally from the military discipline of daily cleaning rituals; how they drew strength from one another; and how they found comfort in their collective religious and patriotic values. More than 90 per cent believed those experiences had helped make them the kind of person they wanted to be; 61 per cent felt that their experiences had helped with their subsequent social relationships, their self-understanding and their sense of optimism.[9] And while one might have expected those who were particularly harshly treated in prison to have subsequently suffered the most in terms of their mental health, the opposite proved to be true. Prisoners who had undergone the most gruelling of times – 'with more physical and psychological suffering, more conflict with the captors over physical and psychological matters, more injuries while in captivity, and greater severity of problems'[10] – reported the greatest benefit from their experience afterwards. All felt that the bonds they built with their fellow prisoners became a defining light in their lives. As with ex-combatants involved in the war in Afghanistan, ex-prisoners from the Vietnam War often returned to an environment where they felt estranged from the people around them. It wasn't prison that damaged them; it was their subsequent disconnection from their group – the prison community. The community kept them together. It kept them sane.

The influence others have on us – for good or ill – has long been recognised. It has, however, been subject to shifting interpretations. For many decades there was a view that societies moved ever upwards on a civilising path, strengthened by the social glue of shared community values. However, this optimistic view was, as Ervin Staub wrote in *The Roots of Evil*, 'shattered by the events of the Second World War, particularly the systematic, deliberate extermination of six million Jews by Hitler's Third Reich'.[11] In its place came a more pessimistic, sombre interpretation of human nature. Staring across the courtroom at former Nazi leader Obersturmbannführer Eichmann at his trial for war crimes in Jerusalem in 1961, the journalist Hannah Arendt was struck by his seeming ordinariness (you will understand why she thought that if you look at footage of the trial on YouTube). She had assumed that he would be 'a man obsessed with a dangerous and insatiable urge to kill', equipped with 'a dangerous and perverted personality'. Instead he looked like a humdrum bureaucrat. She coined the term the 'banality of evil' to describe what she had witnessed.[12] Anyone, it seemed in this post-Nazi world, was capable of acts of appalling barbarity, given the right set of influences and circumstances. The community was a fragile and potentially hostile animal.

This grim notion received a further boost just two years later via the now world-famous obedience experiment conducted by the American psychologist Stanley Milgram. In it volunteers were instructed to ask questions of a 'Learner', who was not visible to them but whom they could hear, with the added injunction that they should administer electric shocks on a rising scale if the answers they were given were incorrect. (In reality, the ever more vocal protestations of the Learner were faked, since he wasn't wired up to any machine.) That 65 per cent of the participants should have followed instructions from a white-coated lab assistant to keep going up to the maximum voltage level, despite the increasingly anguished protestations of the Learner, seemed to confirm the impoverished view of human conduct and influence that the post-war world had constructed. As Milgram wrote in his 1974 book *Obedience to Authority*, 'Arendt's conception of the banality of evil comes closer to the truth than one might dare to imagine. The ordinary person who shocked the person [in his experiment] did so out of a sense of obligation – a conception of his duties as a subject – and not from any peculiarly aggressive tendencies.'[13]

If further proof were needed, it seemingly came in the form of the equally famous 1971 Stanford Prison Experiment (SPE) led by Dr Philip Zimbardo. In this carefully staged simulation of arrest and imprisonment, participants quickly conformed to the role arbitrarily meted out to them. The student volunteers dressed as prison guards became domineering and cruel. The 'prisoners' lapsed into anxiety and stress. It wasn't long before things got out of hand. Soon the guards were going out of their way to taunt the prisoners and humiliate them. They even forced them to clean toilets with their bare hands. Six days into the intended two-week timeframe allotted for the experiment it was felt that the guards' tyranny had gone too far and the exercise was halted.

Given the shattering experience of the Second World War, it's not hard to see why such experiments received so much attention at the time, and why they should have stuck so firmly in the popular consciousness. But it's also very easy to be misled by them. They seem to imply that our behaviour is dictated by the power and influence of others and by the roles that we are given to play. The reality is rather different.

Ironically, the researcher who provided the necessary corrective framework was himself an intellectual product of the Second World War. Henri Tajfel was born into a Jewish family in Włocławek, Poland, shortly after the end of the First World War. Moving to Paris for a university education that, as a young Jewish man, he would have found hard to secure in Poland, he was at the Sorbonne studying chemistry when Germany invaded his homeland in 1939.[14]

Called up to serve in a Polish unit in the French Army, Tajfel was soon captured in 1940. His long-term associate John Turner believed that 'had it been discovered by the German authorities that he was Polish rather than a French Jew he would have been killed'. In fact, as his biographer later established, Tajfel's papers stated that he was Polish and he survived only by hiding his Jewishness altogether, a decision that he later described to one or two of his closest friends as his 'lasting shame'.[15] His friends and relatives were less fortunate. When Tajfel returned to Poland after the war he discovered that they had all perished in the Holocaust.

Tajfel's experiences now prompted him to switch the focus of his study from chemistry to psychology. As Turner says, 'It was always clear that, much more than for most, his social psychology, the problems he studied, the theories he proposed and the approaches he saw as necessary and significant, remained closely bound up with the tragedies and experiences of his earlier life.' No doubt Tajfel's sense of guilt over hiding his identity was an additional spur.[16] At any rate, he now became preoccupied by group behaviour, by the fact that people could so easily become tribal and turn against each other. He wanted to understand why.

What he discovered, through observation and experiment, was that it takes the smallest of differences between people to create bafflingly strong senses of loyalty to those who appear like-minded – and animosity to those who appear different. In one experiment, for example, students who were told that they were being allocated to a particular group simply on the basis of previously expressed picture preferences (they had been shown works by Paul Klee and Vasily Kandinsky) quickly coalesced around their new group identity, showing preference to fellow group members and, even more potently, an aversion towards those in the other group. In truth, most had not previously heard of Klee or Kandinsky and had actually been allocated to their group, not according to their aesthetic preference, but at random. In another experiment, volunteers who had just completed one task together were asked to take part in a further one that involved allocating money at random to other participants.[17] The fact that they happened to have been randomly thrown together for one experiment resulted in 'a large majority' giving more money to those they had already been with than to those who had just joined them. Tajfel also noted that even in these loosely affiliated groups, the repulsion towards 'them' was frequently stronger than the pull towards 'us'.[18] Participants, he wrote, 'were more concerned that outgroup members should get less than ingroup members than they were with the absolute amounts of money they gave to ingroup members'.[19] Tajfel's findings have been replicated dozens of times. Whether it's been teenage boys, women or girls, the results have always remained the same.

The complementary pulls of similarity and difference fascinated Tajfel. People, he discovered, define themselves not only in terms of how they belong to one group, but how they differ from members of another. 'Intergroup discrimination is a feature of most modern societies,' he wrote. 'The phenomenon is depressingly similar regardless of the constitution of the ingroup and of the outgroup that is perceived as being somehow different.'[20] He recounted how a Slovenian friend of his had described the stereotypical traits of his fellow citizens and of their poorer Bosnian neighbours. Tajfel had then relayed these summaries to a group of Oxford students, asking them to guess which nationalities these stereotypes described. All assumed that the positive characteristics that Tajfel's friend felt to be typical of Slovenians referred to English people, and that the negative ones used of Bosnian citizens actually related to recent colonial immigrants to Britain. Discrimination is depressingly similar, wherever it is found. For every English joke at the expense of Irish or Scottish people, there is a Polish joke that mocks Germans and Russians, or a Finnish one that makes fun of Swedes and Norwegians. In each case, the home group represents the intelligent heroes, the other groups the stupid or conceited heels.

Viewed through the Tajfel lens, Hannah Arendt's 'banality of evil' thesis and popular assumptions about the lessons of Milgram's electric-shock experiment, or Zimbardo's Stanford Prison Experiment, the interpretations don't really hold up. People don't commit acts of wickedness simply because they are cogs in the machine, obeying commands and assuming a role imposed on them. They behave as they do because they belong to one group that stands in opposition to another. As Alex Haslam (a former student of Tajfel's associate John Turner) and Stephen Reicher (a former student of both Tajfel and Turner) argue, following the lead of Yaacov Lozowick's book *Hitler's Bureaucrats*, Eichmann and his fellow Nazis did not order the murder of millions because they were bureaucratically and blindly obeying orders. They did so because they belonged to a group for whom mass killing was acceptable and necessary. Members of that group thought hard about what they were doing, worked at it and took the lead over many years.[21] In the words of the British historian Ian Kershaw: 'Nazi killers knew what they were doing, believed in what they were doing, and even celebrated what they were doing.'[22] They were seeking to live up to in-group expectations.

With that in mind, it's worth returning to the Milgram study because, on closer inspection, it's not quite what popular accounts of it make it out to be.

The first thing to point out is that there wasn't a *single* Milgram experiment. There were dozens of them. And although, in some, participants did ratchet up the pain they thought they were inflicting on the Learner to the maximum voltage, this didn't occur in all cases. In a number of instances, each volunteer went to the maximum; in others no one did.[23] The second key point is that even with only three people involved – the Teacher (who administered the shocks), the Learner (who 'received' them in another room) and the Experimenter (who supervised the proceedings) – a group dynamic clearly took hold. Haslam and Reicher, who have studied Milgram's painstaking notes in detail, point to one particularly significant passage: 'The subjects,' Milgram wrote, 'have come to the laboratory to form a relationship with the experimenter, a specifically submissive relationship in the interest of advancing science. They have not come to form a relationship with the [Learner], and it is this lack of relationship in the one direction and the real relationship in the other that produces the results ... Only a genuine relationship between the Victim and the Subject, based on identification ... could reverse the results.' In other words, the participants went along with the grim instructions they were given not because they were simply blindly following orders, but because they identified with the Experimenter (who was in the room with them) rather than with the Learner (who was out of sight).

If further proof were needed, it comes from Teacher reactions to the instructions that the Experimenter gave them. Milgram and his team had established a hierarchy of commands here. If a Teacher hesitated to administer a shock, the Experimenter would say 'please continue'. If they still stonewalled, they were told, 'the experiment requires that you continue', then 'It's absolutely essential that you continue' and finally 'You have no other choice, you must continue now.' One would expect even previously resistant Teachers to buckle at that final command if it really were true that they were blindly obedient. In fact, no participant who was told 'You have no choice, you must continue now' acquiesced. They felt they were willing members of a team exercise (after the experiment, many said how proud they were of their involvement), but they recoiled from a direct order that ran so contrary to their instinct. Interestingly, Milgram had concealed the obedience aspect of his project from participants, noting, 'Even in this experiment we must disguise the character of obedience so that it appears to serve a productive end. Therefore we are not dealing with "blind obedience".' For those involved in the project, it was about teamwork up until that final order broke the bond. 'Tyranny isn't the product of "natural" or "blind" obedience,' Haslam concludes. 'Indeed, it probably isn't the product of obedience at all. Rather it is a product of engaged followership that is predicated upon identification with those in authority – whose cause is believed to be right and who are followed on this basis.'[24]

Where does that leave us with Zimbardo's prison study? In 2002, some thirty years after the Stanford Prison Experiment was abandoned, Alex Haslam and Stephen Reicher set about re-creating it for the BBC. Things had changed a lot in the intervening three decades. When Zimbardo undertook his research, the world had barely moved on from the grainy black-and-white film era of the Eichmann trial. Haslam and Reicher, by contrast, were operating in the emergent era of fly-on-the-wall television, dominated by the extraordinary success of the reality series *Big Brother*, which had first aired just a couple of years earlier. Participants were developing a savviness about the image they might project of themselves. In the first *Big Brother*, one participant, Nick Bateman, who had sought to manipulate his housemates, was horrified to discover when he was ejected from the show that he had acquired the nickname 'Nasty Nick' and that he was being widely vilified. His experience was a lesson not lost on those who agreed to be involved in Haslam and Reicher's *The Experiment* documentary series. Several of those who took the role of guard, for example, were clearly anxious not to come across as authoritarian (as Haslam told me, 'Our argument was always that when you put people in that situation and they're aware that their behaviour is monitored, the capacity for them to look bad becomes pretty obvious'). It's also arguable that the 2000s represented a rather less deferential decade than the 1970s: those involved in *The Experiment* were less likely to follow the dictates of the people in charge than those who had been incarcerated in the mock prison on the Stanford campus.

There were other differences between the 1970s filmed research and the 2000s reality programme, too. Zimbardo had gone out of his way to create a backstory, staging 'arrests' of those who would go on to be his prison volunteers. *The Experiment* did not follow suit. Zimbardo organised briefings for his guards and even went so far as to adopt the role of prison superintendent himself. 'We're going to take away their individuality in various ways,' he told his guards on one occasion, adding that he intended to create a sense of 'power-lessness' in the prisoners.[25] Haslam and Reicher took a back seat, enrolling a clinical psychologist to gather data on elements such as stress levels. Such film footage of the Stanford Experiment that was made public was explosive and confrontational. The BBC experiment witnessed prisoner rebellion, but there was none of the retaliatory hosing down with fire extinguishers or sleep deprivation that had characterised Zimbardo's enterprise. The Dutch historian Rutger Bregman went so far as to describe the BBC documentary to me as 'one of the most boring things I've ever seen'.[26]

But even allowing for all these dissimilarities, the outcome of *The Experiment* was so different from that of the Stanford exercise that inspired it as to bring Zimbardo's assumptions and conclusions into question. Zimbardo was clear that his intent was to show the dark side of humanity. 'I was born in New York City in the South Bronx,' he told an interviewer; 'one of the things of growing up poor is that you're surrounded by evil, meaning people whose job it is to get good kids to do bad things for money. Even as a little kid I was always curious about why some kids got seduced and other kids like me were able to resist.'[27] The upshot of his experiment was confirmation of his suspicions. (It's worth noting, though, that one often-neglected detail from the Stanford Prison Experiment was that not all guards accepted their dictated role; some actually sided with the prisoners. Even this dissent was edited from the publicly presented conclusions of the Stanford jail.[28])

Haslam and Reicher, by contrast, found that what emerged most strongly from their experiment was the vital importance and huge potential benefit of a sense of community. Initially the prisoners were told that if they behaved well they might be promoted to being guards – a promise that led to splits and tensions among them. Once one prisoner had been promoted, however, and it was announced that no further elevations were on the cards, the others coalesced into a group. They cooperated with one another. They showed good humour. They exhibited camaraderie. They even sought collectively to overthrow the guards. The guards, by contrast, failed to unite. They couldn't agree on a common approach to discipline or even to trust one another sufficiently to operate a duty rota system. Their group conversations were disconnected and distrustful. They operated independently, each working long hours and becoming exhausted as a result. By the end of the experiment the clinical psychologist observed that the guards were suffering from burnout.[29]

The psychological and physiological impacts of group dynamics surprised even Haslam. 'What we hadn't really seen or anticipated,' he said later, 'was the link between these social identity processes and stress and health dynamics.' He noted in particular the effect that a lack of group cohesion had on the guards: 'You see massive increases in stress on the part of the guards as their social identity starts to decline, in part because lacking social identity they fail to provide each other with useful forms of social support.'[30]

The implications of all this for individual resilience – or fortitude – are profound. For many years there has been a common assumption that individuals are to be trusted far more than groups. An individual may behave badly, but will generally act rationally. A group is, by its very nature, irrational and dangerous. The psychologist Professor Jolanda Jetten and her colleagues explain it in these terms: ' ... becoming part of a group is [framed as] a process of subversion and loss; as we become part of the mass, we lose our sense of self, we lose our capacity to reason, we shed our moral compass, we lack agency and become like sheep, helplessly following the herd. Fine upstanding citizens morph into a mindless mob. Sensible people become victims of groupthink. Thinkers become zombies.' According to this model, if you want optimal outcomes, the best advice you can give people (and society) is to stand alone and apart from the group.[31]

As Alex Haslam argues, though, 'The simple message that "groups are bad and that we automatically abuse power" is actually misleading in the extreme.'[32] His research, and that of his colleague Stephen Reicher and his inspiration, Henri Tajfel, show that while groups are, of course, capable of irrationality, prejudice and great acts of cruelty, they can also aid people's happiness, strength – and fortitude.[33] Zimbardo's message was that 'groups are bad'. Actually it would be far more accurate to say that groups are the source of great individual strength. That strength may, in extreme cases, be deployed to abuse and persecute others. But it may equally be used to support and help. That is why Haslam talks about the 'agency hypothesis': 'When, and to the extent that, people define themselves in terms of shared social identity, they will develop a sense of efficacy, agency and power.'[34]

Fortitude, in other words, is a collective strength, not something that we can acquire on our own.

The reasons for this group power and resilience lie deep in our DNA. Go back 300,000 years and you will find that there were three distinct versions of human or near-human species wandering the different continents of the planet: *Homo neanderthalensis* in Europe, *Homo erectus* in Asia and *Homo sapiens* in Africa. Advance the clock to quarter of a million years ago and *Homo erectus* had disappeared, leaving the field to *Homo sapiens* and *Homo neanderthalensis*. Some interbreeding took place between the two species – it's estimated that we share approximately 2 per cent of our DNA with our distant Neanderthal cousins.[35] Move further forward to 30,000 years ago and you will find that *Homo neanderthalensis* had gone the way of *Homo erectus*. *Homo sapiens* now reigned supreme.

Why? It's not because *Homo sapiens* was smarter than *Homo neanderthalensis*. If anything, Neanderthal man, with his longer skull, was probably marginally more intelligent. It's because *Homo sapiens* was more sociable. Joseph Henrich, professor of human evolutionary biology at Harvard University, clarifies the difference between the two species: 'Neanderthals,' he writes, 'who had to adapt to the scattered resources of ice-age Europe and deal with dramatically changing ecological conditions, lived in small, widely scattered groups ... Meanwhile the African immigrants [our *Homo sapiens* ancestors] lived in larger and more interconnected groups ... ' Such sociability gave *Homo sapiens* a powerful evolutionary advantage. 'Even if each member of [a] social group has only rudimentary ideas about such things as finding food, making tools or whatever else,' writer Matthew Syed explains, 'the density of such ideas means that any one person – even a smart person – can learn more from the group than they could figure out in a lifetime on their own.'[36] Effectively, learning becomes *recombinant* – each new discovery builds on and enhances the wisdom of those who came before, enabling extraordinary progress in a very short time. According to Henrich, 'The extra edge created by more individual brainpower in Neanderthals would have been dwarfed by the power of social interconnectedness of the collective brain sizes of the Africans.'[37]

If sociability aids the success of a species, it also requires mental effort. 'Ecological problems are solved by living in a group,' says the renowned evolutionary anthropologist Robin Dunbar, 'and living in a group is solved by having a large enough brain to manage the stresses involved … The problem with living in stable, permanent groups,' he clarifies, 'is that considerable diplomatic and social skills are needed to prevent the stresses and niggles of living in close proximity with others from overwhelming us.'[38] Many mammals and birds, he notes, spend time together only for the purposes of mating and raising their offspring. The small size of their brains corresponds with these limited social connections. Monkeys, apes and humans, by contrast, are highly sociable animals living in closely connected groups. Their large brains allow them to cope with the complexity that such social interaction entails. The Social Brain Hypothesis posits that a species' brain size (the cerebral neocortex that is associated with social learning, group size and individual innovation)[39] constrains the size of its social group.

Among monkeys and apes, Dunbar has observed, social cohesion is to a large extent achieved and maintained through hours of mutual grooming – far more than is necessary 'for purely hygienic purposes'. (In support of his contention he points out that short-haired monkeys spend just as much time grooming their companions as long-haired ones do, even though they have less practical cause to do so.) Grooming 'build[s] up a sense of psychological yearning for the individual you groom with', he argues.[40] It stimulates the release of endorphins, a chemical in the brain that acts as a natural painkiller and that triggers pleasure and a sense of well-being. We humans employ various methods to achieve a similar sense of togetherness, and we experience the benefits of a similar endorphin rush as a consequence.

If sociability is a key element of what it is to be human, so its opposite – loneliness – is something that we find hard to bear and so seek to avoid. John Cacioppo, one of the world's leading experts on social neuroscience, points out that our minds interpret isolation as a sign that we have been rejected by our tribe. In his view, 'the social pain of loneliness evolved as a signal that one's connections to others are weakening and to motivate the repair and mainten-ance of connections to others that are needed for our health and well-being and for the survival of our genes'.[41] We accordingly feel threatened and vulnerable. Of course isolation is not a purely phys-ical thing. We might live in a busy street or in a bustling apartment building; we might be surrounded by others at work. However, if we *feel* that we are lonely, then that subjective experience becomes objectively true for us. It's no good sitting at a meal with others if nobody talks to one another.

Loneliness is mentally debilitating. As Dunbar says, 'we tend to underestimate the significance of psychological wellbeing as the bedrock on which our success in life is founded … being part of a group makes us feel properly human'.[42] At the same time it has a physiological effect. Cacioppo and Louise Hawley, who have stud-ied people who reported feeling lonely and compared them with their more contented peers, concluded that the 'correlation between loneliness and blood pressure was sizeable'.[43] Lonely people, they found, didn't smoke, drink or eat more (though they were slightly more inclined to take recreational drugs).[44] They didn't exercise less. But their sleep patterns were less healthy than those of their less socially isolated peers. They were more prone to what are known as micro-awakenings – an indication that their bodies were urging them to be hypervigilant and on their guard against possible risk. Admittedly the measured differences between the sleep patterns of lonely and non-lonely people were small: lonely people were found to wake on average 1.95 times a night as compared with the 1.57 average among non-lonely people.[45] But they were significant nonetheless. Interestingly, urine samples taken from lonely people were shown to contain significantly higher concentrations of epinephrine than those of non-lonely individuals. Epinephrine, which goes by the street name of *adrenaline*, is a 'fight-or-flight' stimulant that places our body in a vigilant state. It's no wonder we sleep less well if we're lonely. And if we sleep less well, we lose out on the powerfully restorative impact on the body's health that we know a good night's sleep to provide.

Cacioppo and Hawley found that lonely people experience other problems, too. Their volunteers reported the same number of stressful life events as non-lonely people did, but recalled more instances of childhood adversity and chronic stress. The diaries they were encouraged to keep showed that they found everyday activities more stressful. They expressed greater feelings of helplessness and threat.[46] They tended to misread the expressions and intentions of other people, thereby adding to their feelings of estrangement. Loneliness, in other words, was a stressful state for them to be in. For clinical psychologist Catherine Haslam and her co-writers, the absence of social relationships lies 'at the very heart of the depressive condition'.[47] For Cacioppo and Hawley, 'perceived social isolation (i.e. loneliness) is a risk factor for, and may contribute to, poorer overall cognitive performance, faster cognitive decline, poorer executive functioning, increased negativity and depressive cognition, heightened sensitivity to social threats, a confirmatory bias in social cognition.' The long list extends as far as an increased likelihood of schizophrenia, as noted by the psychiatrist Robert Faris back in the 1930s.[48]

Ultimately, the increased levels of stress in lonely people add to the wear and tear of the body's nervous system. And since loneliness is associated with elevated systolic blood pressure and may contribute to the development of hypertension (one of the symptoms of high blood pressure), it has a role in cardiovascular disease, the single most common cause of death.[49] Loneliness can kill.

*

If loneliness shortens lives, it seems fair to assume that togetherness prolongs them. And that indeed has been shown to be the case in what has to be the longest-running of all social studies. Back in 1938 Dr Arlie Bock at Harvard University set about tracking the lives of a random subset of the college's students. (The first sample of 268 students of the then all-male institution included future president John F. Kennedy in its ranks.) More recently, alumni, their children and various comparison groups have been added to the mix. Over the more than eight decades in which it has been in operation, the Harvard Study of Adult Development has thus brought together a vast quantity of data about individuals, more or less from cradle to grave: their accomplishments, their family relationships and their physical and mental health. Its conclusion? According to Dr George Vaillant, who took over from Bock as the long-serving director of the study, social connection is everything. Its power is both mental and physical. It makes our memories sharper.[50] More generally, it makes us happier (Vaillant titled one report 'Happiness is love: full stop').[51] At the same time, as he put it in 2017, 'The surprising finding is that our relationships and how happy we are in our relationships has a powerful influence on our health. Taking care of your body is important but tending to your relationships is a form of self-care too.'[52]

The importance of social interconnectedness is something that the American social commentator Robert Putnam picked up on in his now-famous 2000 book, *Bowling Alone*. It was a cause of concern for him that many traditional community organisations – of which bowling clubs were perhaps the most emblematic – had seen their membership decline over the years. Bowling might have become more popular in terms of the total number of people involved, he noted, but between the 1960s and the 1990s membership of leagues had fallen from around 8 per cent of all men to just 2 per cent. The adverse consequences, he argued, were there for all to see. 'Dozens of painstaking studies from Alameda (California) to Tecumseh (Michigan) have established beyond reasonable doubt,' he wrote, 'that social connectedness is one of the most powerful determinants of our well-being.'[53] The decline of the traditional bowling club was one element in the erosion of that well-being.

Two decades later in 2020, when Putnam revisited his original work, he noted how subsequent research had confirmed his findings. 'Over the last twenty years more than a dozen large studies of this sort in the United States, Scandinavia, and Japan have shown that people who are socially disconnected are between two and five times more likely to die from all causes, compared with matched individuals who have close ties with family, friends, and the community.'[54] He also reminded his readers of the extraordinary benefits of group cohesion. 'The more integrated we are with our community,' he concluded, 'the less likely we are to experience colds, heart attacks, strokes, cancer, depression, and premature death of all sorts.' In his view, 'social capital might actually serve as a physiological triggering mechanism, stimulating people's immune systems to fight disease and buffer stress'. And he came up with a strikingly arresting way to prove his point. 'As a rough rule of thumb, if you belong to no group but decide to join one, you cut your risk of dying over the next year in half.' Or to put it another way, 'If you smoke and belong to no groups, it's a toss-up statistically whether you should stop smoking or start joining.'[55]

Research by Alex Haslam a few years back, among those recovering from heart attacks, confirms Putnam's thesis. At the time when Haslam and his team undertook their study, heart operations still involved highly invasive techniques and, as a result, particularly heightened levels of fear and stress for the patient. Indeed, according to one study, recovering heart patients were twice as likely as other patients to develop a psychiatric disorder subsequently.[56] Those who took part in the study, conducted after the patient was no longer in a critical condition, were asked about their relationship with their family and friends. They were also asked about the level of social support they felt they received in hospital, how stressed they felt and how they would describe their general sense of well-being. It transpired that those who reported that they felt they had received strong social support were also more positive about other aspects of their experience. Indeed, the higher the level of support they felt themselves to have received, the greater their positivity about such aspects of their experience as the hospital environment, the lower their stress and the higher their levels of self-esteem were.

Haslam and his colleagues now tracked ex-patients aged fifty-plus over a period of four years, asking them how they felt supported by the groups they were part of. (It's worth noting that one might normally expect such an evaluation to include an assessment of family circumstances and friendships groups, but in this case the research team focused on extra-familial bonds, asking study participants to tell them about membership of social clubs and societies.) The correlations were both fascinating and revealing: 10 per cent of participants reported being depressed at the outset of the study.[57] At the end of it, those who said they didn't belong to a group were 41 per cent more likely to have relapsed into depression. Those who reported being involved with three or more groups were only 15 per cent more likely to have relapsed. The measurable effects were most striking among those who had a previous history of depression. Here, membership of one group reduced the risk of a relapse into depression by 24 per cent; membership of three groups involved a 63 per cent reduction.

Given statistics such as that, it should come as no surprise that a group of experts who examined 148 studies, involving more than 300,000 heart-attack patients over a period of time that averaged seven years, found that the single biggest predictor of heart-attack survival was not 'giving up smoking' (the number-two factor), but stronger social relations.[58]

Similar patterns have been detected elsewhere. Jolanda Jetten and Janelle Jones found that members of tightly knit team sports, such as bobsleigh, luge and skeleton, experience quicker heart-rate recovery after strenuous exertion. They also discovered that people who volunteered for a cold-endurance test (holding their non-dominant hand in a bucket of iced water for as long as they could) were able to keep going longer if they were reminded of their group identities.[59] A broad review of a whole range of different groups, from

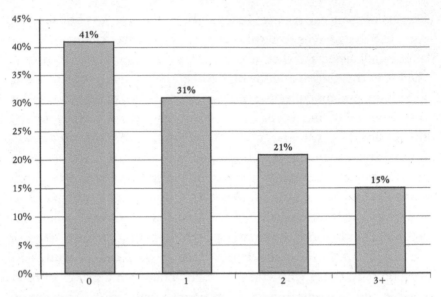

Figure 4: Group membership as a safeguard against depression. This 2013 study shows that those who belonged to three or more groups were significantly less likely to lapse into depression than those who belonged to no groups at all.

heart patients in Norway to school children in Australia, found again and again that people who had high levels of social identification were accordingly less likely to display symptoms of depression. Further independent research in Scotland confirmed that the more groups that a person identified with being part of, the lower the association with depression.[60] Among women diagnosed with breast cancer, those who joined a 1,000-mile motorbike ride to raise funds for fellow sufferers experienced a 'moderate to large' reduction in the cancer-related distress they had previously felt.[61] Among college students, it has been shown, individuals are less likely to be negative about themselves ('I failed because I am stupid') in direct proportion to the number of groups to which they regard themselves as belonging.[62]

The great pioneering social scientist Émile Durkheim coined the term 'collective effervescence' to describe the sense of energy and power that people experience when they come together for a shared purpose. Historian Barbara Ehrenreich describes in *Dancing in the Streets* how dance, song and collective merrymaking (whether for religious or secular reasons) was once the source of great individual strength, and how, as these rituals have tended to decline in many societies, so people have suffered accordingly. 'If the destruction of festivities did not actually cause depression,' she writes, 'it may still be that, in abandoning their traditional festivities, people lost a potentially effective cure for it.'[63] And she quotes a passage from Adam Smith's *The Wealth of Nations*: 'The state, by encouraging, that is by giving liberty to all those who for their own interest would attempt, without scandal or indecency, to amuse and divert the people by painting, poetry, music, dancing ... would easily dissipate, in the greater part of them, that melancholy and gloomy humour.'

Given the overwhelming evidence for the benefits of being part of a group, it's tempting to ask why we don't hear more about it. There are various possible reasons. One – which Alex Haslam puts forward – is that clinicians are uncomfortable with such general, hard-to-categorise truths; they prefer to focus on individual mental and physical conditions than acknowledge 'common structural causes'. As he puts it, 'we can spend a lot of time saying "have you got this disorder or this disorder or this disorder?" but to the extent that you end up compartmentalising all those disorders it blinds you in some sense ... to those commonalities or the social structural variables which can be feeding into those conditions'.[64] He believes that there is a 'horizontal epidemiology' that underpins these conditions – a common thread of social causes that is common to an array of seemingly unrelated illnesses.

It's also the case that complex, networked explanations for common problems are hard to study, and that physicians these days are given so little time to assess, diagnose and prescribe that it's easier to look to individual explanations than consider group factors. The more cynical might additionally suggest that a financial dimension may be involved, too. Pharmaceutical companies make money by selling drugs, not by advocating greater sociability. Even so, Haslam had hope in his voice when he told me, 'I wake up every morning and I think today is the day when Bill Gates knocks on my door and says "go for it!"'[65]

Groups clearly help us, then. But what types of groups do us the most good?

Chapter 9

Team Fortitude

Drawing Strength from Others

When the Luftwaffe embarked on its bombing campaign on London in September 1940, the British authorities worried not only about the death and destruction it would cause, but also about the psychological devastation it might wreak on Londoners. For fifty-seven consecutive nights German planes intensively bombed the city, wiping out individual buildings and destroying whole streets. On the first night alone, 430 people were killed and 1,600 were badly injured.[1] It seemed inconceivable that civilians could withstand the fear and stress that these relentless attacks would cause. 'The experts foretold a mass outbreak of hysterical neurosis among the civilian population ... ' wrote the social scientist Richard Titmuss. 'Under this strain, many people would regress to an earlier level of needs and desires. They would behave like frightened and unsatisfied children.'[2] Winston Churchill feared a public panic that would disrupt defence plans.[3]

It didn't happen. Time and time again, personal diaries kept during the war and shared with the government-commissioned Mass Observation programme display extraordinary levels of resolve and resilience. One survivor commented, 'Once you've been through three nights of bombing, you can't help feeling safe the fourth time.'[4] A woman who had to crawl out of the broken window of a house in Hampstead in North London, after it was bombed, wrote: 'It seems a terrible thing to say, when many people must have been killed and injured last night; but never in my whole life have I ever experienced such *pure and flawless happiness*.'[5] And a twenty-eight-year-old from Maida Vale recorded, 'I feel much more certainty and self-confidence, and much less shyness and "inferiority complex", as a result of the discovery that I am not the coward that I thought.' And she concluded, 'I have a greatly increased feeling of personal responsibility all round.'[6]

Charles Fritz, who was later to pioneer research into how people respond to disasters, described how the Britain that he witnessed in 1943, as a member of the US Air Corps, was a land of bombed-out housing and food and clothing shortages. 'Under those conditions,' he wrote, 'one might expect to find a nation of panicky, war weary people, embittered by the death and injuries to their family members and friends, resentful over their prolonged lifestyle deprivations, anxious and disillusioned about the future, and, more generally, exhibiting personal and social behaviours indicating a state of low morale and esprit de corps ... Instead,' he went on, 'what one found was a nation of gloriously happy people, enjoying life to the fullest, exhibiting a sense of gaiety and love of life that was truly remarkable.'[7] This is perhaps an overly rose-tinted view, and there's no doubt that the so-called Blitz spirit that such testimonies exemplify may have subsequently been exaggerated and glamorised for propaganda purposes. That said, there's no doubt that something extraordinary occurred.

On the other side of Europe, the Soviet writer Aleksandr Fadeev was studying how the youngest survivors of the siege of Leningrad coped with their ordeal. 'The imprint of that terrible winter remained on [children's] faces and was expressed in their games,' he wrote in 1943. 'Many children played by themselves. Even in collective games, they played silently, with serious faces.'[8] They whimpered passively, making no attempt to ask for help. All their energies were focused on the acquisition of food; they would search for it endlessly, hiding microscopic pieces of bread in pockets and matchboxes. Yet, within a matter of months, Fadeev wrote, 'all the children were more or less free from the terrible trauma'. A year later 'the majority of children appeared completely normal and healthy'. An Allied report concurred: 'most of the children who remained in Leningrad developed a sardonic and simple humour that was indestructible,' it noted.[9]

For those who buy into the 'Grit' model of resilience, the survivors of the Blitz and of Leningrad doubtless exemplify the power of the individual to overcome even the most terrible of circumstances. But what they really demonstrate is the extraordinary power of the group. Charles Fritz described how the Blitz created a sense of community: 'The widespread sharing of danger, loss, and deprivation produces an intimate, primarily group solidarity among the survivors ... This merging of individual and societal needs provides a feeling of belonging and a sense of unity rarely achieved under normal circumstances.'[10] He observed that the shared experience was levelling: 'The traditional British class distinctions had largely disappeared. People who had never spoken to each other before the war, now engaged in warm, caring personal relations; they spoke openly with one another about their cares, fears and hopes; and they gladly shared their scarce supplies with others who had greater needs.'[11] He went so far as to suggest that 'people living in heavily bombed cities had significantly higher morale than people in the lightly bombed cities' – their shared experience was more intense. In Leningrad there was a powerful sense of group solidarity among its young survivors, accompanied by 'complete contempt' for the 'invaders'. What individual traumas lurked beneath the surface will probably never be known. But shared experience and a sense of group cohesion helped people weather the storm.

And this solidarity amid conflict demonstrates something else, too. For a group to be effective, there is no need for a narrow common purpose, membership cards and a meeting place. Powerful groups, it turns out, can comprise surprisingly broad affiliations.

Robert Putnam offers an interesting distinction between two forms of group: bonding groups and bridging groups. The former, he says, are socially exclusive; the latter more socially inclusive. Exclusive bonding groups exhibit a strong degree of homogeneity among their members. They might, for example, take the form of a race-based resource group at work or a church-based women's reading group. By their very nature, they will include only those who have something significant in common. Inclusive bridging groups bring together people who might well have very different backgrounds, but have come together for a particular purpose or range of purposes. A civil-rights group or one dedicated to green issues come to mind in this context. We can find kinship with those who are superficially different, but with whom we share common ground.[12]

Of course we are likeliest to form groups with those we regard as being most similar to us. While the corresponding dangers of this bias, sometimes called *homophily*, are often all too apparent, that doesn't make the phenomenon any less ubiquitous. Researchers who have studied 18,000 participants spread across forty-two different countries around the world have concluded that national parochialism is not the preserve of particular cultures or countries. It can be found everywhere. Citizens from all over the world, for example, favour their compatriots over foreigners.[13]

One might expect bonding groups to be more effective in engendering individual fortitude than bridging groups, but as those who experienced the Second World War demonstrate, this is not necessarily the case. It's also the case that it doesn't take that much to create a bond. People who are encouraged to self-categorise themselves as 'elderly' are more likely to self-diagnose hearing loss and accept that they need a hearing aid than their non-group-aware peers. Those who identify themselves as belonging to the medical category of asthma sufferers are more likely to take their medication than those who don't. By the same token, those who receive advice – however well intentioned – from a group of which they do not regard themselves as members are less likely to follow it: something worth bearing in mind in these days of enduring vaccine resistance.[14] A study of African Americans, for instance, demonstrated that they were resistant to dietary advice from sources they regarded as white and middle-class. It's also worth pointing out that different groups exert different levels of influence. Youths who view themselves more as family group members than as part of a teenage peer group are far less likely to take up smoking.[15] For the social scientist Xavier de Souza Briggs, 'Bonding social capital is good for "getting by," but bridging social capital is crucial for "getting ahead".'[16] Bonding and bridging groups are not static, either. There's plenty of evidence to demonstrate that an initially loosely affiliated bridging group can achieve outstanding closeness in exceptional circumstances.

'Exceptional circumstances' include disaster and catastrophe, of course, and that is precisely why so many stories of misfortune also include a catalysing sense of community. Rebecca Solnit, author of *A Paradise Built in Hell*, describes how as people streamed away from the Twin Towers on 9/11 an atmosphere of group solidarity was soon created. She talked to Astra Taylor, then a twenty-something working in a publishing job in TriBeCa on the lower west side of Manhattan, who was there on that day. 'We were all trying to figure this out together,' she told Solnit. 'What was happening to us, should we go home, and what should we do?' At first, the disaster had an isolating effect: 'We were just sort of in the streets, and there was this flood of people coming north, people covered in dust running for their life and not stopping. There were still hundreds of us in the streets feeling oddly insular.'[17] But then, as Taylor and her sixteen-year-old brother first walked to the Village and joined others drinking a beer, then queued to cross the Williamsburg Bridge to Brooklyn, a change took place. 'We were probably milling around for two hours, waiting to cross the bridge, getting hot, and that was the moment where you were feeling your small softness. You're just this small, soft human amongst all these others just wanting to cross this water. Finally we were allowed to cross the Williamsburg Bridge, and the people who met us on the other side were Hasidics [members of the ultra-traditional sect of Jews centred in Brooklyn]. They met us with bottles of water ... The feeling on the street was a sense of community and calmness,' she said. 'There was a sense on the street on September 11 of calm, of trusting in the people around you – kind of being impressed with how intelligently the people around you were handling the circumstances.' Taylor also noted how different the ultimate responses were of those who experienced the horrors of that Manhattan morning at first hand and those who watched them unfold on their TV screens. Amongst the community on the streets, 'There was camaraderie, no hysterics, no panic, you felt that people would come together. That's obviously what happened in the towers, there was a lot of heroism that day.' By contrast, the TV viewers she subsequently spoke to felt very differently: 'you're isolated and you're watching the news and it's hysterical ... they were so overwrought and they're just showing the image again and again of the plane hitting the tower and the tower collapsing. The experience on television was so different than the experience on the street.'

In disaster movies, the moment of catastrophe is invariably shown as a moment of mass panic, as screaming people flee for their lives, their arms flailing in front of them. The reality is more complex. The sociologist Enrico Quarantelli, whose research was funded by a US Department of Defense that assumed in its nuclear-war scenario-planning that a nuclear strike would immediately be followed by mass panic, came to the conclusion that – actually – such an outcome is highly unlikely. 'In general,' Quarantelli and his colleague Russell Dynes suggested in a 1975 paper, 'cooperation rather than conflict is encouraged ... Whereas many stress situations accentuate status and other differences,' they said, 'disasters democratise social life' and lead to a shared 'community identification'.[18] Or as journalist Sebastian Junger put it in his book *Tribe*: 'What catastrophes seem to do – sometimes in the span of a few minutes – is turn back the clock on ten thousand years of social evolution. Self-interest gets subsumed into group interest because there is no survival outside group survival.' So powerful is that social bond, Junger argued, that it 'creates a social bond that many people [subsequently] sorely miss'.[19]

This nostalgia for a period of suffering is a baffling contradiction within the human psyche. When Junger interviewed people who had survived the siege of Sarajevo during the civil war that broke

Yugoslavia apart, and in which thousands upon thousands of people perished, he found that time and again they talked of it as being the worst and the best of times. 'Whatever I say about war, I still hate it,' stated journalist Nidžara Ahmetašević, before going on to say: 'I missed being that close to people, I missed being loved in that way. In Bosnia, as it is now, we don't trust each other anymore; we became really bad people. We didn't learn the lesson of the war, which is how important it is to share everything you have with human beings close to you.'[20] Were people happier during the war? Junger ventured to ask. 'We were *the happiest!*' she exclaimed, adding, 'And we laughed more.' Group identity seemingly out-weighed individual suffering – at least, in retrospect.

Shared adversity creates shared feeling, but the dynamics vary according to the nature of that adversity. When San Francisco was struck by an earthquake and then consumed by fire in 1906, for example, one journalist, Pauline Jacobson, recorded that 'The individual, the isolated self was dead, the social self was regnant. Never even when the four walls of one's own room in a new city shall close around us again shall we sense the old lonesomeness shutting us off from our neighbours.'[21] A natural disaster had evoked a community response. However, when the disaster is caused by other humans, the sense of community is also stoked by a powerful awareness of the in-groups and out-groups I discussed earlier. There's a twin pull of shared experience and hostility to the out-group that is seen as culpable for the anguish.

This is, of course, particularly apparent in war situations. It's also been identified in places such as Northern Ireland where inter-communal tension has often in the past spilt over into unrest and violence. Professor Orla Muldoon, who has produced several analyses of the Protestant and Catholic communities in Northern Ireland over the period of 'The Troubles' (1968–98), found that those people who identified most closely with their own particular community – in this case, the strength of commitment to either styling themselves as 'Northern Irish' (reflecting a connection to the United Kingdom) or 'Irish' (an affinity with a united Ireland) – were likely to suffer less from Post-Traumatic Stress Disorder (PTSD) compared to those who had a weaker connection to such protective identities.[22] Another study of The Troubles found that while two-thirds (145) of the 217 people interviewed reported having witnessed shootings in the street at first hand, there was no evidence to suggest that levels of psychiatric illnesses rose over the three decades when there was constant conflict between the two communities and those sent in to police them. In fact, 'The suicide rate fell sharply, while the homicide rate escalated rapidly.'[23] Interestingly, depressive illness declined particularly 'in areas of severest rioting' – in other words, where in-groups and out-groups were at their most polarised. Examining the research, Catherine Haslam and her colleagues added another strand of thought to the in-group/out-group dynamic: '[The] findings suggest that people are more likely to be traumatised by the violence that flows from intergroup conflict if they do not define themselves in terms of a social identity that allows them to make sense of that conflict.' It's something that we should bear in mind when witnessing events in places such as Gaza or Yemen: people who feel a sense of a shared identity are very likely to see actions that, to outsiders, invite condemnation as the pursuit of a righteous goal. Group allegiance can blinker us to what is taking place before our eyes.

But the benefits of group solidarity don't arise only in extreme circumstances or with potentially negative aspects to them. Émile Durkheim argued in his seminal 1897 book *Suicide* not only that suicide rates fall at times of war and revolution, when collective emotion and shared political passion are inflamed, but that they are lower among groups with particularly strong communal cultures (he noted that the suicide rate for Protestant communities was several times higher than that of the socially and religiously tighter Catholic and Jewish communities) and within large families.[24] That such fortitude can come from affiliation with others who are similar, or in a similar situation, shouldn't surprise us. For decades, Alcoholics Anonymous has recognised that putting strangers with a shared sense of identity in a room together can be a powerful means to help them overcome their addiction. Recognition of the power of the community for the two million members in 150 countries that the organisation caters for, at any given moment, is also baked into its twelve-step programme.[25] It contains, as one would expect, steps that deal directly with the problems that alcohol can cause, but it's interesting to note that it has a pronounced social component. Step eight of the programme involves compiling a list of everyone who has been harmed by the recovering drinker; step nine is contacting them to make amends.[26]

Cohesive groups can arise in the most unlikely and unpromising of environments, as I discovered when I spoke to former police officer Stevyn Colgan. As he himself told me, he wasn't the likeliest of candidates for the career that he chose. Aged eighteen, he had achieved 'a set of grades so low that snakes could slither over them' and his future seemed very far from certain. Fortuitously, a drunken bet with his dad that he couldn't stick six months in the police force resulted in him reporting to Hendon Police College to begin basic training. An unorthodox recruit, Colgan then became an unorthodox officer, constantly asking questions and challenging assumptions. Two particular questions bugged him. First, if members of the force were taught that the primary objective of policing was the prevention of crime, why did his basic training not include a single minute on crime prevention?[27] Second, why were the police so prone to offer theories about the root causes of crime without ever testing them?

He gave me an example: 'There used to be this assumption that burglaries went up during the summer holidays because the kids were off school.' Colgan was unconvinced. 'I could never quite make that jump of how a kid went from being a schoolboy to being a burglar. I could never figure that out, and I started digging.' As he did so, he swiftly discovered that school children didn't make a seasonal adjustment from Latin to larceny. Rather, it was the case that criminals had grown wise to the fact that houses were more likely to be unoccupied in the summer when their owners were on holiday, and had learned to spot such useful tell-tale signs as bins being left out on the street long after the dustmen had emptied them.

Colgan's curiosity and ingenuity led him to be allocated to a tiny team called the Problem Solving Unit that dedicated itself to tackling seemingly intractable problems.[28] One such was the 'fractured community' that occupied a big housing estate in Greenwich. 'There were a lot of absent dads,' he told me, 'and the kids were running riot. Because they didn't have a functioning family to belong to, they made their own. The gang problem was starting to emerge. It was a dysfunctional estate,' he said. 'No one talked to anyone else.' In the aftermath of a fatal stabbing and a much-publicised funeral where the victim's coffin was carried by mask-wearing members of his gang, the then prime minister, Tony Blair, asked the police what could be done, and Colgan and his team duly got to work. They tried various community initiatives. First off was a world food fair – 'a street party with lots of different food'. Virtually no one came. Then they tried setting up a youth centre. It, too, failed.

But Colgan didn't give up. 'One of the things I learned over the course of many years is that if you want to bring a community together you need to find points of commonality – something they can all focus on that they all want.' It was simply a question of finding what point of commonality resonated with this particular community. A wander through the estate provided the answer. Lots of people had dogs. A dog show was therefore launched, which involved local schools, local vets, Battersea Dogs Home, even a display of police dogs. The event was remarkably successful. And it had a lasting impact. 'We knew we'd made a chink in the armour,' Colgan said, 'when we saw this little old lady, who looked like a pepper pot out walking her two tiny dogs, and she was having a go at this six-foot-four black lad, telling him his dog was too fat. I thought, these two people would have crossed the road to avoid each other; she would have been scared of him, and he would have thought she was an interfering old busybody. It was joyous.' The fearfulness of residents was later reported to have declined. A shared love of dogs had been the bridging capital required. The fact is that everyone feels less stressed and anxious when there's a community around them.

The progress towards a sense of shared identity is nicely captured by Catherine Haslam and her colleagues, in what they see as a three-stage process. First, they say, comes *identity reflection*. Then *identity representation*. And, finally, *identity realisation*:

Identity reflection:	The group asks itself (or the leaders of the group ask) *Who are we?* A decision is made on the group's values and its members think about how they represent them.
Identity representation	*What do we want to be?* This is the stage at which the group thinks about what its aspirations are – and what it wants to accomplish.
Identity realisation	This is where the group takes actions that will enable it to accomplish its agreed goals: *How do we become who we want to be?*

It's not hard to map Stevyn Colgan's work with the Greenwich housing estate onto this process. Or to understand why psychologist John Turner, long-term associate of Henri Tajfel, talks of the strange contradiction that sits at the heart of it all. Groups seem to be most effective when their members feel subsumed into them. Members exhibit greater personal strength when they define themselves in terms of group membership rather than their individual traits.

As Stanley Milgram's obedience experiment demonstrated, a community has power even when its membership numbers only two people. But it still has to be a community. Talking to a random stranger about worries and concerns is not enough in itself, in most situations. 'There is little evidence that expression of emotions has any beneficial effect following bereavement,' psychologist Mark Seery points out, 'and there is some evidence that it may even impede successful coping.'[29] When he and his team set about seeking to understand how television viewers had been affected by repeat viewings of the attack on the World Trade Center, they found both that those who were encouraged to talk about their anxieties and concerns were no better off for the experience, and those who chose to internalise their emotions were no worse off. 'The notion that expressing one's thoughts and feelings in the immediate aftermath of a collective trauma is a necessary step in successful long-term adjustment was not supported,' Seery says. 'Instead, people who choose not to express appear able to cope very effectively.' For an interaction to be beneficial, in other words, there has to be some kind of a bond there. There has to be a means by which one individual connects with another.

This raises an interesting question about those who opt for therapy to help them cope with everyday life. If just talking about something doesn't help, why should paying someone to hear you talk be any more effective? Cynics would point to the fact that there are, according to one estimate, at least 500 different types of psychotherapy, and that there is evidence to suggest that none of them is any more effective than any other. They would also argue that therapy is no magical cure-all. Take one of the commonest of all mental afflictions – depression – which is reckoned to affect around one-fifth of all people on the planet at some point during their lives (and the average person with a history of depression will experience four episodes).[30] Many seek professional help for it, but there is nevertheless a high failure rate. Even when people receive what is generally considered to be the most effective treatment (Cognitive Behavioural Therapy, or CBT, combined with antidepressant medication) the chances are that around a quarter will experience a relapse in the first two years.

But that doesn't negate the vitally important role that therapy can play. Good therapists can be hugely beneficial. They have an ability to project empathy, to build rapport and to ensure that they and their patient share objectives. In other words, they offer the possibility of a powerful shared *social* connection with their client.

As for the techniques that therapists use, it is indeed possible that there's not that much to choose between behaviour therapy (adapting unhealthy behaviours), CBT (changing unhealthy ways of thinking), interpersonal therapy (addressing unhealthy interactions with others), person-centred therapy (helping individuals find their own solutions to their problems) or any of the many other therapies that are on offer. Back in 1936, psychologist Saul Rosenzweig coined the term 'the Dodo Bird Verdict' in relation to various forms of therapy offered by his contemporaries – his view being that just as the Dodo in Lewis Carroll's *Alice in Wonderland* says at the end of the Caucus Race it has organised that 'everyone has won, all must have prizes',[31] so all therapies are as good as each other and all deserve to win. Many professionals would strongly disagree, but numerous studies since Rosenzweig's time have reached conclusions not dissimilar to his own. To a large extent, though, that's not the point. The important thing is that they're all predicated on a strong therapist–patient relationship, a relationship that creates a bond known as the 'therapeutic alliance'.[32]

What a strong therapeutic alliance achieves is a reignition of the patient's connection with others. One school of thought holds that depression is not so much a question of a chemical imbalance in the body that needs to be redressed as (in the words of clinical psychologist Tegan Cruwys and her colleagues) 'a fundamentally *social* disorder'.[33] True depression (as opposed to merely feeling a bit low) is characterised by cognitive and behavioural changes that include social withdrawal. It's that withdrawal that needs to be addressed and countered.

The physical activities that some therapies recommend can prove very beneficial in this regard, not because of the exercise involved per se, but because of the further opportunity they offer for social bonding. A group of care-home residents suffering from dementia who undertook a programme of intensive exercises recorded the same lower scores on a standardised depression scale after four months as a comparison group that had been seated throughout, but had been encouraged to chat or sing or listen to music or readings. Both sets of people had been helped not by the regimes they had been told to follow, but by virtue of being in a group. The Swedish researchers who undertook this study also found that a control group of elderly people, who had not been given anything to do, showed no similar improvement in their levels of depression. Other researchers have come up with similar results. According to one: 'Much of the positive effect of exercise on depression in past research is due not only to improved aerobic fitness but also to the social aspect of the exercise conditions.'[34]

Looking more generally at trauma, psychologist Alex Haslam and his co-authors have argued that 'Resilience in the face of trauma is typically associated with processes that help to restore, maintain, or enhance a person's sense of self and their sense of meaningful connection to others.'[35]

And there is a word for the way that is achieved: synchrony.

Chapter 10

Synced, Aligned and Connected
The Power of Synchrony

'When you get traumatised, you get out of sync on the most ele-mentary level,' asserts the psychiatrist Bessel van der Kolk.[1] By the same token, an ability to transcend or come to terms with trauma involves getting back into sync – with ourselves and with others. At a personal level, we re-establish our sense of identity and con-trol; at a social level, we re-establish our connectedness with others and move 'in sync' with them. And the two forces interconnect with and reinforce one another.

It's a process that van der Kolk saw at work in the wake of 9/11. A sense of community ensured that people didn't feel ashamed of themselves, 'because your neighbour may have the same feelings of terror and fear that you have'. It also removed a sense of power-lessness and built an 'internal locus of control' for them ('the key factor in healthy coping throughout life').[2] And with people's bur-geoning sense of identity and control came a reinforcing loop of interconnectedness with the community. 'This recognition and mirrored experience in others helps us feel absorbed into a sympa-thetic community around us, it makes us feel understood and accepted, and you don't feel like you're worthy of exclusion.'[3] For her part, Catherine Haslam and her colleagues describe what hap-pens when the reverse occurs: 'when trauma has an adverse psychological impact, this is because it fundamentally compro-mises a person's social sense of self and their relationship to the world at large'.[4] The US veterans of the Iraq and Vietnam conflicts that I described earlier, who were left traumatised by their experi-ences of war, suffered a loss of synchronisation between themselves and others: 'I drank to try and rid myself of the violent part of me that I really didn't like,' recalled one. 'I mean just numbed it, tried to not feel it.'[5]

When totalitarian regimes seek to crush opponents, they do so by dehumanising them as individuals and removing them from the wider community. Primo Levi describes how captives at Auschwitz were deliberately deprived of cutlery: 'Without a spoon the daily soup could not be consumed in any other way than by lapping it up as dogs do … When the camp at Auschwitz was liberated,' he goes on, 'we found in the warehouse thousands of brand-new transparent plastic spoons, besides tens of thousands of spoons made of aluminium or even silver that came from the luggage of deportees as they arrived. So it was not a matter of thrift, but a precise intent to humiliate.'[6] With similar intent, those who ran the camp had each prisoner tattooed with a number that not only branded them like cattle, but also represented a direct attack on Jewish community identity ('precisely in order to distinguish Jews from the barbarians, the tattoo is forbidden by Mosaic law (Leviticus 19:28)').[7]

The same process has been observed in other wars. Blerina Kellezi, who partnered with one of the creators of the BBC Prison Experiment, Stephen Reicher, to examine the devastating Kosovo conflict of 1998–9, has described how Serbian troops systematically raped Kosovo Albanians.[8] They did so in order to leave individuals traumatised and demoralised. At the same time, they sought to exploit a community taboo about rape that in the past had often seen rape victims ostracised from the community, and their family shamed for not protecting them. In some cases, such tactics were successful. 'He is not sent away from where he lives, but people would not speak to him,' one interviewee said of a male rape victim. 'She is forced to leave the family and cannot help but become involved in prostitution,' said another of a woman who had been violated by Serbian troops.[9] But where trauma could be connected with community well-being, individuals were able to overcome what had been done to them. 'I hid my son inside my breast, and I thought "let the bullets take me, only my son should survive,"' said one woman proudly.

More generally, we as individuals are constantly prompted to behave as community members, and are stigmatised if it's felt that we're not. The writer David Berreby views this reality through the prism of childhood experience. 'A child in any society is a tiny foreigner,' he says. 'Adults laugh at her cute mistakes of behaviour.' That laughter is a gentle way to instruct her in the ways of correct behaviour. Later the tools used to remind her of the importance of particular customs and traditions will be less benign. 'Strong emotions mark the rules as important. Boys don't cry. No one works on the Sabbath. Women cover their hair in the street. The young child soon learns that such patterns are not just regularities in life, like dark following sunset. Instead these have a personal bite; when a child disrupts them, adults (and other kids) make sure that he or she feels shame, guilt, fear, and pain.'[10]

Our sync wiring has a strongly physical element to it. Bessel van der Kolk observed that people suffering from trauma find it very difficult to make eye contact with others, and that when they try to do so, they don't follow the (unconscious) reciprocal patterns of normal body language. He shares an example of where the restoration of physical syncing restored behavioural syncing: 'Steve Gross used to run the play program at the Trauma Center. Steve often walked around the clinic with a brightly coloured beach ball, and when he saw angry or frozen kids in the waiting room, he would flash them a big smile. The kids rarely responded. Then, a little later, he would return and "accidentally" drop his ball close to where a kid was sitting. As Steve leaned over to pick it up, he'd nudge it gently toward the kid, who'd usually give a half-hearted push in return. Gradually Steve got a back-and-forth going, and before long you'd see smiles on both faces. From simple, rhythmically attuned movements, Steve had created a small, safe place where the social-engagement system could begin to reemerge.'[11]

All types of physical interaction can bring about such a result. 'Moving together, dancing together with other people, getting a sense of rhythm, which many people around the world except in the Western world use – drumming together, singing together, making music – helps to reestablish that sense of community and being in sync with the people around you,' van der Kolk asserts.[12] For her part, Barbara Ehrenreich argues that 'such rituals serve to break down the sufferer's sense of isolation and reconnect him or her with the human community': they free him or her 'from the prison of the self', from 'the anxious business of evaluating how one stands in the group or in the eyes of an ever-critical God'. They make individuals feel part of something bigger, something shared.[13]

This pleasurable and reassuring sense of togetherness comes about because, just as with grooming among apes and monkeys, human activities ranging from eating, laughing, dancing, marching and performing rituals together, to sharing stories, all trigger the release of endorphins – those chemicals that, as Robin Dunbar explains, are 'weight for weight thirty times more effective as a painkiller than morphine'.[14] He and fellow researcher Emma Cohen told me of one experiment they conducted that beautifully demonstrates the link. First, they said, they put members of the Oxford University rowing crew through their regular morning workout on individual rowing machines and measured the rowers' increase in these neurotransmitters. Then, a week later, they repeated the exercise with the same crew, but this time setting the rowing machines out in the formation of a virtual boat. The result, they found, was a doubling in endorphin levels over the previous week.[15]

Emma Cohen went on to carry out a similar exercise with the rugby team at Oxford University. Here she got half the team to warm up on their own, and half to perform warm-up exercises in pairs. 'Then,' she explained, 'they performed a really challenging sprint test that is a normal part of their training. It would normally take roundabout four minutes, but they managed to shave off about six and a half seconds from their normal time if they'd warmed up synchronously with a teammate, versus non synchronously.' As she went on to point out, it wasn't as though the sprint test was a communal activity – it was a solo effort. Even so, those who had previously performed a simple act of social bonding did better (a '2.5% improvement') and did so without reporting greater fatigue or experiencing higher heart rates.[16]

Such lifts in endorphin levels don't just occur when we play sport together. They happen when we eat together (an activity that has been shown to correlate strongly with a sense of life satisfaction)[17] and when we have 'meaningful conversations' (as opposed to *small talk*) with others.[18] Robin Dunbar has observed rises in endorphin levels among strangers singing together in choirs – the larger the choir, the greater the endorphin release. In his view, this phenomenon helps to explain why the New Zealand All Black national rugby team is so successful. They may have the theoretical disadvantage of being drawn from a tiny population, but they have the *haka* warm-up ritual on their side. 'It has all the hallmarks of a good ritual, every element of which triggers the endorphin system … The key is surely that, under the influence of raised endorphin levels, the team enters the fray in a heightened state of alertness, with a sense of calmness and elevated pain thresholds that allow them to absorb far more punishment and exhaustion during the game that follows than would otherwise be the case.'[19]

According to Joe Devlin, a doctor at University College London, synchrony even occurs among the strangers who find themselves making up a theatre audience. He told me how when his team monitored the heartbeats of people attending a West End musical, they found that they sped up and slowed down in unison. 'Usually, a group of individuals will each have their own heart rates and rhythms, with little relationship to each other,' he explained. 'But romantic couples or highly effective teammates will actually synchronise their hearts so that they beat in time with each other, which in itself is astounding … It turns out,' he went on, 'that in social species (like humans but others too), part of the autonomic nervous system increases activity when we are with other people. It's part of the system that is involved in emotion as well, so a consequence is that being with other people tends to enhance emotional responses, good or bad. It's one of the reasons we feel an energy in live audience environments that is missing when you're by yourself.'[20] Robin Dunbar points out that touch enhances synchrony, too: hugging, for example, has been shown to increase positive feelings and reduce negative ones on days when people are experiencing relationship difficulties.[21]

Every human group, in fact, whether secular or religious, offers the beneficial power of synchrony (Alex Haslam claims that 'the primary benefits of going to church have got nothing really to do with faith and everything to do with community').[22] For the late Rabbi Jonathan Sacks, groups offer a shared joy that is described by the Hebrew word *simcha* (the *ch* is, as in the word 'Chanukah', sounded in the throat) that appears several times in the Old Testament. It's a word, according to Sacks, that 'has a nuance untranslatable into English' because while happiness or joy can be experienced alone: 'simcha, by contrast, is not a private emotion. It means happiness shared. It is a social state, a predicate of "we," not "I."' The word recognises that there seems to be something transformational about experiencing emotions – most positively, joy – alongside and with others. It shows that we are synchronised with them and can see our own emotions reflected back. As Sacks said: 'There is no such thing as feeling simcha alone.'[23]

Of course, as Cohen pointed out to me, the process can work the other way, too. 'There was,' she related, 'a lovely little study that showed that when you have a friend, you perceive a potentially challenging situation to be easier than if you don't have a friend.'[24] The study she referred to involved getting people on a campus to stand at the bottom of a hill, don a heavy rucksack and then estimate the gradient of the hill. Those who happened to have a friend with them at the time invariably estimated that the hill was less steep than those who were on their own.

Synchrony, then, enthuses us and makes us feel positive and engaged. But does it really enhance that sense of personal control that is so key to our well-being? This is something that Katharine Greenaway and her team set out to understand, and they did so by looking at political affiliations in the US in the lead-up to, and aftermath of, the 2012 Presidential Election. Their working assumption was that it was possible that supporters of Mitt Romney, the Republican candidate, might feel disempowered in the wake of the victory of his rival, the incumbent Democrat president Barack Obama. What they found, though, was that a strong sense of affiliation with a particular party was closely associated with 'significantly greater perceived feeling of personal control', regardless of whether that particular party lost or won. The Republicans might just have suffered a major election defeat, but their closest supporters didn't feel less agency as a result. 'The fact that groups can provide people with a sense of personal control even when the group itself has experienced a profound failure speaks to the powerful psychological protection afforded by social identities,'[25] the researchers concluded.

A sense of individual control among Super Elite sportspeople can also, time and again, be seen to derive to a considerable extent from their relationship to a wider group. Dr Pippa Grange, one of the best-regarded sports psychologists in the world, who worked with Gareth Southgate's England football team as they reached the semi-finals of the 2018 World Cup, and whose simple, unfussy brilliance has been celebrated by the likes of the researcher Brené Brown, is very clear on the topic. 'Certainly the ability to overcome and make sense of a negative event and add it to your resilience locker is a valuable thing,' she told me when I asked for her views on the Great British Medallists survey. 'But what that research doesn't actually show is how many of those young people had a really strong mentor or had family relationships that were very supportive that helped them overcome challenges.'[26]

Not just mentors or family members, either. Grange also mentioned the power of community networks and friendship groups. All these entities, she said, gave individual sportspeople an additional 'factor of stability and coping' that helped them. In her view,

'If we only look specifically at the adversity or the tragedy that somebody went through and don't look at all of the things that help them get through that, we get quite a skewed picture.' It stands to reason. If you find yourself a long way from shore and in danger of being swept further out to sea, then you're more likely to make that additional effort that will get you back to dry land if you can see and hear people there who are willing you on. You're not on your own. Your group is there to support you. It's strange to think how that supportive group is airbrushed out of the picture in so many accounts of individual resilience.

As for synchrony and individual identity, this is something to which the great human behaviour specialist Robert Cialdini has devoted considerable research. 'The experience of unity [is] about identities, shared identities,' he writes in the 2021 edition of his classic book *Influence*.[27] He observes that 'a study of a large Indian bank's records revealed loan officers approved more loan applications and gave more favourable terms to applicants of the same religion'. He describes how simple signals of similarity even inform our assessment of events: 'after a service failure in a Hong Kong restaurant, customers were less willing to blame a server who shared their last name[28] … [P]eople often fail to distinguish correctly between their own traits and those of fellow members, which reflects a confusion of self and other,' Cialdini writes. We subsume group identity into our own, and act accordingly: 'People are inclined to say yes to someone they consider one of them.'

The power even of very simple acts of syncing was fascinatingly demonstrated by three Canadian researchers interested in the workings of unconscious bias, who asked volunteers to watch a 140-second-long video of actors reaching for and sipping glasses of water. The researchers varied the ethnicities of the actors (using Black or white actors) and varied whether or not participants were asked to mimic the sipping they could see onscreen. The survey they subsequently undertook showed that – in the short term, at least – unconscious racial bias was erased among those who synced the actors' sipping with their own. 'Mimicking outgroup members, therefore, reduces implicit bias against that outgroup,' the researchers concluded.[29]

The idea that identity is in part a group attribute may be hard for fully-blown individualists to swallow. Yet research finding after research finding points in that direction. It's also apparent that the fully-fledged group enhances the individual. Researchers at New York University's psychology department found an interesting way to put this to the test. They assigned random volunteers either to a team of four who were told they were in competition with other teams, or to a group of four who were told they were competing as individuals. The volunteers were then presented with various challenges that ranged from memory tasks and sudoku puzzles to word tests and brainstorms (such knotty problems as 'rank-ordering items needed for survival in a wintery plane crash scenario'). Those who worked as groups outperformed those who operated as individuals. Brain-scanning headsets that tracked volunteers' 'neural synchrony' found that at first teams showed no more synchrony than individuals working alone, but that by the end of the experiment the teams exhibited a high degree of being in sync. Indeed, the greater the synchrony, the better the collective decision-making. Being on the same wavelength genuinely led to better work, the only exception being a typing exercise, where working together had the effect of slowing people down.[30]

Most of us will have experienced that flash of irritation that occurs when we're at a show with a friend or partner and find that they're looking at their phone rather than sharing the experience. According to Garriy Shteynberg, a Tennessee-based psychologist, this is because we associate learning something at the same time as other people with what he terms 'intragroup coordination'.[31] In experiments he conducted he found that when those involved in an online event believed that other people like them were participating, their memory of that event improved. As he says, 'people devote greater cognitive resources to any feature of their environment that is thought to be co-attended synchronously with a socially close other'.[32] From scary films to charity ad campaigns, our emotional response to stimuli is heightened when our experience is shared with people with whom we feel a kinship.[33] In the same way, students who have had their brain activity recorded as they attended biology lessons have been found to display marked synchrony if they have been put into pairs or discussion groups or have watched videos together.[34]

When we feel part of a group and in sync with it, we experience a protective glow. Self and other overlap, and our sense of identity flourishes accordingly. Anything that disconnects us from the group has an invisible but potent adverse effect on our well-being and, by extension, on our fortitude. It could be time to get up and dance.

Chapter 11

Three Tales of Fortitude
Finding Strength in Connection

Anna Hemmings was beyond tired. She was overwhelmed by an exhaustion that completely enveloped her. When she made it to the shower, she couldn't stand or lift her arms. All her energy seemed to be channelled into transmitting pain through her aching body. And yet she was only twenty-eight; she was in her prime. She was also a three-times world-champion kayaker. This shouldn't be happening to her.

She'd first realised something wasn't right when she began to experience intense muscle ache after her daily training sessions. A degree of muscle fatigue was only to be expected, and she was used to it. But this was something different. It was painful and exhausting. Doctors told her there was nothing physically wrong with her, but struggled to come up with suggestions as to what she should do. 'I tried conventional medicine, I tried alternative therapies and nothing was working,' she told me. 'I went to see one doctor and he said to me, "There's no treatment, there's no cure, you might get back in a kayak, but you're never going to race at that highest level again."' His diagnosis – that Anna was suffering from Chronic Fatigue Syndrome (also known as ME) – came across as a shrug, a catch-all that said, 'We see you're sick, but don't really know why.'

All the while Anna was missing out on qualifying for events and was fearful that her goal of competing in the following year's Olympics was slipping away from her. Eventually she felt she had no choice but temporarily to throw in the towel. 'That was it, I didn't train again for eighteen months.' She spent the summer of 2004 despondently being a spectator of the Athens Olympic Games, which she had so desperately wanted to be a part of. 'It got worse because when I got ill, I got more isolated,' she recalls. 'When I got ill I wasn't getting out much. I was living alone. I was doing up a flat on my own. I didn't speak to anyone about how I was feeling. I said, "Yeah, yeah, I'm fine" when people asked. But I was physically and emotionally isolated.'[1]

Then, with help from her sponsors, Anna was referred to a new doctor. John Eaton had been refining an approach he termed *Reverse Therapy* – an approach that 'teaches people to identify the triggers which prompt the brain to create symptoms such as fatigue and unexplained pain'.[2] He encouraged Hemmings to unpick every action she had taken that had brought her to her present state and to document fluctuations in her condition. Various patterns emerged, and Hemmings came to realise that her condition had a number of root causes, but it was possible to perceive an underlying problem – she wasn't connecting with others, and she wasn't making it easy for others to connect with her. 'One of the biggest triggers for me was the non-expression of emotions,' she said. People would ask her how she was and she'd just say 'fine'. She hid her emotional lows from even her closest friends and family. 'I didn't really open up to anyone,' recalls the person who styled her own persona *Poker-face Anna*.

She had teamed up with the renowned Canadian coach Frédéric Jobin and had travelled to Canada and Florida to be with him, but 'I wasn't going to stay full time over there and when I came back to the UK I was training on my own.' At home she trained intensively for four or five hours a day, but as she told me, 95 per cent of the time she did so on her own. 'Although I would phone my coach and we would communicate by email, it wasn't the same as having someone on the river bank to talk to after each training session and have that emotional outlet.' (In these days of endless virtual meetings, it's worth noting that life in the virtual world does not achieve the synchrony of being together. As the technology author Douglas Rushkoff says, 'you can't see if someone's breath is syncing up with yours. So the mirror neurons never fire, the oxytocin never goes through your body, you never have that experience of bonding with the other human being.'[3]) Eaton helped her to appreciate the dangers of this approach. 'For me it was all about the training programme. But my mistake was that I didn't realise the importance of environment and connections and being around training partners ... I'm an extrovert but I don't think I'd realised how much I needed that energy from people.' As she became increasingly ill and correspondingly less inclined to seek out company, a vicious circle was created.

With Dr Eaton's help, Hemmings came to appreciate that her limbic system had been signalling red alert and that she had ignored the warnings. Intense physical stress combined with isolation had been interpreted by her body as a sign that something was calamitously wrong, and it had responded accordingly. She needed to dial up the social connections in her life. 'I thought all I needed to do was to follow a great training program and work really hard. Actually I didn't. I'm not a robot. I needed human connection. I needed emotional support and I needed a place to vent.' Her road to recovery was a complex one and involved various strategies. But renewing contact with others proved a vital tonic. 'I realised that for me to survive I need to have really strong connections to people. I was so blinded to my mission, I was just too focussed.'

It took a while for Anna's confidence to catch up with her return to better physical and mental health. When it did so, she embarked on a remarkable trajectory. First she qualified for the European Championships. Then she won the thirty-two-kilometre race with a sprint finish. By the time of the World Championships in October 2005 her self-belief had surged back. She went on to claim the world title, crossing the line nearly a minute ahead of her nearest rival. With six World Championship gold medals to her name, she remains Britain's most successful ever female kayaker. Her comeback was extraordinary.

Damian Scarf didn't have the easiest of starts in life. 'I failed high school, which meant that I couldn't get into uni for a few years,' he told me. 'The consequence of failing was that I spent a year on benefits. When I finally did make it in, I was just very focused on passing. I didn't really have aspirations to do much beyond that.' Even so, in his first year at university Scarf managed to score a mix of B and C grades.[4] Inspired and motivated by his success, he started to work even harder. Soon he was achieving As and Bs. And now he really doubled down on his academic studies, cutting back on socialising to make more room for them and, in his third year, deciding to stop playing rugby, which he now regarded as a distraction.

As his work took over more of his life, so his connection with others weakened. 'I wasn't part of any kind of social groups or recreational groups,' he recalled. 'And then it culminated in not hanging out with family, not going to family birthdays or spending any time with them.' But there was a psychological price to be paid for such self-imposed isolation. 'My anxiety controlled me. Any time I wasn't studying, my head was filled with noise about being a failure, about not working hard enough, about not having what it takes to succeed … By my third year,' he went on, 'my anxiety extended its focus to my physical appearance. I became bulimic; I was regularly binging and making myself throw up. I was getting up at six to go for runs, getting to the library before it opened at eight, studying until it closed at eleven and then cycling home. I kept that schedule seven days a week.' Ultimately, this punishing regime led to physical collapse. Riven with anxiety and having lost fifty pounds in weight, Scarf had to be admitted to hospital and so missed his end-of-year exams.

His fourth year was, if anything worse. Undeterred by the alarm bells that his body had been sounding, he yet again stepped up his academic commitment, rising at three or four in the morning to study and then dashing to the library to be there at opening time. He knew he didn't feel right, but trusted that his mental-health problems would be temporary: 'I had hoped that by the end of the fourth year my anxiety would abate.' The end of exams, however, didn't presage the conclusion of his anxiety. If anything, things got worse. 'Eliminating all those [social] groups had created a hole, and now without study and exams to fill it, depression did.'

It was only at this stage that Damian realised he would have to reach out for help. He knew that he needed to rebuild his relationship with friends and family and restore his links with the world around him. Social connections in themselves would not have enabled him to avoid the problems he experienced: 'at least in my case I don't think maintaining those connections would have prevented me from developing anxiety and depression'. However, he had come to realise that 'I definitely think they would have reduced the impact. I would have been more resilient.'

Today, Damian is Dr Scarf, a senior lecturer at the University of Otago in New Zealand, and a man who has been able not only to assimilate his personal experience, but to draw upon it in his academic studies and help others in the process.

A while back, for example, he became interested in a long-standing social project in New Zealand that involved teenagers living aboard and taking responsibility for a stunning tall ship, the *Spirit of New Zealand*.[5] Working with a team that included his mentor Jackie Hunter, Damian looked at sixty children aged between eight and fifteen who spent ten days on the ship. Each child was tracked for a month before their adventure, on their first day aboard, on their final day and then nine months later, and the results were compared with those from a control group of 120 children who weren't involved with the project.

The regime on the *Spirit of New Zealand* was a rigorous and spartan one. No technology (in particular, no phones) was allowed, branded clothing was prohibited, children slept in bunks in cramped quarters and their cleanliness regime depended strongly on sea-bathing. New crew members were assigned to 'Watch' groups – Blue Watch, Red Watch, and so on – and, over the course of the voyage, were given various responsibilities by the twelve-person professional crew of the boat – for example, 'working with others to clear "mountains of dishes" in a cramped galley, pulling for hours on ropes with others, and standing lookout at 2 a.m'.[6] Each day a different person would be made the Watch leader. Each evening there would be a group discussion about the events of that day and the lessons learned. Many of the children suffered initially from seasickness and often from homesickness.[7]

Scarf was fascinated to see the gradual change that overcame the teenagers. 'From the first day, you've got forty youths standing on a wharf, looking at their shoes, not wanting to talk to one another,' he said. 'And then on the last day, you've got forty youths who are crying because they have to leave one another after ten days.' Their resilience scores matched their mood. On the first day they were no higher than they had been when they were measured for the first time a month before. By the tenth day they had significantly increased. And that improvement was still apparent when the final measurements were taken nine months later.[8] Intriguingly, the more adverse the physical conditions of any given sea expedition, the more the groups bonded and the greater the strength they drew from one another – or, as Scarf put it, 'we actually found some evidence that the worse the weather, the higher the gain of resilience; the rougher the seas, the more they kind of fuse with their group, and lean on their group for support'. And the greater the sense of belonging on board, the greater the resilience measured nine months later.[9]

'The shared identity is the key,' Scarf explained. 'They identify as a member of this Watch group. What does that identity consist of? They can take swims around a boat in freezing-cold water at six o'clock in the morning, they can work together to raise the sails, they can keep watch at two o'clock in the morning, they can deal with seasickness, they can deal with being out on a boat in the middle of nowhere. It's the identity of that Watch group. What that Watch group means, or what that identity is, is kind of what's key here. And in this case, that identity consists of a group of people who are resilient.' He also pointed out that it's not just about group membership in itself, but about acceptance of the individual by the group: 'the people around us accept us for who we are, whether they accept us for the good and the bad, or perhaps parts of us that we hide from others'. That 'unconditional acceptance' is 'probably a key to building resilience and self-esteem'. 'We need to give people a forum where they can be themselves and where there's no parts of themselves that they have to hide.'

More generally, Scarf told me, 'The number of groups we belong to not only bolsters our resilience, but is also protective against developing depression, can be curative of existing depression, and helps to prevent depression relapse ... Even when you're old, groups are critical,' he added. 'The more groups we belong to, the slower our cognitive decline.' He described the 'Men's Sheds' that are pro-liferating worldwide: informal gatherings typically housed in workshop or shed-type locations, where older retired men can join others in hands-on activity. These are people who have tradition-ally been difficult to reach out to and who have been reluctant to forge new connections with strangers. The Men's Sheds project has helped break down their inhibitions and has encouraged them to come together with others (with a convenient excuse that they're working on a woodworking project).

I first came across Damian Scarf via a TEDx Talk he had given, and I was struck then by a particular phrase that he used: 'social cure'. He was explaining how, while we're all given health messages about the dangers of smoking and the wisdom of eating healthily and exercising more, we're never told about the benefits of being part of a group. And yet, he explained, 'building social relationships, having high rather than low social support, has a comparable impact on decreasing mortality as a moderate smoker quitting smoking. It exceeds well-known factors, such as increasing physical activity and eating healthy ... Perhaps,' he concluded, 'our doctors should be asking us about the number of groups we belong to.' This indeed is social cure.[10] Or, as one research subject told the psychologist Catriona Matheson and her colleagues in an adjacent context, 'you can't be resilient on your own, can you?'[11]

I'm on the third floor of the Highgate Wing of the Whittington Hospital, a red-brick building that sits on a winding lane set back from the busy main roads of Archway, North London. It was once the institution's psychiatric ward and before that, according to Florence Nightingale, 'by far the best of any workhouse infirmary we have'.[12] I'm there at lunchtime, and my partner is a mask-wearing junior doctor who is attempting to pat her head and touch her nose while I repeatedly count up to three.

Our host for the day is Dr Heidi Edmundson, an inspirational medic who has led a quirkily brilliant approach to the depressingly familiar problem of burnout. My companions are twelve medical staff who work with Edmundson in A&E – talented people from four continents who are united by a desire to help people. One of them has just completed a night shift, but still manages to be astonishingly alert.

The context at the moment we've got together is that the National Health Service is under immense pressure – and so are the people who work for it. Patient numbers are rising, staff are working long hours and they are often short-handed. Emergency staff, hospital surveys show, face particular challenges, but all have too much work and too little time to relax and recharge their batteries. 'When I worked as a junior doctor,' Edmundson tells me, 'there were more pockets of five minutes downtime when nothing was happening. On night shifts it would get quietish around five o'clock and you could sit for an hour or so and chat with the people you work with.' But those moments have been squeezed out.

The loss of these 'pockets' has become a real concern for her. She feels they fulfilled a valuable twofold task. They were the moments when 'people bonded, they forged a relationship and they were able to offer a little support'. 'In medicine there's certain activities we do as teams,' she explains. 'If somebody comes in in cardiac arrest, there's a teamwork to it. I think we've got very good at practising task-based team activities, but I still think there's a place to just build people getting to know each other and growing together as individuals. You bond with people you laugh with.' At the same time she is acutely aware that these 'pockets' brought people together. When teams become stressed, she says, they start 'retreating into themselves' and stop connecting with one another, creating a vicious circle of isolation and stress.

Edmundson describes to me how she set about dealing with the challenges that presented themselves when she started trying to tackle the problem. 'We didn't have a budget and the other thing we didn't have was time.' She did, however, spot one possible avenue. Each morning in the training department where she worked, ten minutes was set aside for the team to get together to learn about standard procedures or new techniques. 'Some of the slots were empty, so we decided to take over one of the ten-minute slots and dedicate it to wellness.'

Previously Edmundson had run an annual experiment training initiative that linked up with students from the Central School of Speech and Drama to practise an intriguing form of improvisational performance called Forum Theatre. 'It's a style of theatre created by a gentleman called Augusto Boal. It's also known as Theatre of the Oppressed.' Boal was a Brazilian man of the theatre and political activist, who believed that by encouraging an audience to become active participants in a performance he could inspire them to enact change in their own communities. Amongst the resources he has left to us is a book of warm-up exercises and improvisations titled *Games for Actors and Non-Actors*. Edmundson decided to draw on Boal's ideas and techniques in her own work with medical staff: 'if you're engaged in anything that is fun or creative it works in the same way as mindfulness,' she believes. 'You have to be completely in the present; it stops you focusing on the past.'

At first, while some staff were enthusiastic, others reticently held back. But participation grew, and there was positive enthusiasm the day the winner of a knockout tournament of 'Rock Paper Scissors', who was from Chile, chose to mark her triumph by singing the Chilean national anthem. As the team learned more about one another, it wasn't long before they discovered common connections. Most importantly, they started to laugh together.

Building on the success of the first programme, Edmundson added a whole day of training for each member of the team, measuring the participants' wellness and their connection to others at every stage. The results were impressive. Staff proved more resilient in the face of ever-increasing patient numbers. Indeed, although patient attendance had risen by 8 per cent over the previous year, such was staff engagement that waiting times did not. At the same time, and over the same period, sick days among staff declined by 33 per cent. The medics felt better, and they worked better.

Downtime at work would be very familiar territory to previous generations of workers, accustomed to adjourning to a nearby pub on a regular basis. Edmundson, however, had reservations about reintroducing this particular habit. 'I think the problem with going to the pub,' she tells me, 'is that it's not inclusive, for a myriad of different reasons. The other thing about fun – people might trivialise it – but it's actually not as easy to have fun as you might think. So you can go to the pub and you can laugh, but you can go to the pub and end up not laughing and rehashing the same problems from work. I don't think going to the pub is a particularly sure-fire way to have fun.' Dudley Moore may have squealed, 'Isn't fun the best thing to have?' in the 1981 film *Arthur*, but it's more easily desired than achieved. Edmundson's group activities, however, certainly set people on the right road.

Now I'm here to observe Edmundson's project in progress, she has ingeniously hatched a plan to get cabin crew, presently on COVID furlough, to help train emergency staff in the art of dealing with abusive members of the public. Among the various activities that I witness, there are clapping routines, counting games where people have to replace numbers with gestures, and then a game of 'bomb and shield' where, as Edmundson describes it, 'everyone chooses someone to be their bomb and someone to be their shield. They do not tell anyone their choice. They then have to walk round the room, not stopping, trying to make sure their shield is between them and their bomb.'[13]

When the session is over, she reflects on what people seek from their relationship with their jobs: 'Someone said they wanted more sunshine, laughter and cake.' I could certainly see that today's session had helped with the sunshine and laughter. But cake? 'Every Thursday afternoon some of the nursing staff try to have afternoon tea: we buy some cakes and make a huge pot of tea. Once a week we try to have a pause for that, so there's a sense of community.'

It all reminds me of what one of the founders of positive psychology, Christopher Peterson, said when he was asked to summarise his discipline in two words. Positive psychology, he replied, is about 'other people'.[14]

Chapter 12

Fortitude Falling?

Is Fortitude in Retreat?

As we get older, many of us have a tendency to say, 'Things aren't how they used to be' with a touch of nostalgic regret. We remember the best aspects of our past and gloss over unhappier moments. People used to be more friendly, we say. Communities were so safe that you could leave your front door unlocked. There was so much less crime and violence and murder. We don't stop to ask ourselves how accurate those perceptions are. We don't consider the past's less attractive features. And we leave out of our calculations any benefits we now enjoy that weren't around when we were younger.

With that in mind, when we hear the view commonly expressed these days that 'people are much less resilient than they used to be' we need to be on our guard. It is, of course, possible that, as so many politicians, social commentators and journalists assert, there is indeed a 'snowflake generation' around, who lack the grit their parents and grandparents exhibited, are far too easily upset and offended, and less able to bounce back when things get tough. But given our temptation to don rose-tinted spectacles about the past, we should be wary about judging the present too hastily. It is, after all, as common a human fault to decry the 'younger generation' as it is romanticise those who went before. Ancient Egyptians were bemoaning the habits of youth in the third millennium BC. A couple of thousand years later, in the fourth century BC, Aristotle said disapprovingly of young people: 'They think they know everything, and are always quite sure about it ... [they] are high-minded because they have not yet been humbled by life, nor have they experienced the force of circumstances.'¹ 'Youth were never more saucy … the ancient are scorned, the honourable are contemned, the magistrate is not dreaded,' said Thomas Barnes, minister of St Margaret's in the City of London, in 1624.² 'We defy anyone who goes about with his eyes open to deny that there is, as never before, an attitude on the part of young folk which is best described as grossly thought-less, rude, and utterly selfish,' wrote a correspondent for the *Hull Daily Mail* in 1925. People who criticise Simone Biles or Naomi Osaka and regard them as typical products of a problematic genera-tion would do well to bear in mind that such overarching characterisations are nothing new.

In fairness, the assumption that young people aren't what they were is a trap that even the experts fall into. Back in 1972, Walter Mischel, a professor at Stanford, devised the Marshmallow Test to see whether children were able to meet the challenge of delayed gratification by waiting fifteen minutes for two marshmallow treats rather than consuming one marshmallow straight away. More recently – in 2019 – researchers at the University of California asked 260 trained developmental psychologists how they thought young people today would fare if they undertook the challenge; 82 per cent of the trained specialists believed children would either be less able to resist temptation than previous genera-tions or would perform much the same. In fact, independent research shows that results in the Marshmallow Test have been steadily improving for fifty years.³ 'This is a prejudice, this is a bias,' says John Protzko; 'and if people were to make the claims they currently make about young people and children, if instead they make the same claims about ethnic minorities, for example, people would be up in arms, saying "That's ridiculous, you have no objective evidence of this."'⁴ His explanation for this is that the more that adults identify with a particular trait they regard as a strength, the less likely they are to recall how, and over what time period, they acquired it, and the less likely they are to ascribe it to younger people. 'We're likely to assume that our childhood selves had the same abilities that we do today, though in reality we may have spent a lifetime honing those skills … The result is a perceived decline in ability over time, even when none exists.'

That the lives of young people differ from those that their parents and grandparents led is unquestionable. The eminent American social psychologist Jonathan Haidt and the president of the Foundation for Individual Rights in Education (FIRE), Greg Lukianoff, whose 2018 book *The Coddling of the American Mind* was an international bestseller, have identified behavioural shifts in the US that have also been spotted in other countries.[5] They draw attention, for example, to what they believe to be the more interventionist nature of modern parenting. Once children enjoyed long periods of autonomy, they argue. From the age of perhaps seven or eight children were free to go out and play in the street or in the local park. Today's 'helicopter parents' have put paid to that. They endlessly chaperone; they supervise; they seek to eliminate the 'negative experiences, and minor risks' they themselves underwent as children that helped them 'develop into strong, competent, and independent adults'. The authorities have gone along with this new approach to the extent that, in Haidt's words, 'In fact you could be arrested if your nine-year-old is found playing in a park with a friend.'[6]

For both Haidt and Lukianoff, this is a false step. By coddling children, they argue, we remove them from a healthy exposure to the day-to-day challenges and frictions of life. 'We change the way we are with kids, we deprive them of the kinds of experiences of independence of facing risk on their own.' Their view is that such coddling has impaired the development of those born after 1996: 'The normal growth of a human being (or any mammal) is to play constantly and to take risks in play. All of that is to tune up the frontal cortex to develop instincts, to learn how to calibrate, manage and estimate risk,' they suggest. '[I]f you deny them that, if you make them spend their entire childhood preparing for tests and taking violin lessons and doing organised sports where there's a coach watching, you're basically stunting their growth.'

I mentioned earlier the inverted J-curve of lifetime adversity described by Mark Seery. Haidt and Lukianoff are effectively suggesting that the first part of the J has got larger, that more individuals are experiencing too little early adversity in their lives. They should be sitting in the healthy Goldilocks zone between adversity and good fortune. Instead they are lounging in a curated luxury that leaves them unfit to cope with the inevitable setbacks they will experience at some time or other.[7] Rather than suffering Toxic Stress, they are experiencing its opposite: 'Toxic Coddling'.[8]

A further factor in this unhealthy state of affairs, according to Haidt and Lukianoff, is social media. Anyone much over the age of thirty can remember an era when it either didn't exist or you could ignore it. Younger people, though, have grown up in a world of Instagram and text messages, where constant interconnectedness creates anxiety about what other people might be thinking or saying about them. They suggest that this may well be a particular problem for young women, 'because they are more adversely affected by social comparisons (especially based on digitally enhanced beauty), by signals that they are being left out, and by relational aggression'.

For Haidt and Lukianoff, this brave new world of coddling and constant interconnectedness has had unhealthy consequences, manifesting in an unwillingness to accept the pushbacks and challenges that previous generations accepted as an intrinsic part of life. They assert that young people are effectively wrapped in cotton wool from birth and refuse to emerge from it. Add to that a new institutional culture of 'safetyism' ('show students that you care about their [emotional] safety') and the increasing polarisation of society in recent decades – the tendency for people aggressively to adopt absolute stances on political and social issues – and you also have young people who resist intellectual challenge, who adopt hard-and-fast ideological stances that they're not prepared to question, and who refuse to accept that other viewpoints might be worth listening to (it was reports of students demanding that 'offensive' material be removed from college courses that was the trigger point for *The Coddling of the American Mind*). Haidt and Lukianoff talk of instances of the 'ideological vetting' of speakers on college campuses, of people with challenging political or social views being 'disinvited'. And they remind their readers of a principle enunciated by Hanna Holborn Gray, which they think is in danger of being fatally eroded: 'Education should not be intended to make people comfortable; it is meant to make them think.'[9]

The political aspect of the 'coddling' debate is inevitably the one that has most inflamed opinions and received the most media attention. For that very reason it's also the one that has to be approached with the greatest circumspection: inflamed opinions and calm assessment, like nostalgia and objective judgement, don't go hand-in-hand. In reality the level of bans and disinvitations is actually very low: across 4,700 American colleges, in 2020, for example, there were a total of seven 'disinvitations'.[10] It's also worth bearing in mind that whatever individual opinion-formers may say, 'no plat-forming' of people with a different view is not the exclusive preserve of either those on the left or those on the right. It's true that in 2020 the disinvitations to speak on university campuses included protests against Republican vice-president Mike Pence and the president's daughter Ivanka Trump. But it's also true that a quarter of the dis-invitations of 2019 were down to protestors who were to the right of the speakers they sought to ban;[11] and that those targeted in 2021 included Democratic Party president Joe Biden's son Hunter.[12] One shouldn't forget, either, that 'no platforming' and 'cancel culture' are scarcely a new phenomenon. In July 1945, just two months after the Allied victory in Europe, prime minster Winston Churchill was loudly booed by a London crowd who had no desire to hear what he had to say. If you sign up for the cheers, you sign up for the boos, and that was always the case.[13]

And while some worry about the 'snowflake' generation, others very clearly don't. The current president of Columbia University, Lee Bollinger, for example, takes a pretty sanguine view, citing a 2016 survey that reported 78 per cent of college students saying they favoured an open learning environment that includes offensive views (a score twelve points higher than that for the population as a whole). 'It's true,' Bollinger says, 'that, in recent years, there have been more than a few sensational reports ... of misguided demands for censorship on campus, providing a ready, if false, narrative about liberal colleges and universities retreating from the open debate they claim to champion.' But he doesn't accept the overall picture that has been painted. 'First, universities are, today, more hospitable venues for open debate than the nation as a whole. Second, not only have fierce arguments over where to draw the line on acceptable speech been a familiar occurrence in the United States for the past century, but such dialogue has also been indispensable to building a society that embraces the First Amendment.'[14] It's a similar picture in the UK, where a report by the Office for Students found that in 2017 and 2018 only fifty-three out of 62,094 requests for speaker events were rejected by university authorities or student groups: 0.09% of the total.[15]

One needs to be a bit wary, then, before assuming that the no-platforming culture that is supposed to be so emblematic of a snowflake generation is either wholly unique to our times or ubiquitous. It is certainly true that, at a more under-the-radar level, some college lecturers and students have expressed a view that they're constantly 'walking on eggshells' when engaging with others; and a 2017 survey of 1,250 college students by FIRE suggested that a majority of the students who were asked felt they had to self-censor when talking to people who held different ideas from them.[16] These are justifiable matters for concern. The extent to which they are tied up with the existence of a snowflake generation, however, is open to question. After all, not everyone who files spiky Instagram replies is in their teens or twenties, and the polarised nature of debate in many countries today runs through the generations.

To complicate things further, the American psychologist Jean Twenge, who is based at San Diego State University and on whose research Haidt and Lukianoff have drawn heavily, suggests in her book *iGen* that young people might actually be *more* tolerant than their older peers. She found that they were more likely to adopt a laissez-faire attitude to issues such as legalising marijuana, abortion, the death penalty, gun control, national health care and government environmental regulation, even if that involved switching between classically liberal and conservative viewpoints (they're actually less likely to favour gun-control laws than any other demographic).[17]

From the particular perspective of fortitude, it's important to acknowledge something else, too. It's possible to argue that young people who refuse to listen to an alternative point of view do so out of personal weakness. But it's also possible to argue precisely the opposite, and suggest that those who stand in vehement opposition to others are actually asserting their nascent adult voices. Proving a lack of backbone among younger people on the basis of the stances they adopt on issues of the day is, in other words, fraught with problems.

Not all is well with the younger generation, though. Jean Twenge, drawing on a longitudinal study called *Monitoring the Future*, which tracks changing attitudes among American teenagers, has detected a number of worrying trends that seem to be better evidenced. First, young people are feeling less connected to each other than ever before. In 1991, 27 per cent of US school children sampled said they 'often felt lonely'; by 2015 that figure was 32 per cent.[18] In 1990, 83 per cent of sixteen-year-olds said they were actively dating; by 2015 it had fallen to 59 per cent. There are also signs of rising levels of anxiety and a fall in overall levels of contentedness. Between 2012 and 2019, according to a paper that Twenge collaborated on with Jonathan Haidt, rates of depression among American adolescents doubled.[19]

Nor is this a purely US phenomenon. A study undertaken by Haidt and Twenge of data from the Program for International Student Assessment, which had been surveying fifteen-year-olds across thirty-seven countries for more than two decades, showed that in all but one country (South Korea), loneliness has been increasing. Between 2002 and 2012 levels had been 'relatively stable',

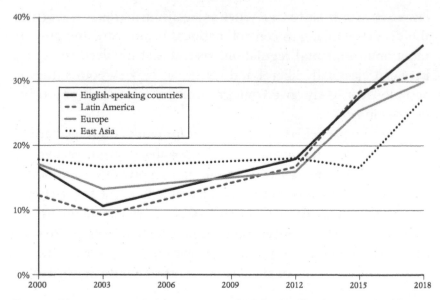

Figure 5: The percentage of students reporting high levels of loneliness at school has increased sharply in recent years.

with 18 per cent of survey participants reporting that they suffered loneliness at school. Post-2012 the numbers skyrocketed. According to Haidt and Twenge, they 'roughly doubled in Europe, Latin America and the English-speaking countries, and rose by about 50 percent in the East Asian countries'. 'Loneliness is certainly not the same as depression, but the two are correlated – lonely teens are often depressed teens, and vice versa,' the pair pointed out.[20]

Why should this be so?

Twenge's view – and, as we've already seen, Haidt's too – is that when it comes to well-being, technology has a lot to answer for. The title of her 2017 *Atlantic* piece is pretty explicit on the subject: 'Have Smartphones Destroyed a Generation?' In the course of the article she pinpoints the advent of the iPhone as an inflection point in the problematic social trends that she has been observing – loneliness, depression, delayed dating (and consequently, on the upside, less teenage pregnancy) and also delayed development in terms of, for example, learning to drive.[21] She also observes that greater electronic stimulation is displacing rest. In 1991 just 26 per cent of those sampled got fewer than seven hours' sleep a night; by 2015 it was 40 per cent (you'll recall from earlier that a lack of personal control in an overly regulated life was credited with the sleep-stealing phenomenon of 'revenge bedtime procrastination', see p.124). 'I had grown accustomed to line graphs of trends that looked like modest hills and valleys,' she wrote in her *Atlantic* article. 'Then I began studying [Gen Z] … the gentle slopes of the line graphs became steep mountains and sheer cliffs.'[22] Declines in family size, changes in GDP, rising income inequality, increases in unemployment – none of these seemed to correlate with those mountains and cliffs. 'Only smartphone access and internet use increased in lock step with teenage loneliness. The other factors were unrelated or inversely correlated.'[23]

Haidt believes that connectivity via electronic devices had displaced face-to-face communication by 2009. '[B]efore that [young people] would often go over each other's houses or they would do something together, after 2011 they're mostly on social media. They might be sitting next to each other but they'll be communicating on their devices. Childhood really changes in those few years.'[24] Twenge reminds us that the Gen Z group that she studies are the first to have grown up with social media accounts and 24/7 messaging apps. The result, she says, has been a decline in hanging out with friends and a concomitant rise in communicating with them online. 'Given that digital media does not produce as much emotional closeness as in-person interaction, the result may be more loneliness in recent years.'[25] In a discussion about their work on an online forum, Haidt and Twenge also point to a problematic group dynamic:[26] *'smartphones and social media don't just affect individuals, they affect groups. The smartphone brought about a planetary rewiring of human interaction. As smartphones became common, they transformed peer relationships, family relationships and the texture of daily life for everyone* – even those who don't own a phone or don't have an Instagram account. It's harder to strike up a casual conversation in the cafeteria or after class when everyone is staring

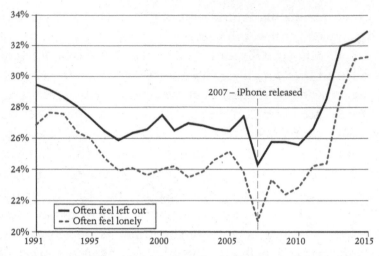

Figure 6: Percentage of 8ᵗʰ-, 10ᵗʰ-, and 12ᵗʰ-graders in the US who agree or mostly agree with the statement 'I often feel left out of things' or 'A lot of times I feel lonely'. This data suggests a link between the advent of the smartphone and a rise in a sense of loneliness.

down at a phone. It's harder to have a deep conversation when each party is interrupted randomly by buzzing, vibrating "notifications" [original emphasis].'[27]

Not all aspects of this new online world are bad. Twenge initially argued that 'All screen activities are linked to less happiness, and all non-screen activities are linked to more happiness.'[28] More recently she has modified her objections, arguing (in collaboration with Haidt) that watching videos – which accounts for a huge amount of screen time – is a relatively benign pursuit, especially if it promotes synchronous activity (one teacher I spoke to told me how a discussion about favourite TikToks offers the children in his class a welcome opportunity to laugh and joke with each other).[29] But Twenge remains adamant that social media is an unalloyed problem. And, so far as she is concerned, the implications are catastrophic: 'It's not an exaggeration to describe [Gen Z] as being on the brink of the worst mental-health crisis in decades.'[30]

★

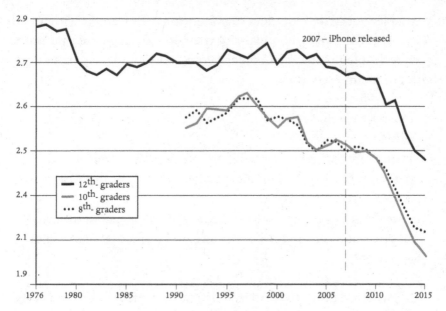

Figure 7: How many times a week school students in the US go out without their parents. The data suggests a sharp decline in sociability after the advent of the smartphone.

Before we're tempted to accept technology as the smoking gun here, some caveats have to be made. In the first place, it's important not to confuse correlation with causation. The fact that teenage loneliness rose at the time smartphones became ubiquitous may mean that the latter caused the former, but it may also be pure coincidence. One could prove things definitively either way only if one could observe the mental health of a control group of non-smartphone-owning teenagers living their lives offline – a control group that these days it would be challenging to find.

Second, it's worth bearing in mind that, to an extent, we've been here before. In the 1970s and 1980s it was often argued that there was a close correlation between a rise in violent crime and the depiction of violence on television and in the cinema. The theory fell apart in the 1990s when the appetite for it, in its fictional form, continued unabated while real-life violence declined. Tying a complex social development to a single cause is fraught with problems. We also need to be wary of the natural suspicion that most new technologies inspire in older people. As Douglas Adams' three rules of technology state:

> 1 Everything that's already in the world when you're born is just normal;
> 2 Anything that gets invented between then and before you turn thirty is incredibly exciting and creative and with any luck you can make a career out of it;
> 3 Anything that gets invented after you're thirty is against the natural order of things and the beginning of the end of civilisation as we know it.[31]

It's worth adding that Adams' third rule included a final sub-clause that speaks to the way in which we can be persuaded about the benefits of new things, even in our dotage, as he added, 'until it's been around for about ten years when it gradually turns out to be alright really'.

Finally, it has to be said that different studies have yielded different results. While some, such as those of Haidt and Twenge, have suggested that smartphones have a socially malign effect, others – such as one conducted among 1,200 teenagers in Holland – have found that teenagers who devote more time to communicating online report stronger friendships than those who spend more time offline. A larger-scale survey in Bermuda yielded similar results.[32] Both surveys concluded that mobile phones played a huge role in shaping young people's developing sense of identity. Another study that looked at 355,358 adolescents concluded that 'The association we find between digital technology use and adolescent well-being is negative but small, explaining at most 0.4% of the variation in well-being.'[33]

That is not to deny that the online world can have a very negative effect on teenagers. Cyber-bullying is a widespread problem. So, too, are issues to do with perceptions of physical appearance. In

2021 the *Wall Street Journal* reported that private data gathered in-house about Instagram by parent-company Facebook suggested that the online service was harmful for young girls: 'when they felt bad about their bodies, Instagram made them feel worse'. It was also recorded that in the UK one in eight girls who felt suicidal attributed their poor mental health to their use of the photo- and video-sharing app.[34] A number of tragic recent high-profile cases bear out this assessment. However, ascribing all the undoubted levels of stress and depression that are apparent among younger people today to this single cause is, problematic. At the very least, it needs to be considered alongside a whole raft of other pressures, from economic (wage stagnation, high cost of living, student debt) to existential worries about the future (60% of young people in a recent worldwide survey, for example, said that they were 'very worried' or 'extremely worried' about climate change: as one 16-year-old put it: 'It's different for young people – for us, the destruction of the planet is personal.')[35]

The recent COVID pandemic has shed some intriguing light, if not on all the reasons for teenage anxiety, at least on some strategies that help to ameliorate them. And – perhaps hardly surprisingly – they are strategies that are hard-baked into the fortitude model.

There's no doubt that the pandemic has proved a time of great suffering and stress for many. Uncertainty, ill health and the economic and social impact of lockdowns have all exacted a toll – for many, a very heavy one indeed. But it's interesting to note that when Twenge and her team surveyed American teenagers in the early months of the crisis in 2020, when 'shelter in place' orders were in force in many US states and home schooling had become the norm for many, the picture that emerged was a surprisingly positive one. 'We had expected mental health to be awful during the pandemic,' Twenge said in an interview, 'but we really didn't find that – we found that teens were relatively okay.'[36] Levels of both teenage loneliness and depression actually declined between 2018 and 2020. And kids got less – not more – lonely in the first months of the pandemic.

Twenge attributed part of the reason for this encouraging picture to the fact that teenagers were sleeping more. Sleep and mental health are, as I have already observed, closely connected. Harvard Medical School director Irving Kirsch has observed that taking medication for depression achieves on average a 1.8-point improvement on the 0–53 scale of the Hamilton Depression Rating Scale (known as HDRS or HAM-D) in comparison to taking a placebo, but that 'a six-point difference can be obtained just by changes in sleep patterns'.[37] Most US schools start before 8.30 a.m. (some as early as 7 a.m.), a time that is out of kilter with the circadian rhythm of children going through puberty (hence perhaps the reason why California enacted a law from 2022 that pushed the school day back to a mandated start time after 8.30 a.m.).[38] So it should come as no surprise that as the pandemic hit and teenagers found they could spend more time in bed, their mental health improved accordingly. 'In 2018, only 55 percent of teens said they usually slept seven or more hours a night,' Twenge recorded. 'During the pandemic, this jumped to 84 percent among those for whom school was still in session.' Her findings were consistent with the paper looking at the impact of smartphones that I cited earlier, which noted that 'simple actions such as getting enough sleep and regularly eating breakfast have much more positive associations with well-being than the average impact of technology use'.[39]

The other key factor was social. Two-thirds of the teenagers Twenge surveyed said they were sad they couldn't see their friends, but the same proportion said they had become closer to their families. They were spending less time on gaming and social media, more time watching TV and video – and more time chatting to their parents and siblings.[40] Fifty-six per cent of teens said they 'were spending more time talking with their parents than they had before the pandemic'; 'Fifty-four percent said their families now ate dinner together more often'; 'Forty-six percent reported spending more time with their siblings'. 'Teens who spent more time with their families during the pandemic and who felt their families had grown closer were less likely to be depressed,' Twenge reported. 'Only 15 percent who said their families had become closer during the pandemic were depressed, compared with 27 percent of those who did not believe their families had become closer ... Thus,' she concluded, 'it appears that one of the primary foundations for teen resilience during the pandemic is family support and connection.'

Twenge is at pains to point out that face-to-face contact is the critical component for well-being: 'For teens it's all about their friends. I think that's really why the smartphone did have such a big impact on their lives. It fundamentally changed how they spent their time outside of school. It shifted hanging out with their friends face-to-face to communicating with friends online.' While the pandemic saw an increase in face-to-face social time, albeit with family, 'pre-pandemic that was not the case. They were replacing face-to-face time with friends with online time and it's a pale substitute.'[41]

Where, if at all, do the other pillars of fortitude that I've talked about – control and identity – fit in? Twenge's analysis of teenagers' sleep patterns suggests an intriguing possibility, at least so far as one of the pillars is concerned. If we accept the notion of 'revenge bedtime procrastination' that I mentioned earlier – the argument that a life excessively curated by others leaves us screaming out for some degree of control at sleep time – then it's possible that during the early months of lockdown, when young people had the windfall of having their daily commuting time returned to them unused, the extra hours gifted some breathing space to their tightly scheduled lives, leaving them feeling unburdened and in greater control as a result. As for identity, it's possible that those early stages of lockdown, when millions of people were at home with their families, removed from school halls the hourly pressure to create a façade of identity on platforms such as Instagram that involved carefully curating how they presented themselves, what they wore and how they compared with others. They could simply be themselves.

Such trends suggest that some of the debate about a 'coddled', internet-reliant generation might be misplaced. We shouldn't be worrying about whether children are being over-protected from adversity or spending too much time on social media per se. Instead we should be considering whether helicopter parenting, self-policing and the constant consumption of friends' idealised online personas are undermining people's feeling of control or the robust feelings of identity that are so crucial to individual well-being. We shouldn't be worrying about existing notions of individual resilience. We should be focusing on social identity. If the accusation is that we have moved from 'Generation We' to 'Generation Me', then we urgently need to find the right ways to restore a sense of 'we'.

Chapter 13

Striding Towards Fortitude
How To Build Collective Strength

Liverpool FC manager Jürgen Klopp is a leader who prides himself on the team spirit he engenders, to the extent that he plays down the importance of leadership in favour of collective identity. In a profession that celebrates and makes icons of those who achieve success – where, for example, José Mourinho once characterised himself as 'the Special One' – the German playfully styled himself 'the Normal One'. So far as he's concerned, it's not about him, it's about the team. 'A coach who doesn't love his players can't be a good coach,' he once told a colleague.[1] According to his biographer Raphael Honigstein, when Klopp was the manager of the German Bundesliga side Borussia Dortmund, he made it clear to everyone in executive roles at the club that they 'had to develop this feeling of "we"'.[2]

He took his obsession with collective identity with him when he joined Liverpool. Keen that the club should embody the together-ness he'd fostered at Borussia Dortmund, Klopp set about learning the names of everyone who worked at the club's training ground, Melwood. Summoning the players to the press conference room, the manager then brought each of the facility's eighty staff to the stage, introducing them – to the players' applause – by name. The club, he made it clear, was, so far as he was concerned, a family. He also told the club's social organisers that they should expect social events to increase in frequency. To the uninitiated, that might seem a distraction from the business of playing and winning matches, but Klopp knew it worked. The legendary long-time coach of the San Antonio Spurs, Gregg Popovich, made a virtue of the dinners

223

he hosted, regarding them as essential to building the team and its collective identity and memory. The record of the Spurs under his leadership speaks for itself: he led them to five NBA championships and has clocked up the most wins of any coach in NBA history.[3]

Klopp's sense of 'us' didn't only mean his players and the support staff. It meant the supporters, too. Each of these three groups was discrete and important in its own way – but they all came together to form a coherent whole. His early decision to get the team to take a bow and to salute the home supporters at a drawn match with a mediocre West Bromwich side may slightly have misfired at the time, but the intention behind it was very much part of his overall vision. 'Very early at his time at the club,' business professor Damian Hughes told me, 'he made criticism of the Liverpool fans, because he felt they'd left early during games when it wasn't going well. He felt that they got on the back of players and if they were getting beaten with ten minutes to go, he noticed that the stadium would empty.' The message that Klopp was seeking to get across with his team gesture to supporters, Hughes said, was: 'I want to create an environment where our fans are supporting the players and even when we're not winning they stay right till the end.'[4]

Klopp's acceptance of the decision to suspend matches during the early days of the COVID-19 pandemic, even though it involved a threat to Liverpool's ascendancy in the Premier League, was of a piece with his worldview and proved that a principle is only a principle we hold when it costs us something. In the statement that he issued to fans on 13 March 2020 he explained his simple reasoning: 'if it's a choice between football and the good of wider society, it's no contest'.[5] It was a far cry from the famous words of a former Liverpool manager, Bill Shankly: 'Some people think football is a matter of life and death. I assure you, it's much more serious than that.' In his 381-word statement Klopp used the words 'we', 'us' and 'our' seventeen times. He was advancing the shared identity of the group even at a time of worry and frustration. 'For leaders this sense of us-ness is the key resource that they need to marshal in order to secure the support and toil of others,' Alex Haslam commented.[6]

There's no doubt that Liverpool has experienced extraordinary success since 2015 under Klopp's guidance: UEFA Champions League finalists in 2018 and winners in 2019; UEFA Super Cup and FIFA Club World Cup winners the following season; and winners, too, of the Premier League, so ending a thirty-year title-drought. Klopp was awarded the FIFA Coach of the Year accolade in both 2019 and 2020. He would doubtless view it as an accolade to be shared.

I started this book with tales of individual resilience and triumph. I'm ending it with the lesson that Jürgen Klopp can teach us about team success. Of course we should all be dazzled by the existence of extraordinary people who overcome all obstacles on their own. And we should all applaud the Simone Bileses, the LeBron Jameses, the Andy Murrays and the Kelly Holmeses of this world. But that applause should not distract us from an awareness of the price these celebrated heroes often have to pay, or from an assumption that what has worked for a handful of individuals will work for all. For most people – and, indeed, for the sporting heroes I've just mentioned – it's not about Grit or mindset; it's about the heady mix of identity, control and the group. Fortitude is the strength that we draw from feeling in close synchrony with those around us, from feeling part of something meaningful that is bigger than us. We lack that strength when life experiences leave us feeling helpless and disconnected from those around us.

So what practical lessons can we learn and apply?

When it comes to reinforcing our sense of identity, it's worth taking a leaf out of the Super Elite athletes' book. We need to develop an understanding of who we are and who we wish to be. For Kelly Holmes, 'sport became my identity'.[7] For Greg LeMond, the victim of childhood sexual abuse who went on to be a three-times winner of the Tour de France, 'Cycling saved my life. I know it did ... It allowed me to reinvent myself.'[8] Models that enable individuals to better understand their experiences – such as the Adverse Childhood Experience framework – can be of immense value here.

As people consider the various categories of trauma, they can seek to reframe their own story in such a way that the trauma no longer defines it. At the same time they may find themselves drawing comfort from the realisation that, as Robert Anda puts it, 'I'm not the only person who experiences these things.'[9] More generally, reframing a narrative is a powerful way to gain a sense of empowerment and direction, as Barack Obama demonstrated in early adulthood.

Dr Nadine Burke Harris has put such theory into practice with the children she treats, and in so doing has demonstrated that even those with very high ACE scores can transform their lives.[10] Her approach involves universal screening for ACE levels as part of a typical doctor's examination, and then a programme for those children identified as being on the upper reaches of the scale that involves encouraging better sleep patterns, involving themselves in mindfulness and meditation, and – crucially – removing themselves from responsibility for whatever caused their trauma, so that they do not identify themselves in terms of what they have experienced. Trauma becomes their experience, not their identity.[11]

Those who have adopted this type of intervention at scale have been impressed by the results. In Washington State's county of Walla Walla, the adoption of an ACE approach to a range of social problems was accompanied by a 33 per cent reduction in domestic violence and a 59 per cent decline in youth suicide attempts. Kitsap County, which applied ACE techniques to the education system, saw a 62 per cent decrease in secondary-school dropouts.[12] Thurston County, which shifted its drugs-policy focus from arrest and imprisonment to counselling, experienced a 39 per cent drop in teenage arrests for drug offences. Okanogan County, which launched an initiative to train all teachers and pupils about the dangers of Toxic Stress and the techniques available to combat it, witnessed a 66 per cent drop in youth arrests for crime. Overall, such programmes were reckoned to have saved $1.4 billion in public expenditure.[13]

Nor is this just a US phenomenon. In Britain a school in the Harpurhey area of Manchester that implemented ACE-based 'trauma training' saw school expulsions fall by 88 per cent. '[I can] honestly say I've never come across a project such as this where I've seen such a positive impact,' local councillor Joanne Green told the *Manchester Evening News*.[14] 'This project has opened our eyes on how agencies should work together with local people,' said her colleague Pat Karney. 'It's had the biggest impact in our area of social intervention for years.'

Jack Shonkoff, the director of Harvard's Center on the Developing Child, who has studied ACEs closely, is clear that interventions that revive individuals' sense of identity can have a transformational effect. People are not destined to live out a bleak life because of adverse formative experiences, he argues. ACE interventions allow people to rewrite their stories in a way that moves them beyond the traumas they experienced.[15] An identity re-owned is an identity renewed.

As we have seen, identity works in tandem with control. The greater certainty we have about our position in the world, the more positive our view of ourselves will be and the greater the leverage we will feel ourselves to possess. Control is not easily won, and for many people it must seem wholly beyond their reach. But there are still techniques that one can learn that will help. As I briefly mentioned in Chapters 6 and 7, and as the experience of many people recovering from illness has shown, self-control strategies such as mindfulness and meditation do genuinely help. Avoiding doomscrolling on our phones, trying not to stay up too late and seeking or granting more autonomy at home and in the workplace are similarly beneficial.

As for the final pillar of fortitude – social identity – perhaps we should take a tip from Jillian Richardson, a 'super-connector' based in Manhattan who used her own experience of loneliness in the city to become a meet-up organiser and ultimately helped thousands of strangers to find moments of community. She's the creator of the Joy List Social, an event designed to bring people together and help them make friends. In Jillian's experience, creating some rules at the outset of the process ends up enabling more meaningful synchrony later on. She explained to me that laying down rules and restrictions might seem to be oppressive, but it can help social connection feel more authentic. At the Joy List Social, for example, 'there's no alcohol in the space, there's no phones in the space'. 'I found,' she told me, 'people are more at ease the more often I repeated "Everyone who is here is here to make a new friend", "Everyone who is here is the sort of person who is willing to go to an event in New York City, be sober and connect".'[16]

In fact Jillian has a set of five rules. 'One is that they happen every week; two – the same people show up consistently; three – there is space for vulnerable conversation; four – there is space for mentorship; five – there is an easily accessible way for people to give back to the community.' One of her approaches is to have a Post-it-covered wall where group members are invited to write their 'asks', or their 'offers' to the group. If any of this seems familiar, it's because Jillian has drawn inspiration from organised religion. She sees her role as taking the best principles of religious congregations and applying them to secular gatherings.

It's worth reiterating here that those twin pillars of identity and control that I have identified as being key to personal fortitude have an inextricable group aspect to them, too. Burke Harris's research on children with high ACE scores shows, for example, that 'in many ways the cure for toxic stress is strong parental buffering' – the more supportive parents are in the moment, the greater the mitigating effect on the trauma.[17] And, as I have already argued, group power can grow from the loosest of initial affiliations and connections. Josh Krichefski, at the time a senior leader at the advertising agency Mediacom, gave me an inspiring example of this from his own workplace, relating how – by getting a number of colleagues to share 'My Mental Health Story' with others during Mental Health Awareness Week – barriers came down and a group identity was forged that served to normalise a topic that is so often regarded as taboo: 'Immediately there was a change in culture, there was a bit of a shift in that we immediately created like an inclusiveness by breaking down barriers.' Josh himself was only too aware of the struggles so many people have to preserve their mental equilibrium. 'It came from a place of understanding myself,' he told me; 'if I don't take time and give myself headspace, looking after myself, I feel it, I struggle.' And he added, 'If I'm particularly stressed or anxious I'll struggle to sleep at night and that's directly connected with work, quite honestly.'[18] The response to 'My Mental Health Story' was overwhelmingly positive: according to Josh, those who wrote the emails got hundreds of emails in return from people relating their own experiences, or thanking them for their honesty. A group had been forged.

The group works everywhere. Organisers of Parkrun, an independent charity that organises free, weekly five-kilometre runs in public parks, commissioned a study that found that those who volunteered as stewards reported improvements in their happiness that were even greater than those who actually did the running.[19] Another study has concluded that those trying to lose weight do so more effectively when they feel a bond with others in the same position.[20] (Incidentally, the study that showed this offers a useful caution to people organising self-help groups: if attendance drops or you sense a degree of disengagement, it's a sign that the stages of identity reflection and identity representation that I mentioned on p.181 haven't been observed and that corrective steps need to be taken.) Those who have high ACE scores benefit from increased community participation. A 2018 report by Public Health Wales found, for example, that among people with an ACE score of four and above who became more involved with the community and with friendship groups, the incidence of mental illness fell from 29 to 14 per cent, and self-harm and suicidal thoughts dropped from 39 to 17 per cent.[21]

Earlier I talked about 'horizontal epidemiology' – a jargon phrase that seeks to capture the notion that many specific disorders have their roots in common social conditions. Those who coined the phrase felt that 'in order to get the data needed to characterise the actual lived experience of people experiencing mental health problems, it makes more sense to go beyond diagnostic differences and collect information "horizontally" across these conditions'.[22] Humans are complex social beings, but in our innate sociability lie many of the remedies for the problems that we experience as individuals. The number and nature make our curious pursuit of resilience understandable. But we shouldn't be distracted from how such riches are achieved – the individual and collective origins of true fortitude. And it's something that we can all help each other to attain.

Notes

Prologue: F**k Resilience! We Just Want to Live!

1 'RAW VIDEO: Beirut blast caught on camera', Sky News on YouTube, 4 August 2020, https://www.youtube.com/watch?v=oKFupx9xo-k&ab&ab_channel=SkyNews

2 'What We Lost That Day', *New York Times*, 1 August 2021, https://www.nytimes.com/interactive/2021/08/01/world/middleeast/beirut-explosion-anniversary.html

3 'Beirut: Anatomy of a lethal explosion', BBC News, 10 August 2020, https://www.bbc.co.uk/news/av/business-53712679

4 '"How much more can we take?" Beirut is in mourning and rejects "resilience"', TRT World, 5 August 2020, https://www.trtworld.com/magazine/how-much-more-can-we-take-beirut-is-in-mourning-and-rejects-resilience-38669

5 'We Lebanese Thought We Could Survive Anything. We Were Wrong', *New York Times*, 3 August 2020, https://www.nytimes.com/2020/08/03/opinion/lebanon-coronavirus-economy.html

6 *Mariella Frostrup show*, Times Radio, 28 September 2020

7 'The Profound Emptiness of "Resilience"', *New York Times* magazine, 1 December 2015, https://www.nytimes.com/2015/12/06/magazine/the-profound-emptiness-of-resilience.html

8 'Is Resilience Overrated?', *New York Times*, 19 August 2020, https://www.nytimes.com/2020/08/19/health/resilience-overrated.html

9 Ibid.

10 Laura Sullivan, 'How Big Oil Misled the Public Into Believing Plastic Would Be Recycled', NPR, 11 September 2020, https://www.npr.org/2020/09/11/897692090/how-big-oil-misled-the-public-into-believing-plastic-would-be-recycled?

11 Ibid.

12 Sian Sutherland, 'A Plastic Planet', Twitter, 1 November 2019, https://www.twitter.com/aplastic_planet/status/1190155273048068097

13 Laura Sullivan, 'How Big Oil Misled the Public Into Believing Plastic Would Be Recycled', NPR, 11 September 2020, https://www.npr.org/2020/09/11/897692090/how-big-oil-misled-the-public-into-believing-plastic-would-be-recycled?

14 Ibid.; and author's interview with Sian Sutherland, 9 March 2020

15 Author's conversation with Professor Alex Haslam, 29 March 2021, edited for clarity

16 John Carvel, 'HSE investigates staff stress at leading hospital', *The Guardian*, 5 August 2003, https://www.theguardian.com/society/2003/aug/05/hospitals.nhsstaff; https://www.hse.gov.uk/foi/releases/westdorsetgen.pdfe

17 Author's conversation with Professor Alex Haslam, 29 March 2021

Chapter 1: I Get Knocked Down But I Get Up Again

1 Linda Stone, 'The Connected Life: From Email Apnea to Conscious Computing', HuffPost, 7 July 2012, https://www.huffpost.com/entry/email-apnea-screen-apnea-_b_1476554

2 Simone Biles, 'The cat got fed instead of us', *The Guardian*, 30 June 2021, https://www.theguardian.com/sport/2021/jun/30/simone-biles-foster-care-adoption-grandparents-gymnastics

3 Simone Biles, *Courage to Soar*, Zondervan, 2016, p.24

4 Ibid.

5 'Training for 2024?', *Daily Mail*, 10 August 2021, https://www.dailymail.co.uk/femail/article-9881303/Simone-Biles-heads-gym-leaving-door-open-Paris-2024.html

6 'Simone Biles says she was molested by gymnastics doctor Larry Nassar', NBC News, 15 January 2018, https://www.nbcnews.com/news/us-news/simone-biles-says-she-was-molested-gymnastics-doctor-larry-nassar-n837806

7   'For Simone Biles "medals are medals" but character transcends gymnastics', *USA Today*, https://eu.usatoday.com/story/sports/columnist/nancy-armour/2021/07/21/simone-biles-more-than-medals-gymnastics-star-olympics/7970885002/

8   'What Simone Biles Understands About Greatness', *The Atlantic*, 28 July 2021, https://www.theatlantic.com/culture/archive/2021/07/simone-biles-olympics-withdrawal-greatness-language/619595/

9   'Childhood scars drove Jonah Lomu to excel on pitch', *Stuff*, 19 November 2015, https://www.stuff.co.nz/sport/rugby/opinion/74223569/brian-moore-childhood-scars-drove-jonah-lomu-to-excel-on-pitch

10 'Why did Andre Agassi hate tennis?', *The Guardian*, 29 October 2009, https://www.theguardian.com/sport/2009/oct/29/andre-agassi-hate-tennis

11 'Siya Kolisi: My sin was exposed – he told me I needed to stop drinking', *The Guardian*, 4 October 2021, https://amp.theguardian.com/sport/2021/oct/04/siya-kolisi-my-sin-was-exposed-he-told-me-i-needed-to-stop-drinking

12 'Marie Curie and the Science of Radioactivity', American Institute of Physics biography of Marie Curie, https://history.aip.org/exhibits/curie/; and Pallab Ghosh, *Great Lives*: 'Marie Curie', BBC Sounds, 24 April 2007, https://www.bbc.co.uk/sounds/play/b0077722

13 Matthew Parris, *Fracture: Stories of How Great Lives Take Root in Trauma*, Profile Books, 2020, p.185

14 Ibid., p.179

15 Mihaly Csikszentmihalyi, 'Family influences on the development of giftedness', in Gregory R. Bock and Kate Ackrill (eds), *The Origins and Development of High Ability*, John Wiley, 1993, p.190

16 'London 2012: Olympic success is key to national pride', BBC News, 1 January 2012, https://www.bbc.co.uk/news/world-16245075

17 Author's interview with Professor Tim Rees, 2 March 2021

18 Owen Slot, *The Talent Lab*, Ebury Press, 2017, p.8

19 Tim Rees, Lew Hardy, Arne Güllich et al., 'The Great British Medalists Project: A Review of Current Knowledge on the

Development of the World's Best Sporting Talent', *Sports Medicine*, vol. 46, 2016, pp.1041–58, https://doi.org/10.1007/s40279-016-0476-2

20 Anders Ericsson, Ralf Krampe and Clemens Tesch-Romer, 'The Role of Deliberate Practice in the Acquisition of Expert Performance', *Psychological Review*, vol. 100, no. 3, 1993, pp.363–406

21 Herbert Simon and William Chase, 'Skill in Chess', *American Scientist*, vol. 61, no. 4, 1973, pp.394–403

22 'Tim Rees explains his research into elite sport performance', YouTube, 29 November 2017, https://www.youtube.com/watch?v= NCAZNiFfL5c&ab_channel=bournemouthuni

23 Slot, *The Talent Lab*, p.71

24 Tim Rees, Lew Hardy et al., 'Great British medalists: Psychosocial biographies of Super-Elite and Elite athletes from Olympic sports', *Progress in Brain Research*, vol. 232, 2017, p.19

25 Nico Van Yperen, 'Why some people make it and others do not: Identifying psychological factors that predict career success in professional adult soccer', *Sports Psychologist*, vol. 23, September 2009, pp.317–29

26 Dave Collins and Áine MacNamara, 'The Rocky Road to the Top', *Sports Medicine*, vol. 42, no. 11, November 2012, pp.907–14

27 Louis de Bernières, 'Readers' boarding school stories', *Sunday Times*, 25 April 2021, https://www.thetimes.co.uk/article/readers-boarding-school-stories-the-cruelty-scarred-me-for-life-at-75-i-am-still-hurting-2jgbw69zx

28 *Andy Murray: Resurfacing* (dir. Olivia Cappuccini, 2019), https://www.imdb.com/title/tt11243364/

29 Ibid.

30 I have used the NBA's Most Valuable Player Award as being the recognised award for 'Player of the Year' here

31 *More Than a Game* (dir. Kristopher Belman, 2008), https://www.imdb.com/title/tt1286821/?ref_=fn_al_tt_1

32 Ibid.

33 Tom Daley, *Desert Island Discs*, BBC Sounds, 30 September 2018, https://www.bbc.co.uk/sounds/play/boblhfpj

34 *World at One*, BBC Radio 4, 27 July 2021, https://www.bbc.co.uk/
    programmes/moooy5f6

35 Owen Slot, *The Talent Lab*, Ebury Press, 2017, p.71

36 Tim Rees inaugural lecture, 29 November 2017, https://www.
    youtube.com/watch?v=eEV50SEWoQI

37 Rees, Hardy, Güllich et al., 'The Great British Medalists
    Project', pp.1041–58, https://doi.org/10.1007/s40279-016-0476-2 (some
    of the notes in square brackets have been edited, for additional
    clarity)

38 Tim Rees, Lew Hardy et al., 'Great British medalists: Psychosocial
    biographies of Super-Elite and Elite athletes from Olympic sports',
    Progress in Brain Research, vol. 232, 2017, p.73

39 Tim Rees, Lew Hardy et al., 'Great British medalists: Psychosocial
    biographies of Super-Elite and Elite athletes from Olympic sports',
    Progress in Brain Research, vol. 232, 2017, p.53

40 Tim Rees, Lew Hardy et al., 'Great British medalists: Psychosocial
    biographies of Super-Elite and Elite athletes from Olympic sports',
    Progress in Brain Research, vol. 232, 2017, p.44

41 'Kurt Vonnegut on the Secret of Happiness', *The Marginalian*,
    16 January 2014, https://www.brainpickings.org/2014/01/16/
    kurt-vonnegut-joe-heller-having-enough/

42 Names and details have been slightly adapted to preserve anonymity.

43 Danny MacKinnon and Kate Driscoll Derickson, 'From resilience to
    resourcefulness: A critique of resilience policy and activism', *Progress
    in Human Geography*, vol. 32, no. 2, 2013

44 Building Your Resilience, American Psychological Association,
    1 February 2020; retrieved from http://www.apa.org/helpcenter/
    road-resilience.aspx

45 Steven Southwick, Preface, in Steven Southwick, Brett Litz,
    Dennis Charney and Matthew Friedman, *Resilience and Mental Health:
    Challenges Across the Lifespan*, Cambridge University Press, 2011

46 Richard D. Kahlenberg, 'Race Based Admissions: The Right Goal, but
    the Wrong Policy', *The Atlantic*, 4 June 2015, https://www.theatlantic.
    com/education/archive/2015/06/race-based-admissions/394784/

47 'EtonX builds resilience in UK teens', Eton School Blog, 13 October 2020, https://www.etoncollege.com/blog/etonx-builds-resilience-in-uk-teens/

48 Angela Duckworth, 'Grit: The power of passion and perseverance', TED Talk, April 2013, https://www.ted.com/talks/angela_lee_duckworth_grit_the_power_of_passion_and_perseverance/transcript?language=en

Chapter 2: *What Doesn't Kill You (Almost Kills You)*

1 Lenore Terr, 'Children of Chowchilla', *The Psychoanalytic Study of the Child*, vol. 34, 1979

2 'Ed Ray, Bus Driver During Kidnapping, Dies at 91', *New York Times*, 18 May 2012, https://www.nytimes.com/2012/05/19/us/ed-ray-bus-driver-who-helped-save-kidnapped-children-dies-at-91.html; further details are drawn from Kaleb Horton, 'The ballad of the Chowchilla bus kidnapping', *Vox*, 23 July 2021, https://www.vox.com/the-highlight/22570738/chowchilla-school-bus-kidnapping

3 CBS News, 'Chowchilla kidnapping: Parole hearing could re-open scars for victims buried alive in 1976', YouTube, 8 October 2019, https://www.youtube.com/watch?v=m6oVcCatlEk&ab_channel=CBSThisMorning; and 'School Bus Driver Who Saved Students "Was a Hero"', NPR News, 22 May 2012, https://www.npr.org/2012/05/22/153308664/school-bus-driver-who-saved-students-was-a-hero

4 Lenore Terr, *Too Scared to Cry*, HarperCollins, 1990, p.182

5 'Conan O'Brien Delivers Dartmouth's Commencement Address', YouTube, 13 June 2011, https://youtu.be/ELC_e2QBQMk?t=1034

6 'Adverse Childhood Experiences (ACE), featuring Dr Robert Anda', YouTube, 6 November 2012, https://www.youtube.com/watch?v=QLfUi4ssHmY&t=3155s&ab_channel=uaajusticecenter

7 Sourced from Nadine Burke Harris, *The Deepest Well*, Bluebird, 2018, p.31; and 'A Tribute to Dr Vincent Felitti', YouTube, 14 June 2016,

https://www.youtube.com/watch?v=q22Zt6aGwsA&ab_channel= HealthHappensHere

8   Dr Vincent Felitti, 'Reflections on the Adverse Childhood Experiences (ACE) Study', YouTube, 23 June 2016, https://www.youtube.com/ watch?v=-ns8k09-ljU&ab_channel=NationalCongressofAmerican Indians

9   Burke Harris, *The Deepest Well*, p.34

10 *Resilience* (dir. James Redford, 2016)

11 'Adverse Childhood Experiences', YouTube, https://www.youtube.com/ watch?v=QLfUi4ssHmY&t=3155s&ab_channel=uaajusticecenter

12 Questions from ACE Resource Network, https://numberstory.org/ explore-your-number/#

13 Burke Harris, *The Deepest Well*, p.38

14 *Resilience* (dir. James Redford, 2016)

15 Linda Hartling, Evelin Lindner, Uli Spalthoff and Michael Britton, 'Humiliation: A nuclear bomb of emotions?', *Psicología Política*, no. 46, 2013, pp.55–76

16 Will Storr, *The Status Game*, William Collins, 2021, p.66

17 Burke Harris, *The Deepest Well*, p.9

18 Alec Roy, Xian-Zhang Hu, Malvin N. Janal and David Goldman, 'Interaction between Childhood Trauma and Serotonin Transporter Gene Variation in Suicide', *Neuropsychopharmacology*, vol. 32, 2007, pp.2046–52, retrieved at https://www.nature.com/articles/1301331; and Alec Roy, 'Relationship of childhood trauma to age of first suicide attempt and number of attempts in substance dependent patients', *Acta Psychiatrica Scandinavica*, vol. 109, no. 2, 2004, pp.121–5

19 'Childhood adversity increases risk for long-term health and behavioral issues', Center for Youth Wellness, https://centerforyouth wellness.org/health-impacts/

20 Rebecca Ruiz, 'How Childhood Trauma Could Be Mistaken for ADHD', *The Atlantic*, 7 July 2014, https://www.theatlantic.com/ health/archive/2014/07/how-childhood-trauma-could-be-mistaken- for-adhd/373328/

21 'Adverse Childhood Experiences', YouTube, https://www.youtube.com/watch?v=QLfUi4ssHmY&t=3155s&ab_channel=uaajusticecenter

22 Gabor Maté, speaking in *The Wisdom of Trauma* (dir. Zaya Benazzo, 2021)

23 Burke Harris, *The Deepest Well*, p.40

24 Ibid., p.40

25 Bessel van der Kolk and R. Fisler, 'Dissociation and the fragmentary nature of traumatic memories: Overview and exploratory study', *Journal of Traumatic Stress*, vol. 8, no. 4, October 1995, pp.505–25

26 Dr Bessel van der Kolk, 'This Conversation Will Change How You Think About Trauma', *New York Times*, 24 August 2021, https://www.nytimes.com/2021/08/24/opinion/ezra-klein-podcast-van-der-kolk.html?showTranscript=1

27 Maria Popova, 'Poet and Philosopher David Whyte on the Deeper Meanings of Friendship, Love and Heartbreak', *The Marginalian*, 29 April 2015, https://www.themarginalian.org/2015/04/29/david-whyte-consolations-words/

28 Tarik Qassem, Paul Bebbington, Nicola Spiers, Sally McManus, Rachel Jenkins and Simon Dein, 'Prevalence of psychosis in black ethnic minorities in Britain: Analysis based on three national surveys', *Social Psychiatry and Psychiatric Epidemiology*, 2015

29 Gabor Maté speaking in the documentary film *The House I Live In* (dir. Eugene Jarecki, 2021)

30 'A Revolutionary Approach to Treating PTSD', *New York Times*, 22 May 2014, https://www.nytimes.com/2014/05/25/magazine/a-revolutionary-approach-to-treating-ptsd.html

31 Sarah M. Marsicek, John M. Morrison, Neha Manikonda, Michael O'Halleran, Zach Spoehr-Labutta and Melissa Brinn, 'Implementing Standardized Screening for Adverse Childhood Experiences in a Pediatric Resident Continuity Clinic', *Paediatric Quality & Safety*, 2019, https://www.ncbi.nlm.nih.gov/pmc/articles/PMC6494230/

32 'Richard Bentall on the causes of mental ill health', *The Life Scientific*, BBC Sounds, 23 February 2021, https://www.bbc.co.uk/sounds/play/m000sj7c

33 Ibid.

34 Richard P. Bentall, Sophie Wickham, Mark Shevlin and Filippo Varese, 'Do Specific Early-Life Adversities Lead to Specific Symptoms of Psychosis? A Study from the 2007 The Adult Psychiatric Morbidity Survey', *Schizophrenia Bulletin*, vol. 38, no. 4, 18 June 2012, https://academic.oup.com/schizophreniabulletin/article/38/4/734/1870335

35 'Adverse Childhood Experiences, featuring Dr Anda', YouTube, 6 November 2012, https://www.youtube.com/watch?v=QLfUi4ssHmY&t=3155s&ab_channel=uaajusticecenter

36 Burke Harris, *The Deepest Well*, p.61

37 Emma Win, Nur Hani Zainal and Michelle G. Newman, 'Trait anger expression mediates childhood trauma predicting for adulthood anxiety, depressive, and alcohol use disorders', *Journal of Affective Disorders*, vol. 228, 1 June 2021

38 C. Rittschof et al., 'Early-life experience affects honey bee aggression and resilience to immune challenge', *Scientific Reports*, vol. 5, 23 October 2015

39 Victor Carrion, Carl Weems, Kit Richert, Bryce Hoffman and Allan Reiss, 'Decreased Prefrontal Cortical Volume Associated with Increased Bedtime Cortisol in Traumatized Youth', *Biological Psychiatry*, vol. 68, no. 5, 1 September 2010

40 Burke Harris, *The Deepest Well*, p.58

41 Gabor Maté speaking in the documentary film *The House I Live In* (dir. Eugene Jarecki, 2021)

42 John Calhoun, 'Philippe Petit: The True Story Behind the Daredevil's World Trade Center Wire Walk', Biography.com, 29 September 2015, https://www.biography.com/news/the-walk-philippe-petit-movie; and Elizabeth Day, Philippe Petit interview: 'There is a child inside me that wants to come out', *The Guardian*, 22 June 2014, https://www.theguardian.com/theobserver/2014/jun/22/philippe-petit-man-on-wire-highwire-creativity-book

43 M. D. Barlow, Tim Woodman, C. Chapman, M. Milton, T. Dodds and B. Allen, 'Who takes risks in high-risk sport? The role of alexithymia', *Journal of Sport and Exercise Psychology*, vol. 37, no. 1, February 2015

44 *Daredevils: The sky walker,* Firecracker films for Channel 4 (dir. M. Soldinger, 2010)

45 Author's conversation with Kyle Ganson, 5 May 2021

46 Catherine Haslam, Jolanda Jetten, Tegan Cruwys, Genevieve Dingle and S. Alexander Haslam, *The New Psychology of Health: Unlocking the Social Cure,* Routledge, 2018, p.115

47 Andrea Danese and Bruce S. McEwen, 'Adverse childhood experiences, allostasis, allostatic load, and age-related disease', *Physiology & Behavior,* vol. 106, no. 1, 12 April 2012

48 Kathryn Ridout, Samuel Ridout, Constance Guille, Douglas Mata, Huda Akil and Srijan Sen, 'Physician-Training Stress and Accelerated Cellular Aging', *Biological Psychiatry,* vol. 86, no. 9, 1 November 2019

49 Gabor Maté, *When the Body Says No – The Cost of Hidden Stress,* Vermilion, 2019, p.37

50 Hans Selye, *The Stress of Life,* McGraw-Hill, 1978, p.45

51 Burke Harris, *The Deepest Well,* p.19

52 Ibid., p.12

53 Maté, *When the Body Says No,* p.43

54 Gabor Maté speaking in the documentary film *The House I Live In*

55 Dr Gabor Maté, 'When the Body Says No: Understanding the Stress-Disease Connection', *Democracy Now!,* 15 February 2010, https://www.democracynow.org/2010/2/15/dr_gabor_mat_when_the_body

56 Marco Balenci, 'Historical-Clinical Pathways to a Cancer Holistic Perspective', *Madridge Journal of Cancer Study & Research,* vol. 3, no. 1, 14 February 2019

57 Ibid.

58 Michael Wirsching, Helm Stierlin, Florian Hoffmann, Gunthard Weber and Barbara Wirsching, 'Psychological identification of breast cancer patients before biopsy', *Journal of Psychosomatic Research,* vol. 26, no. 1, 1982, pp.1–10

59 S. P. Thomas, M. Groer, M. Davis, P. Droppleman, J. Mozingo and M. Pierce, 'Anger and Cancer', *Cancer Nursing,* vol. 23, no. 5, 2000, pp.344–9; and Molly C. McKenna, Michael A. Zevon, Barbara Corn and James Rounds, 'Psychosocial factors and the development of breast cancer: A meta-analysis', *Health Psychology,* vol. 18, no. 5, 1999, pp.520–31

60 Mark Seery, Alison Holman and Roxane Cohen Silver, 'Whatever does not kill us: Cumulative lifetime adversity, vulnerability, and resilience', *Journal of Personality & Social Psychology*, vol. 99, no. 6, December 2010

61 The chart represents the illustrative shape shown in Seery, Holman and Cohen Silver, 'Whatever does not kill us'

Chapter 3: Her 'only competition is herself'

1 Gold Over America tour, https://www.goldoveramericatour.com/goat/tickets.html

2 Simone Biles, 'The cat got fed instead of us', *The Guardian*, 30 June 2021, https://www.theguardian.com/sport/2021/jun/30/simone-biles-foster-care-adoption-grandparents-gymnastics

3 Eren Orbey, 'The radical courage of Simone Biles's exit from the Team USA Olympic finals', *The New Yorker*, 27 July 2021, https://www.newyorker.com/sports/replay/the-radical-courage-of-simone-biless-exit-from-the-team-usa-olympic-finals

4 'Simone Biles Dials Up the Difficulty "Because I Can"', *New York Times*, 24 May 2021, https://www.nytimes.com/2021/05/24/sports/olympics/simone-biles-yurchenko-double-pike.html; and 'Simone Biles Takes Gymnastics to a New Level. Again', *New York Times*, 9 August 2019, https://www.nytimes.com/2019/08/09/sports/olympics/simone-biles-takes-gymnastics-to-a-new-level-again.html

5 Simone Biles, 'Now to prepare for finals', Instagram, https://www.instagram.com/p/CRxsq_kBZrP/

6 'Gymnastics – Women's Team Final', BBC Sport, 27 July 2021, https://www.bbc.co.uk/iplayer/episode/po9pjrs7/olympics-gymnastics-womens-team-final

7 Orbey, 'The radical courage of Simone Biles's exit from the Team USA Olympic finals', https://www.newyorker.com/sports/replay/the-radical-courage-of-simone-biless-exit-from-the-team-usa-olympic-finals

8   'Simone Biles withdraws from Olympics team final after vault miss, proving she's the GOAT', NBC News, 27 July 2021, https://www.nbcnews.com/think/opinion/simone-biles-withdraws-olympics-team-final-after-vault-miss-proving-ncna1275205

9   'Piers Morgan criticized for "nasty" comments about Simone Biles' Olympics withdrawal', *The Independent*, 29 July 2021, https://www.independent.co.uk/sport/olympics/piers-morgan-simone-biles-twitter-b1891787.html; and Orbey, 'The radical courage of Simone Biles's exit from the Team USA Olympic finals', https://www.newyorker.com/sports/replay/the-radical-courage-of-simone-biless-exit-from-the-team-usa-olympic-finals

10 'Simone Biles explains just how bad her twisties got at the Tokyo Olympics', *Huffington Post*, 13 August 2021, https://www.huffingtonpost.co.uk/entry/simone-biles-tokyo-twisties-video_n_61161e06e4b01da700f44770

11 Lauren Starke, 'On the Cover of *New York* Magazine: Simone Biles', *New York* magazine, 27 September 2021, https://nymag.com/press/2021/09/on-the-cover-of-new-york-magazine-simone-biles.html

12 'In a divided US, it's no surprise some see Simone Biles as a villain', *The Guardian*, 28 July 2021, https://www.theguardian.com/sport/2021/jul/28/simone-biles-withdrawal-olympics-gymnastics-tokyo-media-reaction

13 'What Simone Biles Understands About Greatness', *The Atlantic*, 28 July 2021, https://www.theatlantic.com/culture/archive/2021/07/simone-biles-olympics-withdrawal-greatness-language/619595/

14 Piers Morgan, Twitter, 27 July 2021, https://twitter.com/piersmorgan/status/1420027274565390355

15 Ibid., 28 July 2021, https://twitter.com/piersmorgan/status/1420391707330416642?lang=en

16 Matt Walsh, Facebook, 27 July 2021, https://www.facebook.com/MattWalshBlog/posts/simone-biles-quit-on-her-team-because-she-wasnt-having-fun-this-is-called-being-/393112558837798/

17 'In a divided US, it's no surprise some see Simone Biles as a villain', https://www.theguardian.com/sport/2021/jul/28/simone-biles-withdrawal-olympics-gymnastics-tokyo-media-reaction

18 'Charlie Kirk brands Simone Biles "Shame to the country" after Olympics exit', *Newsweek*, 28 July 2021, https://www.newsweek.com/charlie-kirk-brands-simone-biles-shame-country-after-olympics-exit-1613809

19 'Athlete of the Year', *Time* magazine, 9 December 2021, https://time.com/athlete-of-the-year-2021-simone-biles/

20 'Cricketer Ben Stokes becomes the latest high-profile star to take time out from sport', Mail Online, 31 July 2021, https://www.dailymail.co.uk/news/article-9845127/amp/Ben-Stokes-latest-athlete-step-sport-focus-mental-wellbeing.html

21 Andrea Danesea and Bruce McEwen, 'Adverse childhood experiences, allostasis, allostatic load, and age-related disease', *Physiology & Behavior*, vol. 106, no. 1, 12 April 2012

22 Emily Kaier, Lisa DeMarni Cromer, Joanne L. Davis and Kathleen Strunk, 'The Relationship Between Adverse Childhood Experiences and Subsequent Health Complaints in Elite Athletes', *Journal of Child & Adolescent Trauma*, 2015

23 Author's interview with Professor Tim Rees, 2 March 2021

24 Robert Anda, David Brown, Vincent Felitti, Shanta Dube and Wayne Giles, 'Adverse childhood experiences and prescription drug use in a cohort study of adult HMO patients', *BMC Public Health*, vol. 8, 4 June 2008, https://bmcpublichealth.biomedcentral.com/articles/10.1186/1471-2458-8-198

25 Kyle Ganson, Stuart Murray, Deborah Mitchison, Jason Nagata et al., 'Associations between Adverse Childhood Experiences and Performance-Enhancing Substance Use among Young Adults', *Substance Use & Misuse*, vol. 56, no. 6, 16 March 2021

26 Author's conversation with Kyle Ganson, 5 May 2021, edited slightly for clarity

27 'Marion Jones shocked track and field fans two years ago when she said she would try for 5 gold medals in Sydney', *Chicago Tribune*, 10 September 2000, https://www.chicagotribune.com/news/ct-xpm-2000-09-10-0009100445-story.html

28 Paul Gogarty and Ian Williamson, *Winning at All Costs*, JR Books, 2009, p.78

29 'IOC chief says Hunter failed four drug tests', ESPN, 25 September 2000, http://www.espn.com/oly/summer00/news/2000/0925/777764.html

30 'Ex-husband turns on Jones', Associated Press, 24 July 2004, https://products.kitsapsun.com/archive/2004/07-24/4591_ex-husband_turns_on_jones.html

31 Gogarty and Williamson, *Winning at All Costs*, p.81

32 'What am I, if I'm not a good tennis player', She the People, 7 July 2021, https://www.shethepeople.tv/news/naomi-osaka-netflix-documentary-trailer/

33 Simone Biles, Twitter, 29 July 2021, https://twitter.com/simone_biles/status/1420561448883802118

Chapter 4: Crafting Stories of Self

1 Dan P. McAdams and Bradley D. Olson, 'Personality Development: Continuity and Change Over the Life Course', *Annual Review of Psychology*, vol. 16, 10 January 2010

2 Ibid.

3 B. Roberts, N. Kuncel, R. Shiner, A. Caspi and L. Goldberg, 'The power of personality: The comparative validity of personality traits', *Perspectives of Psychological Science*, vol. 2, no. 4, 1 December 2007

4 McAdams and Olson, 'Personality Development: Continuity and Change Over the Life Course'

5 Jia Tolentino, *Trick Mirror*, Random House, 2019, p.174

6 George Herbert Mead, *Mind, Self, and Society*, 1934, p.223

7 Rodica Ioana Damian and Dean Keith Simonton, 'Diversifying Experiences in the Development of Genius and their Impact on Creative Cognition', in *The Wiley Handbook of Genius*, ed. Dean Keith Simonton, Wiley-Blackwell, 2014, p.376

8 Ann Roe, *The Making of a Scientist*, Dodd, Mead, 1953

9 Mihaly Csikszentmihalyi, 'Family influences on the development of giftedness', in Gregory R. Bock and Kate Ackrill (eds), *The Origins and Development of High Ability*, John Wiley, 1993, p.190

10 Matthew Parris, *Fracture: Stories of How Great Lives Take Root in Trauma*, Profile Books, 2020, p.261

11 Dave Collins, Áine MacNamara and Neil McCarthy, 'Super Champions, Champions, and Almosts: Important Differences and Commonalities on the Rocky Road', *Frontiers in Psychology*, 11 January 2016

12 Dave Collins and Áine MacNamara, 'Much Ado about … ? A response to Hardy et al.', *Progress in Brain Research*, vol. 232, 2017

13 'The Novel That Asks, "What Went Wrong With Mankind?"', *The Atlantic*, 15 June 2018, https://www.theatlantic.com/magazine/archive/2018/06/richard-powers-the-overstory/559106/

14 Cited in Tilmann Habermas and Susan Bluck, 'Getting a life: The emergence of the life story in adolescence', *Psychological Bulletin*, vol. 126, no. 5, September 2000, pp.748–69

15 Ibid.

16 Dave Collins and Áine MacNamara, 'The Rocky Road to the Top', *Sports Medicine*, vol. 42, no. 11, November 2012

17 'The tales athletes tell: Narrative structure and identity in Great British medalists', *Progress in Brain Research*, vol. 232, January 2017, https://www.researchgate.net/publication/313031531_The_tales_athletes_tell_Narrative_structure_and_identity_in_Great_British_medalists

18 J. L. Pals, 'Constructing the "Springboard Effect": Causal Connections, Self-Making, and Growth Within the Life Story', in D. P. McAdams, R. Josselson and A. Lieblich (eds), *Identity and story: Creating self in narrative*, American Psychological Association, 2006, p.177

19 Bessel van der Kolk, *The Body Keeps the Score*, Viking, 2014, p.80

20 Collins, MacNamara and McCarthy, 'Super Champions, Champions, and Almosts', https://www.frontiersin.org/articles/10.3389/fpsyg.2015.02009/

21 C. Stewart, B. Smith and A. C. Sparkes, 'Sporting autobiographies of illness and the role of metaphor', *Sport in Society*, vol. 14, 15 July 2011, pp.581–97, doi.org/10.1080/17430437.2011.574358

22 Christopher Peterson, Martin E. P. Seligman and George E. Vaillant, 'Pessimistic Explanatory Style Is a Risk Factor for Physical Illness: A

Thirty-Five-Year Longitudinal Study', *Journal of Personality and Social Psychology*, vol. 55, no. 1, July 1988

23 Leslie P. Kamen and Martin E. P. Seligman, 'Explanatory style and health', *Current Psychological Research & Reviews*, vol. 6, 1987

24 Martin Seligman, *Flourish*, Free Press, 2011, p.185

25 Dan P. McAdams, Ann Diamond, Ed de St Aubin and Elizabeth Mansfield, 'Stories of commitment: The psychosocial construction of generative lives', *Journal of Personality and Social Psychology*, vol. 72, no. 3, 1997

26 Pals, 'Constructing the "Springboard Effect"', in McAdams, Josselson and Lieblich (eds), *Identity and story: Creating self in narrative*

27 Dr Bessel van der Kolk, 'This Conversation Will Change How You Think About Trauma', *New York Times*, 24 August 2021, https://www. nytimes.com/2021/08/24/opinion/ezra-klein-podcast-van-der-kolk. html?showTranscript=1 [SUBSCRIBERS ONLY]; and Pals, 'Constructing the "Springboard Effect"', in McAdams, Josselson and Lieblich (eds), *Identity and story: Creating self in narrative*, p.192

Chapter 5: The Billion-Dollar Resilience Industry

1 'Rutger Bregman Is Hopeful For Humankind', *Eat Sleep Work Repeat* podcast, 20 April 2021, https://eatsleepworkrepeat.com/rutger

2 Natalie Purcell, Christopher J. Koenig, Jeane Bosch and Shira Maguen, 'Veterans' Perspectives on the Psychosocial Impact of Killing in War', *The Counseling Psychologist*, vol. 44, no. 7, 15 November 2016, pp.1062–99, doi.org/10.1177/0011000016666156

3 I. Pivar and N. Field, 'Unresolved grief in combat veterans with PTSD', *Journal of Anxiety Disorders*, 2004

4 Purcell, Koenig, Bosch and Maguen, 'Veterans' Perspectives on the Psychosocial Impact of Killing in War'

5 Stephen Evans, 'How soldiers deal with the job of killing', BBC News, 11 June 2011, https://www.bbc.com/news/world-13687796

6 Martin Seligman, *Flourish*, Free Press, 2011, p.166

7 Jesse Singal, *The Quick Fix*, Farrar, Straus and Giroux, 2021, p.117

8 'One in eight soldiers commits violence on return', BBC News, 24 July 2012, https://www.bbc.com/news/uk-18902195

9 'Why the link between veterans and mass shootings is more complicated than you think', ABC News, 16 November 2018, https://abcnews.go.com/US/link-veterans-mass-shootings-complicated/story?id=59057321

10 Seligman, *Flourish*, p.126

11 'Perma Theory of Wellbeing and Perma Workshops', Penn Arts and Sciences, https://ppc.sas.upenn.edu/learn-more/perma-theory-well-being-and-perma-workshops

12 'Best Advice Ever' by Martin Seligman, Bridge Winners, 11 June 2017, https://bridgewinners.com/article/view/best-advice-ever/

13 Singal, *The Quick Fix*, p.102

14 'The Leadership Lectures: Martin E. P. Seligman', Florida International University, YouTube, 4 December 2017, https://www.youtube.com/watch?v=CzCjsHoIvnI

15 'Penn Resilience Program and Perma Workshops', Penn Arts and Sciences, https://ppc.sas.upenn.edu/services/penn-resilience-training

16 Seligman, *Flourish*, p.127

17 'Martin Seligman: Increasing Well-being in the US Army', addresses WOBI conference, April 2014, YouTube, 23 May 2017, https://www.youtube.com/watch?v=rGSpFFr5oSk

18 Jesse Singal, Twitter, 9 May 2021, https://twitter.com/jessesingal/status/1369299675178762242

19 Singal, *The Quick Fix*, p.124

20 Original page (U.S. Army, 'Justification review document for other than full and open competition: U.S. Army Master Resiliency Trainer program', 2009) now removed. Cited at thewinnower.com/papers/49-a-critical-examination-of-the-u-s-army-s-comprehensive-soldier-fitness-program

21 Angela Duckworth and Martin Seligman, 'Self-Discipline Outdoes IQ in Predicting Academic Performance of Adolescents', *Psychological Science*, vol. 16, no. 12, 1 December 2005

22 'Angela Duckworth on Passion, Grit and Success', *New York Times*, 10 April 2016, https://www.nytimes.com/2016/04/10/education/edlife/passion-grit-success.html

23 Angela Duckworth, Christopher Peterson, Michael Matthews and Dennis Kelly, 'Grit: Perseverance and Passion for Long-Term Goals', *Journal of Personality and Social Psychology*, vol. 92, no. 6, July 2007

24 'How Praise Became a Consolation Prize', *The Atlantic*, 16 December 2016, https://www.theatlantic.com/education/archive/2016/12/how-praise-became-a-consolation-prize/510845/

25 Claudia Mueller and Carol Dweck, 'Praise for intelligence can undermine children's motivation and performance', *Journal of Personality & Social Psychology*, vol. 75, no. 1, July 1998

26 'No clarity around growth mindset', Slate Star Codex, 8 April 2015, https://slatestarcodex.com/2015/04/08/no-clarity-around-growth-mindset-yet/

27 'Stanford University's Carol Dweck on the Growth Mindset and Education', One Dublin.org, 19 June 2012, https://onedublin.org/2012/06/19/stanford-universitys-carol-dweck-on-the-growth-mindset-and-education/

28 'Forget Grit. Focus on Inequality', *Education Week*, 14 April 2017, https://www.edweek.org/leadership/opinion-forget-grit-focus-on-inequality/2017/04

29 It's worth saying that while the draft report was released as an explicit endorsement, subsequent to publication it was chosen to brand the report, as produced, with the support of the Dept of Education rather than published by them; https://studentsatthecenterhub.org/resource/promoting-grit-tenacity-and-perseverance-critical-factors-for-success-in-the-21st-century/

30 Victoria F. Sisk, Alexander P. Burgoyne, Jingze Sun, Jennifer L. Butler and Brooke N. MacNamara, 'To What Extent and Under Which Circumstances Are Growth Mind-Sets Important to Academic Achievement? Two Meta-Analyses', *Psychological Science*, vol. 29, no. 4, 5 March 2018

31 Eleanor Palmer Primary School, 'Growth Mindsets', https://www.eleanorpalmer.camden.sch.uk/curriculum-and-ethos/growth-mindsets/

32 Eton X, 'How students can learn to build resilience', 4 February 2020, https://etonx.com/how-students-can-learn-to-build-resilience/

33 Inverness High School handbook, https://invernesshs.files.wordpress.com/2017/11/inverness-high-school-handbook-2018.pdf, p.26

34 St Joseph's Catholic Primary School, 'Behaviour for Learning', https://www.st-josephs-pri.oxon.sch.uk/pupils/behaviour

35 Northern Ireland Curriculum, 'Assessment for Learning – A Practical Guide', https://ccea.org.uk/downloads/docs/ccea-asset/Curriculum/Assessment%20for%20Learning%20-%20A%20Practical%20Guide.pdf

36 Eric Schmidt and Jonathan Rosenberg, *How Google Works*, John Murray, 2014; Textio, 'How to write a job description in 2020: Best practices from half a billion job postings', https://textio.com/blog/how-to-write-a-job-description-in-2020-best-practices-from-half-a-billion-job-postings/28706464272; and https://webarchive.nationalarchives.gov.uk/https://innovateuk.blog.gov.uk/2016/05/04/why-you-are-probably-hiring-the-wrong-people/

37 Original page (U.S. Army, 'Justification review document for other than full and open competition: U.S. Army Master Resiliency Trainer program', 2009) now removed. Cited at thewinnower.com/papers/49-a-critical-examination-of-the-u-s-army-s-comprehensive-soldierfitness-program

38 R. G. Tedeschi and R. J. McNally, 'Can we facilitate posttraumatic growth in combat veterans?', *American Psychologist*, vol. 66, no. 1, 2011

39 Martin Seligman, 'Effectiveness of Positive Psychology – Setting the record straight', *Chronicle of Higher Education*, 14 June 2021, https://www.chronicle.com/article/effectiveness-of-positive-psychology

40 P. B. Lester, P. D. Harms, M. N. Herian and D. V. Krasikova, 'The Comprehensive Soldier Fitness Program Evaluation Report #3: Longitudinal Analysis of the Impact of Master Resilience Training on Self-Reported Resilience and Psychological Health Data', *Publications of Affiliated Faculty: Nebraska Public Policy Center*, vol. 32, 2011

41 Seligman, 'Effectiveness of Positive Psychology', https://www. chronicle.com/article/effectiveness-of-positive-psychology

42 Rhonda Cornum, Michael Matthews and Martin Seligman, 'Comprehensive Soldier Fitness – Building Resilience in a Challenging Institutional Context', *American Psychologist*, vol. 66, no. 1, January 2011

43 Donald Meichenbaum, 'We Are the Stories We Tell – A Constructive Narrative Perspective of PTSD', 5 May 2017

44 Seligman, 'Effectiveness of Positive Psychology', https://www. chronicle.com/article/effectiveness-of-positive-psychology

45 Tedeschi and McNally, 'Can we facilitate posttraumatic growth in combat veterans?'

46 P. B. Lester, S. McBride and R. L. Cornum, 'Comprehensive soldier fitness: Underscoring the facts, dismantling the fiction', in R. R. Sinclair and T. W. Britt (eds), *Building Psychological Resilience in Military Personnel: Theory and Practice*, American Psychological Association, 2013, pp.193–220

47 Walter Carr, Devvon Bradley, Alan D. Ogle, Stephanie E. Eonta, Bryan L. Pyle and Patcho Santiago, 'Resilience training in a population of deployed personnel', *Military Psychology*, 1 March 2013

48 Ibid.

49 'Suicide Has Been Deadlier Than Combat for the Military', *New York Times*, 1 November 2019, https://www.nytimes.com/2019/11/01/opinion/military-suicides.html

50 Original page (U.S. Army, 'Justification review document for other than full and open competition: U.S. Army Master Resiliency Trainer program', 2009) now removed. Cited at thewinnower.com/papers/49-a-critical-examination-of-the-u-s-army-s-comprehensive-soldierfitness-program

51 Jesse Singal, Twitter, 9 March 2021, https://twitter.com/jessesingal/status/1369299687975575560

52 Steven M. Brunwasser, Jane E. Gillham and Eric S. Kim, 'A Meta-Analytic Review of the Penn Resiliency Program's Effect on Depressive Symptoms', *Journal of Consulting and Clinical Psychology*, vol. 77, no. 6, December 2009

53 Clare Pattison and Robert Lynd-Stevenson, 'The Prevention of Depressive Symptoms in Children: The Immediate and Long-term Outcomes of a School-based Program', *Behaviour Change*, 1 June 2001

54 Anastasios Bastounis, Patrick Callaghan, Anirban Banerjee and Maria Michail, 'The effectiveness of the Penn Resiliency Programme (PRP) and its adapted versions in reducing depression and anxiety and improving explanatory style: A systematic review and meta-analysis', *Journal of Adolescence*, vol. 52, October 2016

55 Singal, *The Quick Fix*, p.109

56 Martin Seligman, Randal Ernst, Jane Gillham, Karen Reivich and Mark Linkins, 'Positive education: positive psychology and classroom interventions', *Oxford Review of Education*, vol. 35, no. 3, June 2009, p.302

57 Seligman, 'Effectiveness of Positive Psychology', https://www.chronicle.com/article/effectiveness-of-positive-psychology

58 Marcus Credé, 'Much Ado about Grit: A Meta-Analytic Synthesis of the Grit Literature', Department of Psychology, Iowa State University, 2014

59 Singal, *The Quick Fix*, p.146

60 'Ying Kao Lee, DuPont inventor of lacquer that kept cars shiny, dies at 87', *The Philadelphia Inquirer*, 15 April 2020, https://www.inquirer.com/obituaries/dr-ying-kao-lee-dupont-chemist-scientist-immigrated-invented-car-lacquer-died-20200415.html

61 'You're no genius', *Quartz at Work*, 26 March 2018, https://qz.com/work/1233940/angela-duckworth-explains-grit-is-the-key-to-success-and-self-confidence/

62 Alfie Kohn, 'Sometimes it's better to quit than to prove your grit', *Washington Post*, 4 April 2014, https://www.washingtonpost.com/opinions/sometimes-its-better-to-quit-than-to-prove-your-grit/2014/04/04/24075a84-b8f8-11e3-96ae-f2c36d2b1245_story.html

63 Alfie Kohn, 'Grit: A Skeptical Look at the Latest Educational Fad', Fall 2014, https://www.alfiekohn.org/article/grit/

64 Jal Mehta, 'The Problem with Grit', *Education Week*, 27 April 2015, https://www.edweek.org/education/opinion-the-problem-with-grit/2015/04

65 Sir Ken Robinson, 'Do Schools Kill Creativity?', TED Talk, February 2006, https://www.ted.com/talks/sir_ken_robinson_do_schools_ kill_creativity

66 For this analysis I am indebted to the study of Duckworth's work undertaken by Alfie Kohn in *The Myth of the Spoiled Child – Challenging the Conventional Wisdom about Children & Parenting*, Da Capo Lifelong Books, 2014

67 Gregory E. Miller and Carsten Wrosch, 'You've Gotta Know When to Fold 'Em: Goal Disengagement and Systemic Inflammation in Adolescence', *Psychological Science*, 1 September 2007, https://journals. sagepub.com/doi/abs/10.1111/j.1467-9280.2007.01977.x

68 '"Inflammation clock" can reveal body's biological age', *Nature*, 13 July 2021, https://www.nature.com/articles/d41586-021-01915-x

69 Wei Chen, Sathanur R. Srinivasan, Shengxu Li, Jihua Xu and Gerald S. Berenson, 'Metabolic syndrome variables at low levels in childhood are beneficially associated with adulthood cardiovascular risk: The Bogalusa Heart Study', *Diabetes Care*, vol. 28, no. 1, January 2005, https://pubmed.ncbi.nlm.nih.gov/15616245/

70 Kenny Rogers, 'The Gambler', written by Don Schlitz, 1976

71 Kaili Rimfeld et al., 'True Grit and Genetics: Predicting Academic Achievement From Personality', *Journal of Personality and Social Psychology*, vol. 111, no. 5, 2016, https://psycnet.apa.org/fulltext/ 2016-06824-001.pdf

72 'MacArthur "Genius" Angela Duckworth Responds to a New Critique of Grit', nprEd, 25 May 2016, https://www.npr.org/sections/ ed/2016/05/25/479172868/angela-duckworth-responds-to-a-new- critique-of-grit?t=1610962876467

73 Chen Zisman and Yoav Ganzach, 'In a Representative Sample Grit Has a Negligible Effect on Educational and Economic Success Compared to Intelligence', *Social Psychological and Personality Science*, 14 July 2020

74 Alfie Kohn, 'The perils of "Growth Mindset" education: Why we're trying to fix our kids when we should be fixing the system', *Salon*, 16 August 2015, https://www.salon.com/2015/08/16/the_ education_fad_thats_hurting_our_kids_what_you_need_to_know_

about_growth_mindset_theory_and_the_harmful_lessons_it_imparts/

75 Yue Li and Timothy Bates, 'Does growth mindset improve children's IQ, educational attainment or response to setbacks? Active-control interventions and data on children's own mindsets', SocArXiv Papers, 23 January, 2017, https://osf.io/preprints/socarxiv/tsdwy

76 'A Mindset "Revolution" Sweeping Britain's Classrooms May Be Based on Shaky Science', BuzzFeed, 14 January 2017, https://www.buzzfeed.com/tomchivers/what-is-your-mindset

77 Victoria Sisk et al., 'To What Extent and Under Which Circumstances Are Growth Mind-Sets Important to Academic Achievement? Two Meta-Analyses', *Psychological* Science, 5 March 2018, https://journals.sagepub.com/doi/10.1177/0956797617739704

78 'Study finds popular "growth mindset" educational interventions aren't very effective', *Science Daily*, 22 May 2018, https://www.sciencedaily.com/releases/2018/05/180522114523.htm

79 'No Clarity Around Growth Mindset', Slate Star Codex, 8 April 2015, https://slatestarcodex.com/2015/04/08/no-clarity-around-growth-mindset-yet/

80 Russell T. Warne, 'The one variable that makes growth mindset interventions work', 3 January 2020, https://russellwarne.com/2020/01/03/the-one-variable-that-makes-growth-mindset-interventions-work/

81 Jaap Glerum et al., 'The effects of praise for effort versus praise for intelligence on vocational education students', *Educational Psychology*, 8 June 2019, https://www.tandfonline.com/doi/full/10.1080/01443410.2019.1625306

82 Seligman, *Flourish*, p.104

83 Interview by Joshua Freedman, 'Six Seconds', *EQ Life*, 2019, cited by Singal, *The Quick Fix*, p.102

84 Seligman, *Flourish*, p.106

85 Inga Saffron, 'Philly didn't become America's poorest big city by chance. Here's how we fix it', *Philadelphia Inquirer*, 12 October 2020, https://www.inquirer.com/business/philadelphia-poverty-unemployment-racism-education-upskilling-20201013.html

86 Duckworth and Seligman, 'Self-discipline outdoes IQ in predicting academic performance of adolescents', https://pubmed.ncbi.nlm.nih.gov/16313657/

87 Chris Cook, 'The social mobility challenge for school reformers', *Financial Times*, 22 February 2012, https://www.ft.com/content/379774ba-f044-3832-aec9-0a4a130a6426

88 Roger Slee cited in M. Maguire et al., 'Behaviour, classroom management and student "control": Enacting policy in the English secondary school', *International Studies in Sociology of Education*, vol. 20, no. 2, June 2010

89 Gene H. Brody et al., 'Is Resilience Only Skin Deep? Rural African Americans' Preadolescent Socioeconomic Status-Related Risk and Competence and Age 19 Psychological Adjustment and Allostatic Load', *Psychological Science*, vol. 24, no. 7, 1 July 2013; and Edith Chen, Gregory Miller, Gene Brody and ManKit Lei, 'Neighborhood Poverty, College Attendance, and Diverging Profiles of Substance Use and Allostatic Load in Rural African American Youth', *Clinical Psychological Science*, vol. 3, no. 5, September 2015

90 *Resilience* (dir. James Redford, 2016)

91 Ibid.

92 Diane Ravitch's blog, 'Christine Yeh. Forget Grit. Focus on Inequality', 16 January 2018, https://dianeravitch.net/2018/01/16/christine-yeh-forget-grit-focus-on-inequality/

93 Mehta, 'The Problem With Grit', https://www.edweek.org/education/opinion-the-problem-with-grit/2015/04

94 'North Philly to Oxford', *Philadelphia Inquirer*, 19 December 2018, https://www.inquirer.com/education/a/hazim-hardeman-rhodes-scholar-temple-north-philly-20181219.html

95 David Yeager, Angela Duckworth, Carol Dweck et al., 'A national experiment reveals where a growth mindset improves achievement', *Nature*, vol. 573, 7 August 2019

96 Author's conversation with Adrian Bethune, 17 January 2021

97 Ann Masten in *Developmental Psychopathology, Risk, Resilience, and Intervention*, ed. Dante Cicchetti, John Wiley, 2016, p.275

98 Ann Masten, 'Ordinary magic: Resilience processes in development', *American Psychologist*, vol. 56, no. 3, 2001

99 Christy A. Denckla et al., 'Psychological resilience: An update on definitions, a critical appraisal, and research recommendations', *European Journal of Psychotraumatology*, vol. 11, no. 1, 10 November 2020

100 Ibid.

101 Author's conversation with Professor Alex Haslam, 29 March 2021

102 David Bakan, *The Duality of Human Existence*, Rand McNally, 1966, p.15

103 Richard M. Ryan and Edward L. Deci, 'Self-Determination Theory and the Facilitation of Intrinsic Motivation, Social Development, and Well-Being', University of Rochester, 2000

104 Edward Deci, 'Self-Determination Theory', YouTube, 17 October 2017, https://www.youtube.com/watch?v=m6fm1gt5YAM&ab_channel=TheBrainwavesVideoAnthology

105 Emmy Werner and Ruth Smith, *Journeys from Childhood to Midlife: Risk, Resilience, and Recovery*, Cornell University Press, 2001, p.58

Chapter 6: Control

1   Christine Miserandino, 'The Spoon Theory', 2003, https://cdn.totalcomputersusa.com/butyoudontlooksick.com/uploads/2010/02/BYDLS-TheSpoonTheory.pdf; and 'The Spoon Theory written and spoken by Christine Miserandino', YouTube, 16 December 2010, https://www.youtube.com/watch?v=jn5IBsm49Rk&ab_channel=ChristineMiserandino

2   Yumie Ono, Hsiao-chun Lin, Kai-yuan Tzen, Hui-hsing Chen, Pai-feng Yang, Wen-sung Lai, Jyh-horng Chen, Minoru Onozuka and Chen-tung Yen, 'Active coping with stress suppresses glucose metabolism in the rat hypothalamus', *Stress*, vol. 15, no. 2, March 2012

3   Ibid.

4   Mark Seery, Alison Holman and Roxane Cohen Silver, 'Whatever does not kill us: Cumulative lifetime adversity, vulnerability, and resilience', *Journal of Personality & Social Psychology*, vol. 99, no. 6, December 2010

5   M. Visintainer, J. Volpicelli and M. Seligman, 'Tumor rejection in rats after inescapable or escapable shock', *Science*, 23 April 1982

6   Deane Shapiro, Carolyn Schwartz and John Astin, 'Controlling ourselves, controlling our world: Psychology's role in understanding positive and negative consequences of seeking and gaining control', *American Psychologist*, vol. 51, no. 12, December 1996

7   B. K. Anand, G. Chinna and Baldev Singh, 'Some Aspects of Electroencephalographic Studies in Yogis', *Indian Journal of Physiology and Pharmacology*, 1 June 1961

8   James Averill and Miriam Rosenn, 'Vigilant and nonvigilant coping strategies and psychophysiological stress reactions during the anticipation of electric shock', *Journal of Personality and Social Psychology*, vol. 23, no. 1, 1972

9   J. R. Averill, 'Personal control over aversive stimuli and its relationship to stress', *Psychological Bulletin*, vol. 80, no. 4, 1973, pp.286–303

10 J. Whitson and A. Galinsky, 'Lacking Control Increases Illusory Pattern Perception', *Science*, vol. 332, no. 115, 3 October 2008, https://rifters.com/real/articles/Science_LackingControlIncreasesIllusory PatternPerception.pdf

11 The method of creating helpless confusion is explained in N. Pittman and T. Pittman, 'Effects of amount of helplessness training and internal–external locus of control on mood and performance', *Journal of Personality and Social Psychology*, vol. 37, no. 1, February 1979

12 Whitson and Galinsky, 'Lacking Control Increases Illusory Pattern Perception', https://rifters.com/real/articles/Science_Lacking ControlIncreasesIllusoryPatternPerception.pdf

13 J. Lammers, J. Stoker, F. Rink and A. Galinsky, 'To Have Control Over or to Be Free From Others? The Desire for Power Reflects a Need for Autonomy', *Personality and Social Psychology Bulletin*, vol. 42, no. 4, 16 March 2016; the ice-cream study is in Ena Inesi, Simona Botti, David Dubois and Derek D. Rucker, 'Power and Choice: Their Dynamic Interplay in Quenching the Thirst for Personal Control', *Psychological Science*, vol. 22, no. 8, 24 June 2011

14 Pittman and Pittman, 'Effects of amount of helplessness training and internal–external locus of control on mood and performance'

15 Snehlata Jaswal and Anita Dewan, 'The relationship between Locus of Control and Depression', *Journal of Personality & Clinical Studies*, January 1997

16 Eric Endlich, 'Depression and Attributions for Problems and Solutions in College Students', *Psychological Reports*, vol. 65, no. 1, 1 August 1989

17 'It appears that depressed individuals show a general tendency to view outcomes as being beyond personal control and, as noted previously, that they blame themselves for failure', Victor Benassi et al., 'Is There a Relation Between Locus of Control Orientation and Depression?', *Journal of Abnormal Psychology*, 1 August 1988, https://pdfs.semanticscholar.org/e75f/4d70b3cfa0039c2a6a89734e256b31dc135d.pdf

18 'The Dangers of Woke Culture – with Sam Harris', *The Prof G Pod with Scott Galloway*, 16 July 2021, https://podcasts.apple.com/us/podcast/the-dangers-of-woke-culture-with-sam-harris/id1498802610?i=1000528950797

19 Phillip T. Marucha, Janice K. Kiecolt-Glaser and Mehrdad Favagehi, 'Mucosal Wound Healing Is Impaired by Examination Stress', *Psychosomatic Medicine*, vol. 60, no. 3, 1998

20 Shapiro, Schwartz and Astin, 'Controlling ourselves, controlling our world'

21 Gabor Maté, *When the Body Says No – The Cost of Hidden Stress*, Vermilion, 2019, p.15

22 John Helliwell, Richard Layard, Jeffrey Sachs et al., *World Happiness Report*, 2017, p.58

23 David Berreby, *Us and Them: The Science of Identity*, University of Chicago Press, 2008, p.266

24 Michael Marmot, 'Status syndrome', Significance, Royal Statistical Society, 13 December 2004, https://rss.onlinelibrary.wiley.com/doi/10.1111/j.1740-9713.2004.00058.x

25 Ibid.

26 Catherine Haslam et al., *The New Psychology of Health: Unlocking the Social Cure*, Routledge, 2018, p.39

27 'Being wealthy adds nine more years of life, says study', *The Guardian*, 15 January 2020, https://www.theguardian.com/

society/2020/jan/15/being-wealthy-adds-nine-years-to-life-expectancy-says-study

28 'Australia: Life expectancy gap between rich and poor almost 20 years', World Socialist Web Site, 14 August 2017, https://www.wsws.org/en/articles/2017/08/14/life-a14.html

29 Vikram Patel et al., 'Income inequality and depression: A systematic review and meta-analysis of the association and a scoping review of mechanisms', *World Psychiatry*, vol. 17, no. 1, February 2018

30 R. Jay Turner and Samuel Noh, 'Class and Psychological Vulnerability Among Women: The Significance of Social Support and Personal Control', *Journal of Health and Social Behavior*, vol. 24, 1983

31 J. Mirowsky and C. Ross, 'Social Patterns of Distress', *Annual Review of Sociology*, vol. 12, August 1986

32 Catherine E. Ross, 'Collective Threat, Trust, and the Sense of Personal Control', *Journal of Health and Social Behavior*, vol. 52, no. 3, September 2011

33 Daan Scheepers and Naomi Ellemers, 'When the pressure is up: The assessment of social identity threat', *Journal of Experimental Social Psychology*, vol. 41, no. 2, March 2005

34 Ibid.

35 M. Kohn and C. Schooler, 'Occupational Experience and Psychological Functioning: An Assessment of Reciprocal Effects', *American Sociological Review*, vol. 38, no. 1, February 1973, pp.114, 116

36 M. Kohn and C. Schooler, 'Job Conditions and Personality: A Longitudinal Assessment of Their Reciprocal Effects', *American Journal of Sociology*, vol. 87, no. 6, May 1982, p.1265

37 Ibid., p.1272

38 Kohn and Schooler, 'Occupational Experience and Psychological Functioning'

39 Kohn and Schooler, 'Job Conditions and Personality'

40 On depression: M. B. H. Yap, P. D. Pilkington, S. M. Ryan and A. F. Jorm, 'Parental factors associated with depression and anxiety in young people: A systematic review and meta-analysis', *Journal of Affective Disorders*, vol. 156, March 2014; on hostility and low self-esteem: Y. Kawabata et al., 'Maternal and paternal parenting styles

associated with relational aggression in children and adolescents: A conceptual analysis and meta-analytic review', *Developmental Review*, vol. 31, no. 4, December 2011: 'controlling parenting ... were associated with increased relational aggression'

41 S. Georgiou, K. Fousiani, P. Michaelides and P. Stavrinides, 'Cultural value orientation and authoritarian parenting as parameters of bullying and victimization at school', *International Journal of Psychology*, vol. 48, no. 1, 2013

42 Ariel Knafo, 'Authoritarians, the Next Generation: Values and Bullying Among Adolescent Children of Authoritarian Fathers', *Analyses of Social Issues and Public Policy*, vol. 3, no. 1, December 2003

43 Ellen Greenberger, Robin O'Neil and Stacy K. Nagel, 'Linking Workplace and Homeplace: Relations Between the Nature of Adults' Work and Their Parenting Behaviors', *Developmental Psychology*, vol. 30, no. 6, 1994

44 Daphne K. Lee, Twitter, 28 June 2020, https://twitter.com/daphnekylee/status/1277101831693275136; and https://twitter.com/KIO404l/status/1277120227919060992

45 Bart Kamphorst, Sanne Nauts, Denise De Ridder and Joel Anderson, 'Too Depleted to Turn In: The Relevance of End-of-the-Day Resource Depletion for Reducing Bedtime Procrastination', *Frontiers in Psychology*, 14 March 2018

46 'Participation at Work in Britain', Skills and Employment Survey 2017, https://www.cardiff.ac.uk/__data/assets/pdf_file/0010/1309456/5_Participation_Minireport_Final.pdf

47 The 2011 Workplace Employment Relations Study, https://dera.ioe.ac.uk/16383/7/13-535-the-2011-workplace-employment-relations-study-first-findings_Redacted.pdf

48 Skills and Employment Survey 2017 – 86 per cent drawn from crosstab analysis of the SES17 survey

49 Author's conversation with James Bloodworth 8 April 2019, also transmitted as 'Culture and Conditions Under the Radar: Tales from the Gig Economy', *Eat Sleep Work Repeat* podcast, 15 April 2019, https://eatsleepworkrepeat.com/culture-and-conditions-under-the-radar-tales-from-the-gig-economy/; more details are at: 'They resent

the fact I'm not a robot', ABC News, 26 February 2019, https://mobile.
abc.net.au/news/2019-02-27/amazon-australia-warehouse-working-
conditions/10807308?nw=0

50 'NHS patients getting less time with their GPs compared to other
developed countries', *The Independent*, 9 November 2017, https://
www.independent.co.uk/news/health/nhs-gp-doctor-appointment-
time-comparison-patients-latest-a8044681.html

51 '15-minute minimum consultations … ', RCGP, 21 May 2019, https://
www.rcgp.org.uk/about-us/news/2019/may/15-minute-minimum-
consultations-continuity-of-care.aspx

52 'Curriculum Overload: A Way Forward', OECD, 25 November 2020,
https://www.oecd-ilibrary.org/education/curriculum-overload_3081ceca-
en (2020)

53 *Children, their World, their Education: Final report and recommendations
of the Cambridge Primary Review*, Routledge, 2009

54 Peter Gray, 'Kindergarten Teachers Are Quitting, and Here Is Why',
Psychology Today, 20 December 2019, https://www.psychologytoday.
com/us/blog/freedom-learn/201912/kindergarten-teachers-are-quitting-
and-here-is-why

55 'Microsoft says video calls in Teams grew 1000% in March',
TechCrunch, 9 April 2020, https://techcrunch.com/2020/04/09/
microsoft-says-video-calls-in-teams-grew-1000-in-march/

56 Microsoft, 'The Next Great Disruption Is Hybrid Work – Are We
Ready?', 22 March 2021, https://www.microsoft.com/en-us/worklab/
work-trend-index/hybrid-work

57 'Microsoft Analyzed Data on Its Newly Remote Workforce', *Harvard
Business Review*, 15 July 2020, https://hbr.org/2020/07/microsoft-
analyzed-data-on-its-newly-remote-workforce

58 'United Express Flight 3411 Review and Action Report', retrieved at
thepointsguy.com/2017/04/united-policy-changes/

59 Derek W. Johnston et al., 'Why does work cause fatigue? A real-time
investigation of fatigue, and determinants of fatigue in nurses
working 12-hour shifts', *Annals of Behavioral Medicine*, vol. 53, no. 3,
3 May 2019

60 Roy E. Baumeister, Ellen Bratslavsky, Mark Muraven and Dianne Tice, 'Ego Depletion: Is the Active Self a Limited Resource?', *Journal of Personality and Social Psychology*, vol. 74, no. 5, 1998, http://faculty.washington.edu/jdb/345/345%20Articles/Baumeister%20et%20al.%20%281998%29.pdf

61 Martin Hagger et al., 'Ego depletion and the strength model of self-control: A meta-analysis', *Psychological Bulletin*, vol. 136, no. 4, July 2010, https://pubmed.ncbi.nlm.nih.gov/20565167/

62 Matthew Gailliot and Roy Baumeister, 'The Physiology of Willpower: Linking Blood Glucose to Self-Control', *Personality and Social Psychology Review*, 1 November 2007, https://journals.sagepub.com/doi/abs/10.1177/1088868307303030

63 Ibid.

64 Mika Kivimäki et al., 'Job strain as a risk factor for coronary heart disease: A collaborative meta-analysis of individual participant data', *The Lancet*, October 2012, https://www.ncbi.nlm.nih.gov/pmc/articles/PMC3486012/

65 Martin Seligman, *Flourish*, Free Press, 2011, p.142

66 Ibid.

67 O. Stavrova, D. Ren and T. Pronk, 'Low self-control: A hidden cause of loneliness?', *Personality and Social Psychology Bulletin*, 15 April 2021, doi.org/10.1177/01461672211007228

68 Shapiro, Schwartz and Astin, 'Controlling ourselves, controlling our world'

69 Erik Giltay, Johanna Geleijnse, Frans Zitman et al., 'Dispositional Optimism and All-Cause and Cardiovascular Mortality in a Prospective Cohort of Elderly Dutch Men and Women', *Archive of General Psychiatry*, vol. 61, no. 11, November 2004

70 S. Greer et al., 'Psychological Response to Breast Cancer: Effect on Outcome', *The Lancet*, 13 October 1979

71 Hans Selye, *The Stress of Life*, McGraw-Hill, 1956/1978, p.370

72 Maté, *When the Body Says No*, p.37; he himself cites S. Levine and H. Ursin, 'What Is Stress?', in S. Levine and H. Ursin (eds), *Psychobiology of Stress*, Academic Press, 1978

Chapter 7: Identity

1 Chris Hunter, *Eight Lives Down: The most dangerous job in the world in the most dangerous place in the world*, Delta, 2009, p.223

2 He explains in the book that his name is a pseudonym; ibid.

3 Ibid., p.283

4 'How to Be Calm Under Pressure', *The Observer*, 2 February 2017, https://observer.com/2017/02/how-to-be-calm-under-pressure-three-secrets-from-a-bomb-disposal-expert/

5 'Laurie Hernandez whispers "I got this" before beam routine – and it's everything', *Entertainment Weekly*, 10 August 2016, https://ew.com/article/2016/08/10/laurie-hernandez-i-got-this/

6 Phillip L. Hammack, 'Theoretical Foundations of Identity', in *The Oxford Handbook of Identity Development*, ed. Kate C. McLean and Moin Syed, Oxford University Press, 2015, p.14

7 Robyn Fivush and Widaad Zaman, 'Gendered Narrative Voices: Sociocultural and Feminist Approaches to Emerging Identity in Childhood and Adolescence', in *The Oxford Handbook of Identity Development*; and B. H. Fiese and N. L. Bickham, 'Pin-curling grandpa's hair in the comfy chair: Parents' stories of growing up and potential links to socialization in the preschool years', in M. W. Pratt and B. H. Fiese (eds), *Family Stories and the Life Course*, Routledge, 2004

8 Michelle Janning and Maya Volk, 'Where the heart is: Home space transitions for residential college students', *Children's Geographies*, vol. 15, no. 4, January 2017

9 Erik Erikson, *Identity, Youth and Crisis*, W. W. Norton, 1968, p.50

10 Erik Erikson, *Childhood and Society*, W. W. Norton, 1950

11 E. Reese, C. Yan, F. Jack and H. Hayne, 'Emerging identities: Narrative and self from early childhood to early adolescence', in K. McLean and M. Pasupathi (eds), *Narrative Development in Adolescence: Creating the Storied Self*, Springer, 2010, pp.23–43; and Kate McLean and Michael Pratt, 'Life's little (and big) lessons: Identity statuses and meaning-making in the turning point narratives of emerging adults', *Developmental Psychology*, vol. 42, no. 4, August 2006

12 Kate C. McLean and Moin Syed, 'The Field of Identity Development Needs an Identity: An Introduction', *The Oxford Handbook of Identity Development*

13 Natalie Purcell, Christopher Koenig, Jeane Bosch and Shira Maguen, 'Veterans' Perspectives on the Psychosocial Impact of Killing in War', *The Counseling Psychologist*, vol. 44, no. 7, 15 November 2016

14 Ibid.

15 Tilmann Habermas and Christin Köber, 'Autobiographical Reasoning is Constitutive for Narrative Identity: The Role of the Life Story for Personal Continuity', in *The Oxford Handbook of Identity Development*

16 Barack Obama, *Dreams from my Father*, Three Rivers Press, 1994, p.82; the Obama story is also discussed in Dan McAdams, 'Life Authorship: A Psychological Challenge for Emerging Adulthood, as Illustrated in Two Notable Case Studies', *Emerging Adulthood*, vol. 1, no. 2, 1 June 2013

17 McAdams, 'Life Authorship'

18 Dr Bessel van der Kolk, 'This Conversation Will Change How You Think About Trauma', *New York Times*, 24 August 2021, https://www.nytimes.com/2021/08/24/opinion/ezra-klein-podcast-van-der-kolk.html?showTranscript=1

19 Catherine Haslam et al., *The New Psychology of Health: Unlocking the Social Cure*, Routledge, 2018, p.115

20 'Rare cancer seen in 41 homosexuals', *New York Times*, 3 July 1981

21 Steve Cole, Margaret Kemeny and Shelley Taylor, 'Social identity and physical health: Accelerated HIV progression in rejection-sensitive gay men', *Journal of Personality and Social Psychology*, vol. 72, no. 2, 1997

22 M. Schmitt, N. Branscombe, D. Kobrynowicz and S. Owen, 'Perceiving Discrimination Against One's Gender Group has Different Implications for Well-Being in Women and Men', *Personality and Social Psychology Bulletin*, vol. 28, no. 2, 1 February 2002

23 Diane Quinn and Jennifer Crocker, 'Vulnerability to the Affective Consequences of the Stigma of Overweight', in J. K. Swim and C. Stangor (eds), *Prejudice*, Academic Press, 1998

24 H. Tajfel (ed.), *Differentiation between social groups: Studies in the social psychology of intergroup relations*, Academic Press, 1978; and Margie

Lachman and Suzanne Weaver, 'The sense of control as a moderator of social class differences in health and well-being', *Journal of Personality and Social Psychology*, vol. 74, no. 3, 1998

25 H. Landrine and E. Klonoff, 'The Schedule of Racist Events: A Measure of Racial Discrimination and a Study of Its Negative Physical and Mental Health Consequences', *Journal of Black Psychology*, vol. 22, no. 2, 1 May 1996

26 Lachman and Weaver, 'The sense of control as a moderator of social class differences in health and well-being'

27 Tom Daley, *Desert Island Discs*, BBC Sounds, 30 September 2018, https://www.bbc.co.uk/sounds/play/boblhfpj

28 *Resilience* (dir. James Redford, 2016)

29 Nadine Burke Harris, *Toxic Childhood Stress*, Bluebird, 2018, p.108

30 *Resilience* (dir. James Redford, 2016), timestamp 49.00

31 S. Hemenover, 'The good, the bad, and the healthy: Impacts of emotional disclosure of trauma on resilient self-concept and psychological distress', *Personality and Social Psychology Bulletin*, vol. 29, no. 10, 1 October 2003

32 Nadine Burke Harris, *The Deepest Well*, Bluebird, 2018, p.110

33 Alberto Bandura, 'Social Cognitive Theory and Exercise of Control over HIV Infection. AIDS Prevention and Mental Health', in R. DiClemene et al., *Preventing AIDS*, Springer Science, 1994

34 J. Kelly, S. Kalichman, M. Kauth, H. Kilgore, H. Hood, P. Campos, S. Rao et al., 'Situational factors associated with AIDS risk behavior lapses and coping strategies used by gay men who successfully avoid lapses', *American Journal of Public Health*, vol. 81, no. 10, October 1991

35 Dr Bessel van der Kolk, 'This Conversation Will Change How You Think About Trauma', *New York Times*, 24 August 2021, https://www.nytimes.com/2021

Chapter 8: Community

1 '9/11 Survivor Marcy Borders – The Dust Lady', Vimeo, https://vimeo.com/287672681

2   Image of Marcy Borders by Stan Honda, Agence France-Presse, 11 September 2001

3   'The "dust lady" of 9/11 dies', Mail Online, 26 August 2015, https://www.dailymail.co.uk/news/article-3211020/The-dusty-lady-9-11-Marcy-Borders-dies-stomach-cancer-ash-Twin-Towers-decade-long-battle-depression.html

4   ITV News, '9/11 "Dust Lady" dies from stomach cancer aged 42', YouTube, 27 August 2015, https://www.youtube.com/watch?v=lL3oaQdgDjM&ab_channel=CNNCNNVerified

5   Ralf Schwarzer, Rosemarie Bowler and James Cone, 'Social integration buffers stress in New York police after the 9/11 terrorist attack', *Anxiety, Stress, & Coping*, vol. 27, no. 1, January 2014

6   Chris Brewin, Bernice Andrews and John Valentine, 'Meta-analysis of risk factors for posttraumatic stress disorder trauma-exposed adults', *Journal of Consulting and Clinical Psychology*, vol. 68, no. 5, October 2000

7   Author's conversation with Professor Alex Haslam, 29 March 2021

8   Sebastian Junger, 'Why veterans miss war', TED Talk, 23 May 2014, YouTube, https://www.youtube.com/watch?v=TGZMSmcuiXM&ab_channel=TED

9   William Sledge, James Boydstun and Alton Rabe, 'Self-concept Changes Related to War Captivity', *Archives of General Psychiatry*, vol. 37, no. 4, April 1980

10 William Sledge, James Boydstun and Alton Rabe, 'Self-concept Changes Related to War Captivity', *Archives of General Psychiatry*, vol. 37, no. 4, April 1980

11 Ervin Staub, *The Roots of Evil: The Origins of Genocide and Other Group Violence*, Cambridge University Press, 1992, p.3

12 Cited in Alexander Haslam and Stephen Reicher, 'Beyond the banality of evil: Three dynamics of an interactionist social psychology of tyranny', *Personality and Social Psychology Bulletin*, vol. 33, no. 5, 1 May 2007

13 Stanley Migram, *Obedience to Authority: An Experimental View*, Harper & Row, 1974

14 *Social Groups and Identities: Developing the Legacy of Henri Tajfel*, ed. W. Peter Robinson, Psychology Press, 1996

15 Rupert Brown, *Henri Tajfel: Explorer of Identity and Difference*, Routledge, 2019

16 *Social Groups and Identities*, ed. Robinson, p.4

17 Henri Tajfel, 'Experiments in intergroup discrimination', *Scientific American*, vol. 223, no. 5, November 1970

18 Ibid.

19 Henri Tajfel and Michael Billig, 'Social categorization and similarity in intergroup behaviour', *European Journal of Social Psychology*, January/March 1973

20 Tajfel, 'Experiments in intergroup discrimination'

21 Haslam and Reicher, 'Beyond the banality of evil', http://bbcprisonstudy. org/pdfs/pspb%20(2007)%20banality%20of%20evil(2).pdf

22 Cited in ibid., p.617

23 Stephen Reicher, Alexander Haslam and Joanne Smith, 'Working Toward the Experimenter: Reconceptualizing Obedience Within the Milgram Paradigm as Identification-Based Followership', *Perspectives on Psychological Science*, vol. 7, no. 4, 29 June 2012

24 Alex Haslam, The Psychology of Tyranny: Did Milgram Get It Wrong? YouTubehttps://www.youtube.com/watch?v= HxXMKg8-700

25 Haslam and Reicher, 'Beyond the banality of evil'

26 'Rutger Bregman Is Hopeful For Humankind', *Eat Sleep Work Repeat* podcast, 20 April 2021, https://eatsleepworkrepeat.com/ rutger/

27 'The Influence You Have: Why We Fail to See Our Power Over Others', NPR, 24 February 2020, https://www.npr.org/2020/02/ 20/807758704/the-influence-you-have-why-were-blind-to-our-power-over-others?t=1625504969070

28 Stephen Reicher and S. Alexander Haslam, 'Rethinking the psychology of tyranny: The BBC prison study', *British Journal of Social Psychology*, vol. 45, 2006

29 Alexander Haslam, Stephen Reicher and Michael Platow, *The New Psychology of Leadership*, Routledge, 2020, p.99

30 Ibid., p.69; and Professor Alex Haslam, 'Social identity and the new psychology of mental health', The British Psychological Society,

YouTube, 26 February 2015, https://www.youtube.com/watch?v=TWWZd8lrraw

31 Jolanda Jetten, Stephen Reicher, Alexander Haslam and Tegan Cruwys, *Together Apart – The Psychology of COVID-19*, Sage Publications, 2020, p.19

32 'The Experiment – Critical Social Psychology', OpenLearn from the Open University, YouTube, 26 July 2011, https://www.youtube.com/watch?v=WaZCHpqEeio&t=214s&ab_channel=OpenLearnfromTheOpenUniversity

33 Reicher and Haslam, 'Rethinking the psychology of tyranny'

34 Catherine Haslam et al., *The New Psychology of Health: Unlocking the Social Cure*, Routledge, 2018, p.31

35 David Buss, *Evolutionary Psychology*, Psychology Press, 2014, p.22

36 Matthew Syed, *Rebel Ideas*, John Murray, 2019, p.244

37 Cited in ibid., p.245

38 Robin Dunbar, *Friends*, Little, Brown, 2021, p.55

39 Robin Dunbar, 'Neocortex size as a constraint on group size in primates', *Journal of Human Evolution*, vol. 22, no. 6, June 1992

40 Dunbar, *Friends*, p.137

41 John T. Cacioppo and Louise C. Hawkley, 'Perceived social isolation and cognition', *Trends in Cognitive Sciences*, vol. 13, no. 10, October 2009

42 Dunbar, *Friends*, pp.11, 15

43 Louise Hawkley, Christopher Masi, Jarett Berry and John Cacioppo, 'Loneliness is a unique predictor of age-related differences in systolic blood pressure', *Psychology and Ageing*, vol. 21, no. 1, March 2006

44 John Cacioppo, Louise Hawkley, Elizabeth Crawford et al., 'Loneliness and Health: Potential Mechanisms', *Psychosomatic Medicine*, vol. 64, no. 3, May–June 2002

45 John Cacioppo, Louise Hawkley, Gary Berntson et al., 'Do Lonely Days Invade the Nights? Potential Social Modulation of Sleep Efficiency', *Psychological Science*, vol. 13, no. 4, July 2002

46 Louise C. Hawkley and John T. Cacioppo, 'Aging and Loneliness: Downhill Quickly?', *Current Directions in Psychological Science*, vol. 16, no. 4, 1 August 2007

47   Haslam et al., *The New Psychology of Health*, p.162

48   John Mirowsky and Catherine Ross, 'Paranoia and the Structure of Powerlessness', *American Sociological Review*, vol. 48, no. 2, May 1983

49   Louise C. Hawkley, Christopher M. Masi, Jarett D. Berry and John T. Cacioppo, 'Loneliness is a unique predictor of age-related differences in systolic blood pressure', *Psychology and Aging*, vol. 21, no. 1, March 2006, pp.152–164, doi.org/10.1037/0882-7974.21.1.152

50   George Vaillant, *Triumphs of Experience: The Men of the Harvard Grant Study*, Harvard University Press, 2012, p.370

51   George E. Vaillant, *Happiness is love: full stop*, Harvard Medical School and Brigham and Women's Hospital, https://www.duodecim.fi/xmedia/duo/pilli/duo99210x.pdf

52   'Good genes are nice, but joy is better', *The Harvard Gazette*, 11 April 2017 https://news.harvard.edu/gazette/story/2017/04/over-nearly-80-years-harvard-study-has-been-showing-how-to-live-a-healthy-and-happy-life/

53   Robert Putnam, *Bowling Alone*, Simon & Schuster, 2020, p.293

54   Ibid., p.516

55   Ibid., p.298

56   S. Alexander Haslam, Anne O'Brien, Jolanda Jetten, Karine Vormedal and Sally Penna, 'Taking the strain: Social identity, social support, and the experience of stress', *British Journal of Social Psychology*, vol. 44, September 2005

57   Tegan Cruwys, Genevieve A. Dingle, Catherine Haslam, S. Alexander Haslam, Jolanda Jetten and Thomas A. Morton, 'Social group memberships protect against future depression, alleviate depression symptoms and prevent depression relapse', *Social Science & Medicine*, vol. 98, December 2013

58   J. Holt-Lunstad, T. Smith and J. Layton, 'Social Relationships and Mortality Risk: A Meta-analytic Review', *PLOS Medicine*, vol. 7, no. 7, 27 July 2010

59   J. M. Jones and J. Jetten, 'Recovering From Strain and Enduring Pain: Multiple Group Memberships Promote Resilience in the Face of Physical Challenges', *Social Psychological and Personality Science*, vol. 2, no. 3, 2011, pp.239–44

60 Fabio Sani, Vishnu Madhok, Michael Norbury, Pat Dugard and Juliet R. H. Wakefield, 'Greater number of group identifications is associated with lower odds of being depressed: Evidence from a Scottish community sample', *Social Psychiatry and Psychiatric Epidemiology*, vol. 50, no. 9, September 2015; and Tegan Cruwys, Alexander Haslam, Genevieve Dingle, Catherine Haslam and Jolanda Jetten, 'Depression and Social Identity: An Integrative Review', *Personality and Social Psychology Review*, vol. 18, no. 3, 1 August 2014

61 B. A. Morris, S. K. Chambers, M. Campbell, M. Dwyer and J. Dunn, 'Motorcycles and breast cancer: The influence of peer support and challenge on distress and posttraumatic growth', *Supportive Care in Cancer*, vol. 20, no. 8, August 2012

62 Tegan Cruwys, Erica I. South, Katharine H. Greenaway et al., 'Social Identity Reduces Depression by Fostering Positive Attributions', *Social Psychological and Personality Science*, vol. 6, no. 1, 1 January 2015

63 Barbara Ehrenreich, *Dancing in the Streets*, Metropolitan Books, 2006

64 Haslam, 'Social identity and the new psychology of mental health', https://www.youtube.com/watch?v=TWWZd8lrraw&ab_channel =TheBritishPsychologicalSociety

65 Author's conversation with Professor Alex Haslam, 29 March 2021

Chapter 9: Team Fortitude

1 Rebecca Solnit, *A Paradise Built in Hell*, Viking, 2009, p.98

2 Richard Titmuss, *Problems of Social Policy*, Greenwood Press, 1971, p.338

3 Solnit, *A Paradise Built in Hell*, p.99

4 Ibid., p.101

5 Tom Harrisson, *Living Through the Blitz*, Schocken, 1989, p.81

6 Olivia Cockett, *Love & War in London: A woman's diary, 1939–1942*, Wilfrid Laurier, 2005, p.150

7   Charles Fritz, *Disasters and Mental Health: Therapeutic Principles Drawn From Disaster Studies*, University of Delaware Disaster Research Center, 1996, p.4

8   Lisa A. Kirschenbaum, 'The Meaning of Resilience: Soviet Children in World War II', *Journal of Interdisciplinary History*, vol. 47, no. 4, 2017

9   Boris Skomorovsky and E. G. Morris, The Siege of Leningrad: The Saga of the Greatest Siege of All Time as Told by the Letters, Documents, and Stories of the Brave People Who Withstood It, 1944. Cited in Lisa A. Kirschenbaum, 'The Meaning of Resilience: Soviet Children in World War II', *Journal of Interdisciplinary History*, vol. 47, no. 4, 2017

10 Fritz, *Disasters and Mental Health*, p.63

11 Ibid., p.4

12 BBC Worklife, 'What makes strangers click?', 21 September 2020, https://www.bbc.com/worklife/article/20200917-what-makes-strangers-click

13 Angelo Romano, Matthias Sutter, James H. Liu, Toshio Yamagishi and Daniel Balliet, 'National parochialism is ubiquitous across 42 nations around the world', *Nature Communications*, vol. 12, 22 July 2021

14 A. Haslam, J. Jetten, T. Postmes and C. Haslam, 'Social Identity, Health and Well-Being: An Emerging Agenda for Applied Psychology', *Applied Psychology*, vol. 58, no. 1, January 2009

15 Ibid.

16 Robert Putnam, *Bowling Alone*, Simon & Schuster, 2020, pp.29, 619

17 Solnit, *A Paradise Built in Hell*, p.193

18 Russell Dynes and Enrico Quarantelli, 'Community Conflict: Its absence and its presence in natural disasters', Disaster Research Center, 1975; and 'The Lives They Lived', *New York Times*, 28 December 2017 https://www.nytimes.com/interactive/2017/12/28/magazine/the-lives-they-lived-enrico-l-quarantelli.html

19 Sebastian Junger, *Tribe*, Twelve, 2016, p.66

20 Ibid., p.70

21 Solnit, *A Paradise Built in Hell*, p.148

22 Orla Muldoon and Ciara Downe, 'Social identification and post-traumatic stress symptoms in post-conflict Northern Ireland', *British Journal of Psychiatry*, vol. 191, no. 2, August 2007

23 H. Lyons, 'Civil violence – The psychological aspects', *Journal of Psychosomatic Research*, vol. 23, no. 6, 1979

24 Fabio Sani, 'Group Identification, Social Relationships, and Health', in Jolanda Jetten, Alexander S. Haslam and Catherine Haslam, *The Social Cure: Identity, Health and Well-Being*, Psychology Press, 2015, p.22

25 D. Groh, L. Jason and C. Keys, 'Social Network Variables in Alcoholics Anonymous: A Literature Review', *Clinical Psychology Review*, vol. 28, no. 3, March 2008

26 AA, 'The Twelve Steps of Alcoholics Anonymous', https://www.alcoholics-anonymous.org.uk/about-aa/the-12-steps-of-aa

27 From the author's conversation with Steve Colgan, 12 September 2018, also transmitted as 'Learning from the Police' (2 episodes), *Eat Sleep Work Repeat* podcast, 11 and 13 December 2018, https://eatsleepworkrepeat.com/learning-from-the-police-2-episodes/

28 Ibid.

29 Mark Seery, Roxane Cohen Silver, Alison Holman, Whitney Ence and Thai Chu, 'Expressing thoughts and feelings following a collective trauma: Immediate responses to 9/11 predict negative outcomes in a national sample', *Journal of Consulting and Clinical Psychology*, vol. 76, no. 4, August 2008

30 Tegan Cruwys, Alexander Haslam, Genevieve Dingle, Catherine Haslam and Jolanda Jetten, 'Depression and Social Identity: An Integrative Review', *Personality and Social Psychology Review*, vol. 18, no. 3, 1 August 2014

31 Saul Rosenzweig, 'Some Implicit Common Factors in Diverse Methods of Psychotherapy', *American Journal of Orthopsychiatry*, vol. 6, no. 3, July 1936

32 Bruce E. Wampold, Gregory W. Mondin, Marcia Moody, Frederick Stich, Kurt Benson and Hyun-nie Ahn, 'A Meta-Analysis of Outcome Studies Comparing Bona Fide Psychotherapies: Empirically, "All Must Have Prizes"', *Psychological Bulletin*, vol. 122, no. 3, November 1997

33 Cruwys, Haslam et al., 'Depression and Social Identity'

34 G. Boström, M. Conradsson, C. Hörnsten, E. Rosendahl, N. Lindelöf, H. Holmberg and H. Littbrand, 'Effects of high-intensity functional exercise on depressive symptoms among people with dementia in residential care facilities: A randomised controlled trial', *Physiotherapy*, vol. 31, no. 8, August 2016; and J. McNeil, E. LeBlanc and M. Joyner, 'The effect of exercise on depressive symptoms in the moderately depressed elderly', *Psychology and Aging*, vol. 6, no. 3, September 1991

35 Catherine Haslam, Jolanda Jetten, Tegan Cruwys, Genevieve Dingle, S. Alexander Haslam, *The New Psychology of Health – Unlocking the Social Cure*, 2018, p.115

Chapter 10: Synced, Aligned and Connected

1   Dr Bessel van der Kolk, 'This Conversation Will Change How You Think About Trauma', *New York Times*, 24 August 2021, https://www.nytimes.com/2021/08/24/opinion/ezra-klein-podcast-van-der-kolk.html?showTranscript=1

2   Bessel van der Kolk, *The Body Keeps the Score*, Viking, 2014, p.112

3   van der Kolk, 'This Conversation Will Change How You Think About Trauma', https://www.nytimes.com/2021/08/24/opinion/ezra-klein-podcast-van-der-kolk.html?

4   Catherine Haslam et al., *The New Psychology of Health*, Routledge, 2018, p.115

5   Natalie Purcell, Christopher Koenig, Jeane Bosch and Shira Maguen, 'Veterans' Perspectives on the Psychosocial Impact of Killing in War', *The Counseling Psychologist*, vol. 44, no. 7, 2016

6   Primo Levi, *The Drowned and The Saved*, Simon & Schuster, 1988, p.91, cited in Stephen Reicher and Blerina Kellezi, 'The Social Cure or Social Curse? The Psychological Impact of Extreme Events During the Kosovo Conflict', 2015; Jolanda Jetten, Alexander, S. Haslam and Catherine Haslam, *The Social Cure: Identity, Health and Well-Being*, Psychology Press, 2015

7   Levi, *The Drowned and The Saved*, p.95

8   Reicher and Kellezi, 'The Social Cure or Social Curse?'

9   Ibid.

10 David Berreby, *Us & Them: The Science of Identity*, University of Chicago Press, 2008, p.186

11 van der Kolk, *The Body Keeps the Score*, p.85

12 van der Kolk, 'This Conversation Will Change How You Think About Trauma', https://www.nytimes.com/2021/08/24/opinion/ezra-klein-podcast-van-der-kolk.html?showTranscript=1

13 Barbara Ehrenreich, *Dancing in the Streets*, Metropolitan Books, 2006, Chapter 7

14 Robin Dunbar, *Friends*, Little, Brown, 2021, pp.144, 138

15 Author's conversations with Robin Dunbar (17 March 2021) and Emma Cohen (7 August 2019), the latter transmitted as 'Why you need to understand the "self/other overlap"', *Eat Sleep Work Repeat* podcast, https://eatsleepworkrepeat.com/why-you-need-to-understand-the-self-other-overlap/; also Dunbar, *Friends*, p.165

16 From the author's conversation with Emma Cohen, 7 August 2019; the original paper is Arran Davis, Jacob Taylor and Emma Cohen, 'Social Bonds and Exercise: Evidence for a Reciprocal Relationship', *PLOS One*, vol. 10, no. 8, 28 August 2015

17 Robin Dunbar, 'Breaking Bread: the Functions of Social Eating', *Adaptive Human Behavior and Physiology*, vol. 3, 11 March 2017

18 Matthias R. Mehl and Simine Vazire, 'Eavesdropping on Happiness: Well-being is Related to Having Less Small Talk and More Substantive Conversations', *Psychological Science*, vol. 21, no. 4, 1 April 2010

19 Dunbar, *Friends*, p.169

20 'Audience members' hearts beat together at the theatre', *UCL News*, 17 November 2017, https://www.ucl.ac.uk/news/2017/nov/audience-members-hearts-beat-together-theatre

21 Michael Murphy, Denise Janicki-Deverts and Sheldon Cohen, 'Receiving a hug is associated with the attenuation of negative mood that occurs on days with interpersonal conflict', *Public Library of Science One*, vol. 13, no. 10, 3 October 2018

22 Professor Alex Haslam, 'Social identity and the new psychology of mental health', The British Psychological Society, YouTube, 26 February 2015, https://www.youtube.com/watch?v=TWWZd8lrraw

23 Jonathan Sacks, 'Collective Joy', https://rabbisacks.org/collective-joy-reeh-5779/

24 Author's conversation with Emma Cohen, 7 August 2019

25 Katharine Greenaway, Alexander Haslam, Tegan Cruwys, Nina Branscombe, Renate Ysseldyk, Courtney Heldreth, 'From "we" to "me": group identification enhances personal control with consequences for health and well-being', *Journal of Personality and Social Psychology*, 2015

26 From the author's conversation with Pippa Grange, 17 September 2019, partly transmitted as 'Talking Teams – an exclusive interview with Pippa Grange', *Eat Sleep Work Repeat* podcast, 9 October 2018, https://eatsleepworkrepeat.com/interviewing-pippa-grange-head-of-team-culture-at-the-england-football-team/

27 Robert Cialdini, *Influence: The Psychology of Persuasion (new and expanded)*, Harper Business, 2021, p.364

28 Ibid., p.369

29 Michael Inzlicht, Jennifer Gutsell and Lisa Legault, 'Mimicry reduces racial prejudice', *Journal of Experimental Social Psychology*, vol. 48, January 2012

30 Diego Reinero, Suzanne Dikker and Jay Van Bavel, 'Inter-brain synchrony in teams predicts collective performance', *Social Cognitive and Affective Neuroscience*, vol. 16, nos 1–2, January–February 2021

31 G. Shteynberg, 'Shared Attention', *Perspectives on Psychological Science*, vol. 10, no. 5, 1 September 2015

32 Ibid.

33 G. Shteynberg, J. Hirsh, E. Apfelbaum, J. Larsen, A. Galinsky and N. Roese, 'Feeling more together: Group attention intensifies emotion', *Emotion*, vol. 14, no. 6, August 2014

34 S. Dikker et al., 'Brain-to-Brain Synchrony Tracks Real-World Dynamic Group Interactions in the Classroom', *Current Biology*, vol. 20, no. 9, May 2017, https://www.sciencedirect.com/science/article/pii/S0960982217304116#!

Chapter 11: Three Tales of Fortitude

1 Author's conversation with Anna Hemmings, 9 March 2021, additionally enhanced with quotations from 'The Diary of a CEO: interview with Stephen Bartlett', YouTube, 19 January 2021, https://www.youtube.com/watch?v=GGTtZpswgfg; and 'Canoeing – Hemmings reflects on remarkable return', *Surrey Live*, 4 January 2006, https://www.getsurrey.co.uk/sport/other-sport/canoeing–hemmings-reflects-remarkable-4841610

2 'Reverse Therapy: A radical new approach to recovery' developed by Dr John Eaton, https://www.reverse-therapy.com/

3 Douglas Rushkoff, 'How to be "Team Human" in the digital future', Ted Salon, September 2018, https://www.ted.com/talks/douglas_rushkoff_how_to_be_team_human_in_the_digital_future

4 From the author's conversation with Damian Scarf, 25 January 2021, with additional quotations taken from Damian Scarf, 'Anxiety is an Expert Strategist', TEDx Talk, YouTube, 9 November 2015, https://www.youtube.com/watch?v=cbHBZWbEk8A&t=1s&ab_channel=TEDxTalks

5 Damian Scarf, Saleh Moradi, Kate McGaw, Joshua Hewitt, Jillian Hayhurst, Mike Boyes, Ted Ruffman and Jackie Hunter, 'Somewhere I belong: Long-term increases in adolescents' resilience are predicted by perceived belonging to the in-group', *British Journal of Social Psychology*, vol. 55, no. 3, September 2016

6 Ibid.

7 Author's conversation with Dr Damian Scarf, 25 January 2021, also transmitted as 'The root of resilience? Groups', *Eat Sleep Work Repeat* podcast, 26 January 2021, https://eatsleepworkrepeat.com/the-root-of-resilience-groups/

8 Scarf, 'Anxiety is an expert strategist', https://www.youtube.com/watch?v=cbHBZWbEk8A&ab_channel=TEDxTalks

9 Scarf et al., 'Somewhere I belong'

10 Scarf, 'Anxiety is an expert strategist', https://www.youtube.com/watch?v=cbHBZWbEk8A&ab_channel=TEDxTalks

11 Catriona Matheson, Helen D. Robertson, Alison M. Elliott, Lisa Iversen and Peter Murchie, 'Resilience of primary healthcare professionals working in challenging environments: A focus group study', *British Journal of General Practice*, vol. 66, no. 648, July 2016

12 Lynn McDonald, *Florence Nightingale on Public Health Care: Collected Works of Florence Nightingale*, Wilfrid Laurier, 2004, p.447

13 'Play: Tales of success from an NHS hospital', *Eat Sleep Work Repeat* podcast, edited for clarity, 22 April 2019, https://eatsleepworkrepeat. com/play-tales-of-success-from-an-nhs-hospital/

14 Martin Seligman, *Flourish*, Free Press, 2011, p.20

Chapter 12: Fortitude Falling?

1 Aristotle, *Rhetoric*, 2004, p.85

2 H. Rose, *A New General Biographical Dictionary Projected and Partly Arranged by the Late Rev. Hugh James Rose*, B. Fellowes, 1848, vol. 3, cited in John Protzko and Jonathan Schooler, 'Kids these days: Why the youth of today seem lacking', *Science Advances*, vol. 5, no. 10, 16 October 2019

3 'Why We've Been Hating on "Kids These Days" for Thousands Of Years', *Discover magazine*, 16 October 2019, https://www. discovermagazine.com/mind/why-weve-been-hating-on-kids-these-days-for-thousands-of-years

4 'Why old people will always complain about young people', *Vox*, 12 November 2019, https://www.vox.com/science-and-health/2019/11/12/20950235/ok-boomer-kids-these-days-psychology

5 Haidt has since described his initial uncertainty about the title – which was one proposed by the publishers – and conceded that some have regarded it as an exaggeration. 'Jonathan Haidt on making free speech better', *Dialogues with Richard Reeves*, Apple Podcasts, 20 April 2021, https://podcasts.apple.com/us/podcast/jonathan-haidt-on-making-free-speech-better/id1564095051?i=1000518047348

6   'Jonathan Haidt on Making Free Speech Better', YouTube, 1 May 2021, https://www.youtube.com/watch?v=SZ9O-tGEdIU&ab_channel=RichardReeves

7   Mark Seery, Alison Holman and Roxana Silver, 'Whatever does not kill us: Cumulative lifetime adversity, vulnerability, and resilience', *Journal of Personality and Social Psychology*, vol. 99, no. 6, December 2010

8   'Jonathan Haidt on Making Free Speech Better', https://www.youtube.com/watch?v=SZ9O-tGEdIU&ab_channel=RichardReeves; the 'toxic coddling' phrase is at 23 minutes 30

9   Jonathan Haidt and Greg Lukianoff, *The Coddling of the American Mind*, Penguin Books, 2018, p.55

10 Successful disinvitations from US college campus speaking events, Foundation for Individual Rights in Education, 2021, https://www.thefire.org/research/disinvitation-database/

Year	2005	2006	2007	2008	2009	2010	2011	2012	2013	2014	2015	2016	2017	2018	2019	2020	2021
Attempted disinvitations	24	20	18	19	32	16	22	24	34	31	24	43	18	18	41	21	26
Successful disinvitations	12	4	11	11	17	3	12	10	15	12	9	24	27	12	21	7	9

11 Ibid.

12 'Tulane University misidentifed Hunter Biden's expertise', *Washington Examiner*, 28 April 2021, https://www.washingtonexaminer.com/opinion/tulane-university-misidentified-hunter-bidens-expertise

13 Video: 'Winston Churchill booed at Walthamstow Stadium during election rally', Mail Online, https://www.dailymail.co.uk/video/news/video-2404610/Video-Winston-Churchill-booed-Walthamstow-Stadium-election-rally.html

14 Lee Bollinger, 'Free Speech on Campus Is Doing Just Fine, Thank You', *The Atlantic*, 12 June 2019, https://www.theatlantic.com/ideas/archive/2019/06/free-speech-crisis-campus-isnt-real/591394/

15 'Evaluation Report', Office for Students, 21 June 2019, https://www.officeforstudents.org.uk/media/860e26e2-63e7-47eb-84e0-49100788009c/ofs2019_22.pdf

16 'NEW SURVEY: Majority of college students self-censor, support disinvitations ...', FIRE, 11 October 2017, https://www.thefire.org/new-survey-majority-of-college-students-self-censor-support-disinvitations-dont-know-hate-speech-is-protected-by-first-amendment/

17 Jean Twenge, *iGen*, Atria Books, 2017, p.402

18 Jean Twenge, 'Have Smartphones Destroyed a Generation?', *The Atlantic*, September 2017

19 'This Is Our Chance to Pull Teenagers Out of the Smartphone Trap', *New York Times*, 31 July 2021, https://www.nytimes.com/2021/07/31/opinion/smartphone-iphone-social-media-isolation.html

20 Ibid.

21 Twenge, 'Have Smartphones Destroyed a Generation?', https://www.theatlantic.com/magazine/archive/2017/09/has-the-smartphone-destroyed-a-generation/534198/

22 Ibid.

23 'This Is Our Chance to Pull Teenagers Out of the Smartphone Trap', https://www.nytimes.com/2021/07/31/opinion/smartphone-iphone-social-media-isolation.html

24 'Jonathan Haidt on Making Free Speech Better', https://www.youtube.com/watch?v=SZ9O-tGEdIU&ab_channel=RichardReeves

25 Twenge, Haidt et al., 'Worldwide increases in adolescent loneliness', https://www.sciencedirect.com/science/article/pii/S0140197121000853

26 Jean Twenge and Jonathan Haidt, 'Response to Critics of Haidt-Twenge NYT Essay on School Loneliness', 5 August 2021, https://docs.google.com/document/d/1QWXn_pWkAPzBOkjqzjrjS19LCKPoudETzWV__C6xK8I

27 'This Is Our Chance to Pull Teenagers Out of the Smartphone Trap', https://www.nytimes.com/2021/07/31/opinion/smartphone-iphone-social-media-isolation.html

28 Twenge, 'Have Smartphones Destroyed a Generation?', https://www.theatlantic.com/magazine/archive/2017/09/has-the-smartphone-destroyed-a-generation/534198/

29 Twenge and Haidt, 'Response to Critics of Haidt-Twenge NYT Essay on School Loneliness', https://docs.google.com/document/d/1QWXn_pWkAPzBOkjqzjrjS19LCKPoudETzWV__C6xK8I

30 Twenge, 'Have Smartphones Destroyed a Generation?', https://www.theatlantic.com/magazine/archive/2017/09/has-the-smartphone-destroyed-a-generation/534198/

31 Douglas Adams, 'How to Stop Worrying and Learn to Love the Internet', https://douglasadams.com/dna/19990901-00-a.html

32 P. M. Valkenburg and J. Peter, 'Online communication and adolescent well-being: Testing the stimulation versus displacement hypothesis', *Journal of Computer-Mediated Communication*, vol. 12, no. 4, 1 July 2007, pp.1169–82; and K. Davis, 'Young people's digital lives: The impact of interpersonal relationships and digital media use on adolescents' sense of identity', *Computers in Human Behavior*, vol. 29, no. 6, 2013

33 Amy Orben, Andrew Przybylski, 'The association between adolescent well-being and digital technology use', *Natural Human Behaviour*, 2019, https://www.nature.com/articles/s41562-018-0506-1

34 'Facebook Knows Instagram Is Toxic for Teen Girls, Company Documents Show', *Wall Street Journal*, 14 September 2021, https://www.wsj.com/articles/facebook-knows-instagram-is-toxic-for-teen-girls-company-documents-show-11631620739

35 https://www.bbc.co.uk/news/world-58549373

36 'In Pursuit of Happiness', *The Atlantic* interview with Jean Twenge, YouTube, 20 May 2021, https://www.youtube.com/watch?v=QyqzOhpfc-4&t=9852s&ab_channel=TheAtlantic, timestamp 2:46.17

37 Irving Kirsch, 'Antidepressants and the Placebo Effect', *Zeitschrift für Psychologie*, vol. 222, no. 3, 2014

38 'California just pushed back school start times – you weren't dreaming. Now what?', CalMatters, 28 October 2019, https://

calmatters.org/education/k-12-education/2019/10/how-school-start-time-law-will-work-in-california/

39 Amy Orben and Andrew K. Przybylski, 'The association between adolescent well-being and digital technology use', *Nature Human Behaviour*, vol. 3, 14 January 2019 – the three-times figure is taken from online correspondence between Haidt and Przybylski: https://docs.google.com/document/d/1w-HOfseF2wF9YIpXwUUtP65-olnkPyWcgF5BiAtBEy0/edit#heading=h.d7r5kepyjd4n

40 Jean Twenge, Sarah Coyne, Jason Carroll and Bradford Wilcox, 'Teens in Quarantine: Mental Health, Screen Time, and Family Connection', Institute for Family Studies, 2020

41 'In Pursuit of Happiness', https://www.youtube.com/watch?v=QyqzOhpfc-4&t=9852s&ab_channel=TheAtlantic, timestamp 2:50.49

Chapter 13: Striding Towards Fortitude

1 Raphael Honigstein, *Klopp: Bring the Noise*, Yellow Jersey, 2017, p.86

2 Ibid.

3 'Michelin restaurants and fabulous wines: Inside the secret team dinners that have built the Spurs' destiny', ESPN, 25 July 2020, https://www.espn.com/nba/story/_/id/26524600/secret-team-dinners-built-spurs-dynasty

4 Author's conversation with Damian Hughes, 5 June 2019

5 'Jürgen Klopp's message to supporters', Liverpool FC, 13 March 2020, https://www.liverpoolfc.com/news/first-team/390397-jurgen-klopp-message-to-supporters#

6 Alex Haslam, 'Leadership', in Jolanda Jetten, Stephen Reicher, Alexander Haslam and Tegan Cruwys, *Together Apart – The Psychology of COVID-19*, Sage Publications, 2020, p.26

7 'Dame Kelly Holmes opens up about self-harming during her career', *The High Performance Podcast*, 22 May 2020, YouTube, https://

www.youtube.com/watch?v=E864arwOo1I&feature=youtu.be&t=
500&ab_channel=TheHighPerformancePodcast

8   'Greg LeMond vs. The World', *Men's Journal*, https://www.mensjournal.
com/health-fitness/greg-lemond-vs-the-world-20130318/

9   *Resilience* (dir. James Redford, 2016), timestamp 49.00

10 Ibid., 44.40

11 Nadine Burke Harris, *Toxic Childhood Stress*, Bluebird, 2018, p.110

12 'The impact of showing Resilience', Resilience Challenge, https://
resiliencechallenge.org.uk/Groups/330094/The_impact_of.aspx

13 *Resilience* (dir. James Redford, 2016), timestamp 54 mins

14 'How "trauma training" at a Harpurhey school saw exclusions
plummet', *Manchester Evening News*, 25 October 2019, https://www.
manchestereveningnews.co.uk/news/greater-manchester-news/how-
trauma-training-harpurhey-school-17145382

15 *Resilience* (dir. James Redford, 2016)

16 Author's conversation with Jillian Richardson, also transmitted as
'Community 4: A champion community builder shares her advice',
Eat Sleep Work Repeat podcast, 19 October 2020, https://
eatsleepworkrepeat.com/community/

17 *Resilience* (dir. James Redford, 2016)

18 'Mental health & emotions – practical ways of fixing work', *Eat Sleep
Work Repeat* podcast, 8 April 2019, https://eatsleepworkrepeat.com/
mental-health-emotions-practical-ways-of-fixing-work/

19 'Not just a run in the park', Parkrun, 5 October 2019, https://blog.
parkrun.com/uk/2019/10/05/not-just-run-park/

20 L. Nackers, P. Dubyak, X. Lu, S. Anton, G. Dutton and M. Peri,
'Group dynamics are associated with weight loss in the behavioral
treatment of obesity', *Obesity*, vol. 23, no. 8, August 2015

21 'Adverse Childhood Experiences Increase Risk of Mental Illness,
But Community Support Can Offer Protection', Bangor University,
https://www.bangor.ac.uk/news/archive/adverse-childhood-experiences-
increase-risk-of-mental-illness-but-community-support-can-offer-
protection-35429

22 Alarcos Cieza and Jerome E. Bickenbach, 'Laidback Science: Messages from Horizontal Epidemiology', in Richard Williams, Verity Kemp, Alexander Haslam, Catherine Haslam, Kamaldeep S. Bhui and Susan Bailey, *Social Scaffolding: Applying the Lessons of Contemporary Social Science to Health and Healthcare*, Cambridge University Press, 2019

Bibliography

Sue Bailey and Richard Williams, 'Towards partnerships in mental healthcare', *Advances in Psychiatric Treatment*, vol. 20, no. 1, January 2014

David Berreby, *Us and Them: The Science of Identity*, University of Chicago Press, 2008

Augusto Boal, *Games for Actors and Non-Actors*, Routledge, 1992

Rutger Bregman, *Humankind: A Hopeful History*, Little, Brown, 2019

Rupert Brown, *Henri Tajfel: Explorer of Identity and Difference*, Routledge, 2019

Robert Cialdini, *Influence: The Psychology of Persuasion*, Harper Business, 2021 update

Anthony Costello, *The Social Edge: The Power of Sympathy Groups for our Health, Wealth and Sustainable Future*, Thornwick, 2018

Marcus Credé, 'What Shall We Do About Grit? A Critical Review of What We Know and What We Don't Know', *Educational Researcher*, vol. 47, no. 9, 2018, pp.606–11

Tegan Cruwys, Genevieve A. Dingle, Catherine Haslam, S. Alexander Haslam, Jolanda Jetten and Thomas A. Morton, 'Social group memberships protect against future depression, alleviate depression symptoms and prevent depression relapse', *Social Science & Medicine*, vol. 98, December 2013, pp.179–86

——, S. Alexander Haslam, Genevieve A. Dingle, Catherine Haslam and Jolanda Jetten, 'Depression and Social Identity: An Integrative Review', *Personality and Social Psychology Review*, vol. 18, no. 3, 1 August 2014

Robin Dunbar, *Friends*, Little, Brown, 2021

Barbara Ehrenreich, *Dancing in the Streets: A History of Collective Joy*, Metropolitan Books, 2006

Francis Fukuyama, *Identity: The Demand for Dignity and the Politics of Resentment*, Farrar, Straus and Giroux, 2018

Paul Gogarty and Ian Williamson, *Winning at All Costs: Sporting Gods and Their Demons*, JR Books, 2009

Jonathan Haidt and Greg Lukianoff, *The Coddling of the American Mind*, Penguin Books, 2018

Catherine Haslam, Jolanda Jetten, Tegan Cruwys, Genevieve Dingle and S. Alexander Haslam, *The New Psychology of Health – Unlocking the Social Cure*, Routledge, 2018

S. Alexander Haslam, Jolanda Jetten, Tom Postmes, Catherine Haslam, 'Social Identity, Health and Well-Being: An Emerging Agenda for Applied Psychology', *Applied Psychology*, vol. 58, no. 1, January 2009

——, Anne O'Brien, Jolanda Jetten, Karine Vormedal and Sally Penna, 'Taking the strain: Social identity, social support, and the experience of stress', *British Journal of Social Psychology*, vol. 44, September 2005

——, Stephen D. Reicher and Michael J. Platow, *The New Psychology of Leadership: Identity, Influence and Power*, Routledge, 2020

Noreena Hertz, *The Lonely Century: Coming Together in a World that's Pulling Apart*, Sceptre, 2020

Robert Hogan and Daniel Weiss, 'Personality Correlates of Superior Academic Achievement', *Journal of Counseling Psychology*, vol. 21, no. 2, 1 March 1974

Jolanda Jetten, *Together Apart – The Psychology of COVID-19*, Sage Publications, 2020

——, Catherine Haslam and S. Alexander Haslam (eds), *The Social Cure: Identity, Health, and Well-Being*, Psychology Press, 2015

S. J. Jung, A. Winning, A. L. Roberts, K. Nishimi, Q. Chen, P. Gilsanz et al., 'Posttraumatic stress disorder symptoms and television viewing patterns in the Nurses' Health Study II: A longitudinal analysis', *PLOS ONE*, vol. 14, no. 3, 21 March 2019

Ezra Klein, *Why We're Polarized*, Avid Reader Press/Simon & Schuster, 2020

Alfie Kohn, *The Myth of the Spoiled Child – Challenging the Conventional Wisdom about Children and Parenting*, Da Capo Lifelong Books, 2014

Matthew Parris, *Fracture: Stories of How Great Lives Take Root in Trauma*, Profile Books, 2020

Tim Rees, S. Alexander Haslam, Pete Coffee and David Lavallee, 'A Social Identity Approach to Sport Psychology: Principles, Practice, and Prospects', *Sports Medicine*, vol. 45, no. 8, August 2015

Stephen Reicher and S. Alexander Haslam, 'Rethinking the psychology of tyranny: The BBC prison study', *British Journal of Social Psychology*, vol. 45, 2006

Jesse Singal, *The Quick Fix: Why Fad Psychology Can't Cure Our Social Ills*, Farrar, Straus and Giroux, 2021

Joanne R. Smith, *Social Psychology: Revisiting the Classic Studies*, Sage Publications, 2017

Rebecca Solnit, *A Paradise Built in Hell*, Viking, 2009

Niklas K. Steffens, S. Alexander Haslam and Stephen D. Reicher, 'Up close and personal: Evidence that shared social identity is a basis for the "special" relationship that binds followers to leaders', *The Leadership Quarterly*, vol. 25, no. 2, February 2014

Jean Twenge, *iGen*, Atria Books, 2017

J. C. Turner, 'Towards a cognitive redefinition of the social group', in H. Tajfel (ed.), *Social Identity and Intergroup Relations*, Cambridge University Press, 1982, pp.15–40

——, Penelope Oakes, S. Alexander Haslam and Craig Garty, 'Self and Collective: Cognition and Social Context', *Personality and Social Psychology Bulletin*, vol. 20, no. 5, 1 October 1994

Richard Williams (ed.), *Social Scaffolding: Applying the Lessons of Contemporary Social Science to Health and Healthcare*, Cambridge University Press, 2019

Acknowledgements

Immense love and thanks to those I love most dearly: my partner Coco, the little ones Arlie and Wes, and my brilliant buccaneers Billy and Tula. My mom and my sister, Jo, for their enduring love, humour and support. My friends Matt Pennington and Dan Cable who gave me far more laughter than anyone deserved during those weird two years of coronavirus – and who have given me invaluable suggestions when it comes to the ideas I've played around with while writing this book. I also owe a debt of gratitude to the patience and insight of Nigel Wilcockson at Penguin Random House for helping to transform a vast, unwieldy manuscript into something altogether more coherent.

Finally I want to give thanks to Alexandra Elbakyan, the maverick creator of Sci-Hub. I've spent two years working my way through thousands of scientific papers. Through some legacy of tired old business models, these papers sit hidden behind oppressively priced pay-walls – even though the academics doing the work earn nothing from their research being kept from public display. Sci-Hub enables anyone to access these papers. Despite Alexandra being described by *Nature* as one of the ten people who matter most in science, she is on the Interpol arrest list and is in hiding as a consequence. This book couldn't have been researched or written without Alexandra's creation. Much love to the original pirate.

Picture Permissions

Figure 1: author's own.

Figure 2: Chris Cook, 'The social mobility challenge for school reformers', *Financial Times*, 22 February 2012. www.ft.com/content/379774ba-f044-3832-aec9-0a4a130a6426

Figure 3: Jean M. Twenge PhD, *iGen*, Atria Books, 2017. Data drawn from the Monitoring the Future report.

Figure 4: Tegan Cruwys et al., 'Social group memberships protect against future depression, alleviate depression symptoms and prevent depression relapse', *Social Science & Medicine*, vol. 98, December 2013, pp.179–186.

Figure 5: Jean Twenge, Jonathan Haidt et al., 'Worldwide increases in adolescent loneliness', *Journal of Adolescence*, vol. 93, December 2021, pp.257–269. Available under Creative Commons licence Attribution 4.0 International (CC BY 4.0).

Figure 6: Jean M. Twenge PhD, *iGen*, Atria Books, 2017.

Figure 7: Jean M. Twenge PhD, *iGen*, Atria Books, 2017. Data drawn from the Monitoring the Future report, 1976–2015.

The author and publisher gratefully acknowledge the permission granted to reproduce the copyright material in this book. Every effort has been made to trace copyright holders and to obtain their permission. The publisher apologises for any omissions and, if notified, will make suitable acknowledgment in future reprints or editions of this book.

About the Author

Bruce Daisley is a writer, consultant and one of the UK's most influential voices on the intersection of life and work. His research into better working practices has featured in publications including the *Guardian, Telegraph, Wired UK, Washington Post, Harvard Business Review* and the *Wall Street Journal*. His podcast *Eat Sleep Work Repeat* has been an Apple number one business podcast and has featured psychologists, neuroscientists and workplace experts including Daniel Pink, Scott Galloway, Noreena Hertz and Rutger Bregman. He was previously the European Vice-President for Twitter, the firm's most senior employee outside of the US. His first book, *The Joy of Work*, was a *Sunday Times* bestseller and has been translated into sixteen languages.

Index

Academic Mindsets meeting (2013), 85–6

Adams, Douglas, 218

addiction, 28, 36, 46, 80, 143, 148, 178–9

Adler, Nancy, 119

adrenaline, 164

Adverse Childhood Experiences (ACE), 27, 31–7, 41, 43, 55, 57, 99, 122, 141–2, 225–9

adversity; trauma, 5–8, 11–18, 21, 25–50, 55–61, 99, 122, 225–9
  ageing and, 45, 101
  coddling and, 210
  community and, 148–52, 171–3, 175–9, 182
  control and, 122
  drug use and, 35, 36, 57–60, 148
  education and, 34, 99
  elite performance and, 5–8, 11–18, 55, 71, 105, 225
  identity and, 71, 74, 140–43, 225–9
  J-curve, inverted, 49, 68, 210
  loneliness and, 164
  memory of, 37
  mental illness and, 7, 27, 28, 32, 33, 35, 36, 38, 39–41
  obesity and, 28–31, 100

physical illness and, 28, 33, 36, 38, 39, 42, 44–8
psychotic disorders and, 40–41
shame and, 38, 71, 140
sports and, 3–6, 11–18, 43–4
synchrony and, 185–7

Afghanistan War, 88–9, 131

Agassi, Andre, 6

ageing, 45, 101

agency, 106, 118

agency hypothesis, 161

Ahmetašević, Nidžara, 177

AIDS (acquired immunodeficiency syndrome), 140, 143

Alabama, United States, 100

alcohol, 3, 28, 36, 100, 143, 148, 178–9

Alcoholics Anonymous, 143, 178–9

alexithymia, 42–3

Alice in Wonderland (Carroll), 183

almosts, 68

Alzheimer's disease, 36, 46

Amazon, 125–6

American Civil War (1861–5), 77–8

American Psychological Association, 21, 80

American Psychologist, 87, 88, 89

anabolic steroids, 58, 59